From Enlightenment to Risk: Social Theory and Contemporary Society

Also by Simon Clarke:

Social Theory, Psychoanalysis and Racism*

*Also published by Palgrave Macmillan

From Enlightenment to Risk: Social Theory and Contemporary Society

Simon Clarke

palgrave
macmillan

First published 2006 by
PALGRAVE MACMILLAN
Houndmills, Basingstoke, Hampshire RG21 6XS and
175 Fifth Avenue, New York, N. Y. 10010
Companies and representatives throughout the world

PALGRAVE MACMILLAN is the global academic imprint of the Palgrave Macmillan division of St. Martin's Press, LLC and of Palgrave Macmillan Ltd. Macmillan® is a registered trademark in the United States, United Kingdom and other countries. Palgrave is a registered trademark in the European Union and other countries.

ISBN-13: 978–1–4039–3952–4   hardback
ISBN-10: 1–4039–3952–7   hardback
ISBN-13: 978–1–4039–3953–1   paperback
ISBN-10: 1–4039–3953–5   paperback

This book is printed on paper suitable for recycling and made from fully managed and sustained forest sources.

A catalogue record for this book is available from the British Library.
A catalog record for this book is available from the Library of Congress.

10   9   8   7   6   5   4   3   2   1
15 14 13 12 11 10 09 08 07 06

Printed in China

For Wilkin

Contents

Acknowledgements

I would like to thank Emily Salz and the publishing team at Palgrave for their help in the production of this book. The book was developed within the vibrant research culture of the Centre for Psycho-Social Studies at the University of the West of England which provides a base for interdisciplinary theoretical and empirical social research. My special thanks go to Paul Hoggett, John Bird, and Julia Long. In particular I would like to thank Bill Hill for the many hours he spent discussing the content of the chapters on Globalisation and Risk with me and Jem Thomas for many years of discussion of sociological theory. Finally I would like to thank Chris Bryant and Kirsten Campbell for their critical reading of the original typescript and their helpful and insightful comments.

1

From Enlightenment to Risk: An Introduction

'Do we now live in an *enlightened age*?' the answer is, 'No,' but we do live in an *age of enlightenment*… 'Our age is, in especial degree, the age of criticism, and to criticism everything must submit'. (Kant, 1784)

This book is an exploration of key ideas and thinkers in contemporary sociological and critical theory. It has at its heart an emphasis on the construction of identity and the idea of rationality; the idea of different epochs – high, late, post modernity; and finally the idea that Enlightenment ideals have somehow gone wrong, and, indeed, that we have witnessed the end of Enlightenment. In it I chart a critical path from the work of Max Weber, then on to the early Frankfurt School, through to the work of Michel Foucault, the concept of Postmodernism, and finally the debates surrounding globalisation, risk and network society. I conclude by arguing for a critical theory of society that incorporates psycho-social elements which take seriously the ideas of self reflection and the psychological and sociological analysis of the structuring of society, which constantly challenge ideas of rationality and irrationality. From this flows the idea that central to a critical sociological theory is a recognition of the power of the human imagination and of emotion. In particular, the way in which one person's *fiction* is another's *fact*, one person's *rationality* is another's *irrationality* and vice-versa. This in some sense incorporates a critique of positivistic and scientific discourses which discount the interpretive and hermeneutic elements of social life. Without critical self reflection and confrontation then information becomes disinformation and vice-versa, it is difficult to tell the two apart. This book seeks to provide a clear and lucid introduction to sociological thought while retaining a critical and often cynical position vis-à-vis theories and practices. It also seeks to contrast various ideas and look for continuities as well as inconsistencies, for example in the debate between Jurgen Habermas, Michel Foucault and Jean François Lyotard on the nature of post and high modernity.

So we have four clear themes:

1. The idea of rationality/irrationality, tied into the notion of science, positivism and interpretation.
2. Identity and identity construction.
3. The idea of modernities.
4. The end of Enlightenment.

We have many theories to explain these themes which are covered in depth throughout this book. In this first chapter, I want to briefly discuss the nature of Enlightenment thinking and the traditions of thought and theory in sociology that have grown from it before going on to provide a general overview of these themes. It makes sense therefore to start with Immanuel Kant (1784) and ask: just what is Enlightenment? For Kant:

> Enlightenment is man's release from his self-incurred tutelage. Tutelage is man's inability to make use of his understanding without direction from another. Self-incurred is this tutelage when its cause lies not in reason but in lack of resolution and courage to use it without direction from another. Sapere aude! 'Have courage to use your own reason!' – that is the motto of enlightenment. (Kant (1784), 1963, p 3)

The importance of the Enlightenment in the formation of many traditions of thought and indeed the way in which we think about and view the world cannot be understated. The work of a small group of French philosophers and writers; Rousseau, La Mettrie, Diderot, d'Alembert, Voltaire and d'Holbach represent a body of work which has become known as 'progressive' thought. This thought represents a shift from religious dualism to a scientific world view. Classically, questions of life and death; Why are we here? Why do some people die and others live? How did we get here? had been given a religious answer which was explained in terms of good and bad, typified by authority and the unquestioning power of classical religious texts. Progressive thought represents a rejection of supernatural or spiritual explanations of phenomena and instead emphasises empirical observation and reason. The spread of enlightenment thought in the eighteenth century throughout Europe and in particular France culminated in a series of texts which were to form the basis for the way in which we both think about and investigate society today. The *Encyclopedia* under the editorship of Diderot and d'Alembert was more than just a collection of material; rather it was the highest point that human knowledge could reach:

> All things must be examined, debated, investigated without exception and without regard for anyone's feelings... We must ride roughshod over all these ancient

puerilities, overturn the barriers that reason never erected, give back to the arts and
sciences the liberty that is so precious to them (Diderot in Crocker, 1969, p 292)

The *Encyclopedia*, as Anchor (1967) notes, has a threefold purpose; a work of
reference providing information on the arts and sciences, a work of instruction
in all areas of knowledge, and finally, a point of dissemination of new ideas.
It not only expressed but changed and shaped public opinion (Anchor, 1967,
p 69). Tancock (1966) argues that it soon became clear from the *Prospectus*
written by Diderot and the *Discours Preliminaire* by d'Alembert that the work
contained within was to be highly materialistic, progressive in thought and
hostile to religious interests. The *Encyclopedia* represents an integrated world
view that can answer societal questions without relying on sacred religious
texts. Most importantly, from a methodological standpoint good explanation
is grounded in empiricism; all knowledge comes from the senses in the observation of material things. This process is causal and material. Thus we can
trace the origins of much of the statistical and empirical analyses which still
permeates social research and indeed everyday life back to a period of enlightenment and rejection of religious ideas. These themes of eighteenth century
enlightenment thought were brought together by Auguste Comte in the *Cours
de Philosophie Positive* between 1830–1842 marking the birth of sociology and
what was to become the dominant world view – scientism. Comte, as is well
known, coined the terms 'sociology' and 'positive science' arguing that empirical sociological laws could literally be used to administer away misery; rationally planned social reforms would result in stability, social reconstruction
and harmony. This of course is concurrent with the creation in the enlightenment period of Cartesian rational man: Knowledge stems from things that can
be measured; religious dualism is replaced by the mind substance-body
matter dichotomy.

Halfpenny (1982) argues that Comtean sociology found a lasting embodi-
ment in the work of Emile Durkheim. Durkheim adopted Comte's ideas of
empiricism, sociologism and scientism, adding a further dimension – statistics.
Suicide is often heralded as the classic example of the statistical analysis of
quantitative knowledge of a societal problem. Durkheim provides a summary
of sociology as a science in *The Rules of Sociological Method*: 'Sociological explanation consists exclusively in establishing relations of causality, that it is a
matter of connecting a phenomena to its cause, or rather a cause to its effects'
(Durkheim, 1964, p 125).

Durkheim's 'rules' are centred on the notion of a 'social fact'. Social facts are
ways of thinking or feeling which exist outside the individual but place a coer-
cive constraint on that individual. Social facts control us (which is reminiscent
of the notion of the unconscious), Durkheim uses the example of an industrialist using the techniques of a former century, s/he is free to do so, 'but by
doing so, I should invite certain ruin' (Durkheim, 1964b, p 3). Popular opinion
is a social fact; when we eat, how we bring up or socialise our children are

social facts. A social fact 'is every way of acting' and for Durkheim 'The first and most fundamental rule is: *Consider social facts as things.*' (Durkheim, 1964b, p 14). If we treat a social fact as a 'thing', we can then distinguish between 'normal' and 'pathological' variants. This enables classification of 'social types'. Causal explanation of one social fact by and in reference to another enables us to build laws of social life. Durkheim's method suggests a comparative sociology grounded in scientific rules or laws. There are some limitations however to this method. If we were to compare different societies of the same type where would we find them? The contrast between cultures in Europe is quite distinct and that is even before we start travelling between continents. If we were to compare cultures which would be normal and which pathological? (See discussion of Winch in Chapter Four). Perhaps the biggest problem with Durkheim's method is separating the social from the psychological. Durkheim defines a social fact as a 'thing', 'existing in its own right independent of its individual manifestations' (Durkheim, 1964, p 13). How can a thing exist independently of its own manifestation? In other words, how can a social fact be separated from a psychological fact? This allows very little room for the agency of the individual actor, but by Durkheim's own admission there is resistance on the part of the individual and this has psychological consequences: '(if) I do not conform to the customs observed in my country and in my class, the ridicule I provoke, the social isolation in which I am kept' (Durkheim, 1964, p 2).

The point I am trying to make here is that Durkheim's work symbolises a rejection of the inner world of imagination and emotion in sociological methodology. It is paradoxical in that Durkheim's notion of a social fact can actually serve as a good example of the mediation between inner and outer worlds, suggesting that Durkheim was in fact aware of the affective component of social life. A social fact cannot be independent of the psychological. He uses the example of the socialisation of a child. Customs and conventions constrain a child until these are internalised: eating, drinking and sleeping at regular hours become habitual and in doing so Durkheim exemplifies *a psychosocial dynamic* between the child, its parents and society. Again, this demonstrates why the positivist sociological method is unable to explain certain phenomena satisfactorily. Something as fundamental as the psyche is cut out of the equation in the search for objective knowledge.

What statistical information and empirical observation can do, is point to a problem, make us aware that a problem exists, and try to link a cause to an effect as Durkheim demonstrated in *Suicide*. There is however a lack of depth in this form of knowledge, so that we may argue for instance, that unemployment causes stress, stress leads to racism, but why racism and not something else. Statistics are useful and have a place to help understand social phenomena by arriving at fairly general and reliable 'pictures' of society. What statistics fail to do, is provide any form of empathetic understanding of phenomena, or take into account imaginative and emotional dimensions of experience. The culmination of the positivist tradition found an outlet in the logical positivism of Carnap, Hempel and Ayer (see Halfpenny, 1982) and in the philosophical discussion of the scientific method by Popper (1959) and Kuhn (1970), but of course the discussion of this would form the basis of another book.

Positivistic research methods give a particular form and quality of data which we may or may not be able to generalise from. What statistics do not tell us about, after Winch (2000), is the nature of meaningful behaviour, of empathic understanding, and of the unconscious dimensions of human experience; something, that the theorists discussed in this book do engage with in their contemporary critiques of contemporary society(s).

Key Themes

This has just been a brief history of the development of Enlightenment thought and its impact on sociological method, theory and the way in which we study things, objects and phenomena in society. Along with the theories of Karl Marx, this is what we could call classical sociological theory and it is now that I want to turn to contemporary social and critical theories which are the subject of this book. In Chapter Two I introduce the work of Max Weber who many consider to be the greatest classical social theorist. I start with Weber (1978) because he introduces us to concepts around understanding and meaning that are the crux of many contemporary theories and contra to those that I have just described. Weber forms a backdrop to the work of the Frankfurt School and ideas around reason and rationality. In this chapter I ask questions such as how do we understand the meaning behind a certain action? Is the action social? Is the action rational or emotional, or both? What is the Culture Industry? Horkheimer and Adorno's (1994) work forms a logical (rational?) progression from Weber's early work and introduces us to the concept of critical theory. They examine the way in which capitalism and instrumental rationality have a devastating effect on modern culture and the way in which these processes also have specific ramification for notions of self and selfhood.

Modern genocide is embedded in the structures of society, in the nature of capitalism, and in modernity itself. This is the argument in Chapter Three where I look at the notion of modern genocide through two quite distinct referents: first, through the critical theory of the Frankfurt School in which Max Horkheimer and Theodor Adorno use both structural and psychological tools in their analysis of the affective components of anti-Semitism. Second, it is looked at through the lens of Zygmunt Bauman's (1989, 1990, 1991) social theory where genocide is very much located in the structures of modern society, and in particular those that Weber describes in Chapter Two – bureaucracy, technical reason and instrumental rationality. I also introduce Bauman's (building on Simmel (1950)) concept of the stranger, as I feel that it is critical to a contemporary sociology of the imagination. Both theories start to show us how self develops in relation to others and our changing relationship with nature. In this chapter we see the idea of the end of Enlightenment, the lack of self reflection that leads to racism and anti-Semitism and the idea that rationality and positivistic science have begun to dominate the world that we live in. In Chapter Four we see the re-invention of modernity through the work of Jurgen Habermas (1971b, 1981, 1985, 1987). Habermas, in many ways, shares the same concerns as his colleagues before him, but is far less pessimistic about the future. Modernity, far from being in its dying moments, is actually an incomplete project. The rationalisation process has merely gone wrong; this can be put right by sustained self reflection on our practice and method.

Habermas, is, one of the most influential thinkers of our time and his output has been tremendous. This chapter seeks to outline some of his main theories and ideas and relate them to questions of identity and rationality. The two key texts that I look at are *Knowledge and Human Interests* and *The Theory of Communicative Action*. Habermas is one of the most important thinkers as he delves into the dark side of modernity and brings it back into the 21st century. He may have returned to some of the enlightenment ideas, for example, the self reflection model, but in doing so he has laid the field open to develop his notions of the ideal speech situation and communicative rationality: lodged in our very essence as language users there is a form of communicative reason. On this basis we can move toward a more rational society, where rationality means freedom and consensus rather than oppression. Habermas has engaged theoretically with two other thinkers in this book, Foucault (1967, 1977), and Lyotard (1974, 1984, 1988), and I will compare and contrast their positions in Chapters Five and Six. Michel Foucault gives us a radically different vision of history and the creation of self. Foucault's critical melange of sociology, history, psychology and philosophy takes us on a voyage from the origins of madness to disciplinary society. For Foucault, the processes and historical circumstances that give rise to the modern self are bound up with the objectification of the other. The key themes in this chapter are the processes of rationalisation that shape the modern self, that create the modern madman, and that describe the modern deviant. In particular, it is about the ways in which we have been objectified, normalised and observed by modern expert discourses that have their origin in the kind of positivistic outlook that I outlined earlier in this introduction. There are certain similarities in the work of Foucault to those of earlier theorists I will discuss in this book. Foucault takes a micro analytic stance in his work which means he focuses on the specifics of modernity and key events in history that are read through a power knowledge lens. In doing so he provides us with a social history of rationality that implies that the rational is not always a good thing. For example, he challenges the notion that the mad or mentally ill are treated in a more humane way than they were in the past and in doing so, he challenges key ideas about thinking and human existence. The social construction of sexuality challenges questions of self and identity: are we really the makers of our own self, or the passive carriers of Bio-power? Foucault's work in some sense provides a primer for the following chapter on postmodernism, postmodernity and hyperreality.

Chapter six then examines the idea that we live in a postmodern age. It asks what exactly is postmodernism? What is the relationship between post-modernism and postmodernity? Are we talking about a new epoch in history, a new way of thinking, a new way of feeling and seeing? Are these theories, practices or both? In trying to make sense of the postmodern debate I address in some detail the works of Lyotard (1984) and Jean Baudrillard (1970, 1983) in order to examine the way in which consumption, fragmentation and the notion of the decentred self have come to the fore in social and cultural analyses. In particular I focus on Lyotard's critique of knowledge and scientific discourse and his idea of parology, that is, a postmodern science. I also try to link the thought of Lyotard with Foucault and then Baudrillard. Baudrillard's early writings are reminiscent of the Adorno and the early Frankfurt School analysing the dysfunctional nature of the culture industry. However, there is more of an emphasis in Baudrillard's work on the creation of self and the way in which we literally insert 'ourselves' into society. I argue in this chapter that if Foucault did not convince us of the often absurd nature of the construction of the self, then Baudrillard will finish the job as we all become simulations of simulations in the world of hyperreality. In parallel, Lyotard offers us one of the most damning critiques (after Horkheimer and Adorno) of modernist rationality and science. I end this chapter by looking at the work of David Harvey (1989) on postmodernity as an introduction to the world of globalisation which follows in Chapter Seven. Time space compression is the condition of postmodernity and has changed the world we live in. In the global village, *the present is all there is* (Harvey, 1989, p 240).

Globalisation has become a huge area of academic study and in Chapter Seven I outline some of the key debates in this contentious area. These include the work of Anthony Giddens (1990, 1991) who argues that modernity (note not postmodernity) is inherently globalising and this is evident in the reflexivity and disembeddedness of key institutions. Again we return to the question of time and space and the way, for Giddens, in which they have become distanciated in the late modern world. Again I question and examine the nature of rationality in the globalisation debate as Giddens outlines the way in the separation of time and space enables the distinct and rational organisations to appear and function in a way that would not be possible in pre-modern times. Globalisation can be viewed as a social, cultural, political and economic phenomena, and I will concentrate on the cultural through the work of Roland Robertson (1992) and Arjun Appadurai (1990). Appadurai provides a complex model of global cultural flows in which the imagination plays a crucial role. For example, mediascapes allow us to construct imagined lives and are the basis for the movement of peoples, but conversely, they also help us construct imagined homelands that can be the basis of new forms of ethnic conflict. These global cultural fields are the cornerstones of imagined worlds that help us to think of possible futures and broader horizons. I then go on to look at the future of the nation state, a question which is central to most debates on globalisation. In particular I focus on the work of David Held (1988, 1996) who analyses the disjuncture between the actual power of a nation state to determine its own future, and practice between state and economy at a global level. In other words, I question the power and role of the nation state in late modernity. The nation state was at the heart of the colonial project, and as such I go on to look at the relationship between nation state, globalisation and post colonialism. Again, I am cynical about the nature of identity construction in the modern globalised world, and pose the question of who has access to the benefits of this global village, if indeed it exists at all.

Global Risk Society and debates around information, misinformation and networks are the focus in the final chapter of this book. In an analysis of Beck's (1992, 1995a,b, 1996, 2000) risk thesis, I examine the ways in which 'we' exist in late modernity and the implications our modern lifestyle has for identity construction. I question the notion that we are all reflexive practitioners in a global risk society and pose the question 'who takes what risk and on whose behalf?' I believe that the opportunities offered in terms of global identity construction still remain in the realm of the privileged (Western) few and certainly in terms of risk, very few people are able to actively engage either politically or socially with the risks they are exposed to. I also engage with the idea of a network or information society primarily through the work of Castells (1996, 1997, 1998) and Lash (1994, 2002). Lash's work gives us an informed critique of the nature of information and disinformation, and again addresses a central theme of this book, the way in which the most rational formulations can have the most irrational consequences. Finally, I take a brief visit into the virtual; into cyberspace to look at the way that new information technologies may impact on our sense of self on the one hand, on the other create new hierarchies of command and control in a continuation and refinement of Foucault's disciplinary society. I conclude the book by reiterating the importance of critical and sustained self reflection in our practice and methods. I outline what I think a contemporary critical theory of society could look like. In doing so, I argue for the inclusion of interpretive sociological ideas that address imagination, meaning and emotion which are critical if we are to understand both the revolving hermeneutic of rational and irrational and identity construction in the 21st century.

2
Reason, Rationalisation and the Culture Industry

Introduction

We are constantly reminded throughout our lives that we must be reasonable, rational and weigh things up in a logical and carefully considered way. The reason as we have seen in the previous chapter is at the heart of Enlightenment thinking, and in many ways at the core of our individual freedom as human social beings. Perhaps the most important sociologist to address ideas of rationality in the social and political sphere, in our actions and systems is Max Weber. In the following sections of this chapter I want to address Weber's work and in particular I want to look at rationality in contra to the emotional and the processes of rationalisation that actually threaten to burden and imprison rather than emancipate us. How do we understand the meaning behind a certain action? Is the action social? How do we know whether a person performs a certain action because he or she has to, or wants to, or really has not thought about it consciously at all. Most importantly why would we want to know this? At the risk of letting the cat out of the bag I would suggest that often the reason for wanting to know the motive behind a certain action is to be able to deem that action rational or not, and therefore, measure it against some social norm. This, if we are to believe Foucault (1967) this is part of the project of the creation of Cartesian rational man. Rationality delivers to us the ideas of norms, of rules and processes and also gives a yardstick from which to measure the norm, and in doing so creates the idea of the pathological, the deviant, and the madman.

The Frankfurt School and particularly the work of Theodore Adorno, Max Horkheimer and Herbert Marcuse develop a particular way of analysing society that has become known as critical theory. Critical theory draws on the work of Karl Marx, Max Weber and the psychoanalytic thinking of Sigmund

9

Freud. What distinguishes critical theory from other or traditional theories, is the lack of objective distance between the subject and the object that is the focus of research. Critical theorists regard themselves as part of the research process, a process that is dialectical and self reflexive, hence the Freudian theory – critical theory is critical of itself. Thus we could ask questions such as, why have I chosen to study one particular area in a field and not another? What motivates me to do this? Built into the very notion of critical theory is a critique of positivistic sociology and the scientific method in general. In this chapter I examine Max Horkheimer and Theodor Adorno's work on mass culture and the culture industry and a logical progression from Weber's early work. Marcuse introduces us to these themes by asking for what reason and in what way is technology used in capitalist society? It could easily be used in the pursuit of social justice and change, but appears to be gaining an increasing hold over the lives of individuals. But is technology neutral, value free? Or has it become a means of social control? Horkheimer and Adorno's work is one of the greatest critiques of modern society and culture. They examine the way in which capitalism and instrumental rationality, and the elements that go with them – standardisation, rationalisation, and calculation, have a devastating effect on modern culture and encroach in a pervasive way into our private lives and our leisure time. The culture industry encourages us to line up behind those who have power and to loose our sense of self identity and join in with the crowd.

Understanding Meaning in Action

Max Weber (1921, 1978) was the first great theorist of rationality and in his work we can see how thinking about rationality has developed in tandem with processes of rationalisation, and how these have impacted on the modern world. If we look at what essentially is the text book of Weberian Sociology, *Economy and Society* (1978), the very first chapter addresses how we might define a method for the understanding of meaning in action – in other words motivation. Weber is clear that action is social when it takes into account the behaviour of others and is orientated toward this. So, to use one of Weber's examples, if I were to put up an umbrella in the street because it had just started raining, as had many others, this would not be social action, merely a reactive reaction to rain. If however, I took my umbrella down to avoid hitting someone with it, then this would be a social action. If we look at the meaning between these types of action then we have one which is based on purely reactive terms or reactive behaviour, and one which is based on the meaningful understanding of our social environment.

Weber argues that if we are to understand the relationship between social action, meaning and motivation, then we have to delineate two types of understanding (*Verstehen*). First, we have the direct observational understanding of our subjective interpretation of the meaning of an act, which for Weber includes verbal utterances. What this means is that we basically understand on face value, what we see is what we understand, and what we understand is based on observation. So, confronted by someone with a smiling face and jovial manner we will assume that certain facial expressions and utterances equate to happiness in that particular individual. A second form of understanding is that of explanatory understanding where we look at the motive behind the meaning that a social actor attaches to an action. In other words, what is the reason for someone acting in a particular way, at a precise moment, in a certain context? To illustrate this Weber uses the example of a woodchopper and someone aiming a gun. So, imagine a woodchopper in a clearing chopping wood with an axe. Imagine also, someone aiming a gun:

> ... We understand the chopping of wood or aiming of a gun in terms of motive in addition to direct observation if we know that the woodchopper is working for a wage or is chopping a supply of firewood for his own use or possibly is doing it for recreation. But he might also be working off a fit of rage, an irrational case. Similarly we understand the motive of a person aiming a gun if we know that he has been commanded to shoot as a member of a firing squad, that he is fighting against an enemy, or that he is doing it for revenge. (Weber, 1978, p 8)

The latter examples for Weber are affectually determined and based in irrational motives. The main point however, is that an action can be understood only within a sequence of events where if we understand motivation then we can understand the behaviour and actions of a social actor. Thus for Weber 'explanation requires a grasp of the complex of meaning in which an actual course of understandable action thus interpreted belongs' (Weber, 1978, p 9). This is what Weber describes as *intended* meaning.

Weber reminds us that however clear cut or transparent an action may seem in terms of meaning, the analysis of this by a sociologist can never be a causally valid interpretation. It can only be just that – *an interpretation*. In this matter Weber reveals a curiously psychoanalytic understanding of motive – 'conscious motives may well, even to the actor himself, conceal the various "motives" and "repressions" which constitute the real driving force of his action' (Weber, 1978, p 9). This is why many sociologists, including Clarke have argued that only a psychoanalytic sociology can address the motivation behind many social and political acts, particularly with regard to racism and ethnic hatred. (See Clarke, 2003; Craib, 1989, Richards, 1989, and Rustin, 1991). Weber goes on to argue that in such cases it is the task of the sociologist to be aware of this motivational situation and to analyse it 'even though it has not actually been concretely part of the conscious intention of the actor; possibly not at all, at least not fully' (Weber, 1978, p 10). It is from these ruminations that Weber presents us with four types of social action based on his conception of *formal* and *substantive* rationality, that is, and we shall return to this later. Formal rationality is a matter of *fact*, substantive rationality a matter of

value. In this small section from *Economy and Society*, Weber outlines the types
of social action:

1. *Instrumentally Rational* (*zweckrational*), that is, determined by the expectations
   as to the behaviour of objects in the environment and of other human beings;
   these expectations are used as 'conditions' or 'means' for the attainment of
   the actor's own rationally pursued and calculated ends.
2. *Value-rational* (*wertrational*), that is, determined by a conscious belief in the
   value for its own sake of some ethical, aesthetic, religious, or other form of
   behaviour, independently of its prospects of success.
3. *Affectual* (especially emotional), that is, determined by the actor's specific
   affects and feeling states.
4. *Traditional*, that is determined by ingrained habituation.
   (Weber, 1978, p 25)

Weber points out at length that these are actually *ideal types*, or models of
social action and in our everyday reality, action and actions may cross over
the boundaries of each type. It is important to try and understand what he
means by each type as it gives a clear indication of the difference between
formal and substantive rationality. If we look first at instrumentally rational
action then we can align this with a type of formal rationality. So, for Weber
'action is instrumentally rational when the end, the means, and the secondary results are all rationally taken into account and weighed. (Weber,
1978, p 26). For example, if we were to decide that we wanted to manufacture a washing machine, then we would look at the best possible means to
achieve that end, taking into consideration alternative means. This would
involve issues of raw materials, production and labour costs and profit. This
is about calculation and has nothing to do with feeling or affectual states,
ethical values about using certain types of labour force, or situating a factory
on a site of natural beauty. It is the best means to meet the optimum ends
through often ruthlessly efficient calculation.

Value rational action however is more to do with substantive wants and
needs, action is determined by beliefs in certain ethical ways of thinking,
philosophies, religious beliefs – it matters little if the end is successful. What
matters is that your action is consciously determined by your values. The
example Weber uses is thus: 'actions of persons who, regardless of possible
cost to themselves, act to put into practice their convictions of what seems to
them to be required by duty, honour, the pursuit of beauty, a religious call, a
personal loyalty, or the importance of some "cause" no matter in what it consists' (Weber, 1978, p 25). So, you could say for example that the actions of a
Good Samaritan are based on value rationality. The reality of this situation in
modern life is that these distinctions become blurred. If we take production
and consumption and use again the example of the washing machine, then
on one hand the process of production may have been worked out in a pur-

posely rational way, the means to a given end by designers, accountants, planners, etc. But also there is an ethical and environmental factor in the action: that people are more environmentally aware, more sensitive to the exploitation of the labour force and place aesthetic demands on design of household appliances. So, we get washing machines that are 'greener'; they are more energy efficient. The manufacturing process often takes place in the third world where labour can still be exploited, and products become fetishised as objects of desire. The boundary between the formal and substantive starts to blur in the mass market of consumption.

Traditional action for Weber is a matter of habit. We do it because we have always done it, and quite often we do not think about what we are doing; we just do it. This is very similar to the type of reflexivity Harold Garfinkel (1967) describes in *Studies in Ethnomethodology*. We are constantly suspending doubt about the way things are; they appear as they are because we expect them to be as they are. This is what makes life ordered and therefore rational. So, I expect, because you expect – you expect because I expect – I expect because you expect. We constantly suspend doubt and preserve our naive realism. We continue to do things because we have always done them that way and for Weber the great bulk of everyday action to which people have become habitually accustomed is of this type. Affectual action that is emotionally charged action stands on the borderline for Weber of what can be considered 'meaningful'. It is often uncontrolled and merely a reaction to some form of stimuli. When it is released as a form of conscious display of emotion, it is well on the way to being rationalised.

What Weber offers us is both a model and a method for the study of social action. We can start to try and work out the motivation that I talked of earlier behind an action; we can start to understand. There is no doubt whatsoever that these are ideal types and that in practice the types overlap considerably. I think Weber does not emphasise enough the way in which we act and are motivated by emotions. As a sociologist he starts to make the connections, but there is a complex web of meaning that has been weaved between emotion, tradition, values, religion and practice. So, for example, if we take an industrialist who appears to employ instrumentally rational methods to attain the maximum profit through a given means, there is always an element of the emotional and the irrational. There comes a point where enough money has been made to secure a future and a living, pleasure is obtained through profit and the enormous economic power generated by it – there is an element of the affectual even in what appears to be the formally rational economic sphere. There is, I would argue, also a strong link between the affectual and traditional both in social and political life. People form strong attachments to particular ways of life, to communities, either real or imagined (see Anderson, 1983). Emotional attachment is often rationalised as value systems develop, and thus we have a combination of purpose rational action, which is steeped in tradition and often argued about from the heart. This of course is the source of many ethno-national conflicts and pogroms. If we look at the political realm, something I want to explore in more detail later in this book, we have almost irrational attachments to political systems. Horkheimer and Adorno (1994) and Adorno (1991) for example have shown how fascism attracted people to act against their better judgement; instead of acting in their own rational interests people chose to become part of the fascist crowd. They were lured by something far more powerful than rational thinking; that of the emotional and affective dimensions of tradition, community, dependency and authoritarianism.

In this section we have seen how we might distinguish types of action and how they might be rational in a formal or substantive sense. There is also a hint that what appears to be a seemingly irrational feeling, or feeling state, may motivate a rational action. How does this relate to society as a whole and the analysis of modernity? In the next section I want to look at Weber's classic analysis of capitalism as a precursor to an examination of what Theodor Adorno (1947 and 1994) described as the 'culture industry'.

Capitalism, Rationality and Bureaucracy

As Derek Sayer (1991) has noted, Weber's last word on capitalism written in the last year of his life was to describe it as present wherever the industrial provision for the needs of a human group is carried out by the method of enterprise, in other words by private business. (Sayer, 1991, p 92). Weber provides many descriptions of capitalism, some broader than others (see Weber, 1930, 1978). The essence of modern capitalism, however, for Weber is its *rationality* (Brubaker, 1991, p 10). The rationality of the modern market is based in calculability – a purely instrumental action in market exchange. The use of accounting procedures and scientific calculability form the backbone of what Weber describes as the 'peculiar modern Western form of capitalism' (Weber, 1930, 1992, p 24). The idea of rational accounting and in particular double entry book keeping was a key condition for the development of Western capitalism – it enabled the development and expansion of large-scale industry and commerce based on a 'norm' of calculable rules and law. Think of this as multiple industries, private businesses and commercial developers all using the same computer package. If they used different ones they would not be able to communicate effectively. Using the same one produces an industry standard, or norm from which people can work together. In tandem with this, for Weber, calculable law enabled industry and production to become more rational. This is because, another of Weber's key concepts, the *bureaucratic* organisation and administration, allowed industry and production to escape from the fetters of tradition. In other words, the rationalisation process allows high levels of predictability and calculation based on the best means to a given end.

Bureaucratic administration is crucial to Weber's analysis of capitalism; it is the typical form of domination in the modern state (see Parkin, 1982, p 87), and is characterised (see Weber, 1991, p 196) by fixed and official jurisdictional areas ordered by rules and laws; activities are distributed in a fixed way as official duties and there develops hierarchical layers of authority all of which are based, and this is very important, on written documents – the rule book. Organisation is based on domination by knowledge, and for Weber, this is what makes bureaucracy specifically and formally rational (Schroeder, 1992, p 115). All aspects of modern social life are subject to bureaucratisation including the church, the state, and as we have seen, the economic sphere. The formalisation of bureaucratic rules is as Brubaker (1991) notes, expressed in a distinctive ethos:

> Devoted to 'impersonal and functional purposes', the bureaucratic official acts in a spirit of formalistic impersonality… without hatred or passion, and hence without affection or enthusiasm… without regard for persons. (Brubaker, 1991, p 21)

Bureaucracy is therefore an intrinsic part of modern Western capitalism. It is formally rational because of the very fact of its impersonal formalism; because it is based in knowledge and calculation, and finally, because it is based in fact not value. It is instrumental in its rationality – people become faceless, they become objects. This transposes from economic to political spheres and can be seen in what Weber describes as the *legal rational domination* of the modern state, the state being defined by a set of social institutions based on law and 'officialdom'. The government, local government, the judiciary and the police force all use formal rules and procedures to administer the state. In the paper *The Social Psychology of World Religions*, Weber describes the rationality of legal authority in the modern state: 'submission under legal authority is based upon and impersonal bond to the generally defined and functional law of office… [And] is fixed by rationally established norms, by enactments, decrees, and regulations' (Weber, 1991, p 229).

So, we have rather a pessimistic view of the world where wonder and magic have disappeared and have been replaced by the ruthless onslaught of a formally rational and instrumental type of capitalism – an *iron cage* where substantive wants and needs are ignored in the relentless drive for profit, where people are alienated and become objects to be manipulated in a system of ruthless calculation. The question is how did we arrive at such a state? What is it that has made this peculiar form of Western capitalism so successful and long lived? The answer for Weber is to be found in what is probably his most famous, controversial and important work: *Die Protestantische Ethik und der Geist des Kapitalismus*. (1904–5, 1930, 1992).

The Protestant Ethic and the Spirit of Capitalism

> The Puritan wanted to work in a calling; we are forced to do so. For when asceticism was carried out of monastic cells into everyday life, and began to

dominate world reality, it did its part in building the tremendous cosmos of the modern economic order. (Weber, 1992, p 181).

In *The Protestant Ethic and Spirit of Capitalism*, as Reinhard Bendix (1966) has noted, Weber traced the influence of religion on the action and behaviour of 'men', and in doing so, he directly challenged Karl Marx's ideas that 'man's' consciousness is determined by social class. The process of rationalisation that we have examined in the previous section of this chapter is not a gradual process according to Weber, but required some kind of breakthrough, a change in ways of thinking and attitude. It is in the *Protestant Ethic* that Weber describes this change: the psychological internalisation of a way of thinking – 'worldly asceticism', provides a decisive 'impetus' in the development of the economic and social structure of the Western world. In this multi-layered analysis of religion and the development of capitalism, Weber describes a process of inner rationalisation towards the world of work and the elimination of magic and ritual from everyday life. Brubaker (1991) elucidates:

> The logical and psychological pressures generated by the ideas of Luther and Calvin led to the development of what Weber calls 'worldly asceticism'... the inner rationalisation of the personality in the direction of unrelenting work and methodical self control, Weber argues, provides a decisive impetus to the development of modern industrial capitalism. (Brubaker, 1991, p 24)

There is, in some sense here the notion of formal rationality supplanting the substantive in the inner rationality of Protestantism. What Weber noticed was that with spread of Protestantism and particularly in the teaching of John Calvin (1509–64), certain ways of thinking and being favoured the spread of the rational pursuit of economic gain and therefore capitalism. These key ideas in Calvin's teaching included the notion of *predestination*; the idea of work as a *calling*; and the rejection of the sensuous and emotional elements of culture which led to the development of work ethic that placed an emphasis on rational accumulation, self control and calculability. The Calvinist doctrine of predestination basically relates to man's state of grace in relation to God. This state of grace is predestined by God's choice and cannot be changed – we are quite literally saved or damned – you can neither loose it nor attain it:

> There was not only no magical means of attaining the grace of God for those to whom God had decided to deny it, but no means whatever. Combined with the harsh doctrines of absolute transendentality of God and the corruption of everything pertaining to the flesh, the inner isolation of the individual contains, on the one hand, the reason for the entirely negative attitude of Puritanism to all sensuous and emotional elements in culture and in religion, because they are of no use toward salvation and promote sentimental illusions and idolatrous superstitions. (Weber, 1992, p 105).

In other words, we are either in God's grace or not – saved or damned and there is nothing that can be done to save this situation or change it, therefore pessimistically there is no point in trying to change the situation. This of course caused great anxiety – *salvation anxiety*, as there was no way of knowing whether you were saved or damned. Despite this, in the teachings of Calvin all men were to assume themselves chosen; doubt was seen as temptation of the devil and thus all the magical elements of attaining salvation were quashed. Life was rationalised and this for Weber explained the affinity between Calvinism and the spirit of capitalism particularly when viewed in tandem with the notion of a *calling*. The idea of work as a *calling* in Protestantism took religious practice out of the church and into everyday activities. Idleness was considered a deadly sin, whereas to work in your calling for glory of God was proof of a man's state of grace. Every hour wasted was an hour taken away from this devotion to God. If work was an act of worship, then to do well in one's work was a sign of God's grace. The Puritan ascetic was then to lead a simple hardworking life, living on a simple diet, shunning the accumulation of personal material objects, luxuries, and to work hard in one's calling for the grace of God. The ascetic shunned all forms of spontaneous enjoyment in life, and as Weber notes: 'the Puritan idea of the calling and the premium it placed upon ascetic conduct was bound directly to influence the development of a capitalistic way of life' (Weber, 1992, p 166).

There is a paradox if we look at the acquisition of wealth and material things. The real objection to the accumulation of wealth was not in the accumulation itself but in the notion that wealth may lead to idleness and temptations of the flesh. As I have mentioned, wasting time and idleness were seen as one of the deadliest sins, but as a performance of a calling, it was not only morally permissible, but also a matter of duty. The specific forms and types of a calling for Weber heralded a division of labour and specifically justified the activities of the businessman. Although Puritanism shunned the ownership of material things, to invest and reinvest in one's calling is to invest in the glory of God, and thus we have the basis of investment banking, in rational economic accumulation, in capitalism:

> When the limitation of consumption is combined with this release of acquisitive activity, the inevitable practical result is obvious: accumulation of capital through ascetic compulsion to save. The restraints which were imposed upon the consumption of wealth naturally served to increase it by making possible the productive investment of capital. (Weber, 1992, p 172).

For Weber, the Puritan outlook quite simply stood at the cradle of modern economic man. The businessman blessed with God's grace could rest easy at night knowing that religious asceticism provided him with a sober and willing workforce; the workers calling meant that their job was their life's purpose and willed by God. There was also, for Weber, a comforting assurance for the middle class businessman, in that the unequal distribution of goods in the world was a special dispensation of Divine Providence. Poor people were only obedient to God when they remained poor and for Weber this was at the heart of some of the basic ideas of the capitalist economy. For Weber, one of the fundamental elements of the spirit of modern capitalism and modern culture – that is rational conduct on the basis of a *calling*, developed out of Christian asceticism. Modern capitalism however, as we have seen, becomes wholly rational without the religious element because the end, the means and the alternatives are rationally taken into account and weighed up.

Weber concludes *The Protestant Ethic and the Spirit of Capitalism* with some seemly pessimistic comments on the future of modern society. We are born into a machine, the Puritan wanted to work in a calling, we are forced to do so. The modern economic order is bound to the technical and economic conditions of machine production which determines the lives all individuals – 'perhaps it will so determine them until the last ton of fossilised coal is burnt' (Weber, 1992, p 181). It is at this point that Weber talks of the 'iron cage' which has been so often cited by sociologists:

> No one knows who will live in this iron cage in the future, or whether at the end of this tremendous development entirely new prophets will arise, or there will be a great rebirth of old ideas and ideals, or, if neither, mechanised petrification, embellished with a sort of convulsive self-importance. For of the last stage of cultural development, it might well be truly said: 'Specialists without spirit, sensualists without heart; this nullity imagines that it has attained a level of civilization never before achieved' (Weber, 1992, p 182).

These are damning words for the processes of rationalisation and production of material things. For Max Weber material goods have gained an inexorable power over the lives of people, something that had never been seen at the start of the twentieth century. Capitalism no longer needs the spirit of religious asceticism, we are all obsessed with material goods that should, says Weber, after Baxter, only rest on our shoulders like a cloak. In other words, we should be able to cast the material away, but the cloak indeed has become an iron cage. Our lives revolve around the production, consumption and desiring of goods, and rational banking systems, credit and loans finance our obsessions.

It is not difficult to criticise Weber with the hindsight we have now, and indeed Anthony Giddens provides a useful overview of some of these criticisms in the introduction to the 1992 edition of the book the summary of which follows. First, that Weber's characterisation of Protestantism was in some sense faulty; that he was mistaken in his interpretation of the idea of a *calling*, and that in fact Calvinist ethics were actually anti-capitalist. Second, Weber misinterpreted Catholic doctrine, did not study it in any detail and asserted that Catholicism actually involved elements favourable to capitalism. Third, Weber's links between Puritanism and modern capitalism were not based on any cogent empirical materials. Fourth, Weber was not justified in drawing such a sharp line between modern and earlier types of capitalism – Weber slanted his account of modern capitalism to conform to the elements of Puritanism he focused on, and finally Weber was mistaken in making some form of causal relationship between Puritanism and modern capitalism – there was no causal relationship (Giddens, 1976 in Weber 1992). Giddens notes, however, that Weber's critics are often self contradictory in their claims, but there is a problem in his work, particularly with the distinctiveness of the notion of a calling and the lack of affinity between Catholicism and organised entrepreneurial activity. Despite this, Gidden's notes that it would take a sociologist with the scholarly range of Max Weber to untangle the relationship between world religions and rationalisation of culture if there were to be any hope of success.

Frank Parkin (1982) gives us a slightly different position in appraising the *Protestant Ethic*. He argues that there is both a strong and weak thesis in Weber's works, the strong thesis being that 'Calvinist teachings were an active, determinate force in the creation of the capitalist spirit' (Parkin, 1982, p 43). In other words, as Giddens noted, there appears a strong causal link between the protestant ethic and the idea of a calling, and the capitalist mindset. The weak thesis seems more probable – That the Puritan ethic did not give rise to capitalism but the two outlooks were in harmony with each other – 'the capitalist spirit can be shown to have a special affinity with the Protestant ethic, but not that it was born from it' (Parkin, 1982, p 43). The real significance for Parkin is that the Calvinist outlook did not hamper the development of the rational economic mentality. This is a view supported by Giddens (1971) in *Capitalism and Modern Social Theory* where he argues that there is an 'elective affinity' between certain Calvinist beliefs and the activity associated with modern capitalism. Indeed for Giddens, 'The distinctive feature of the work is that it seeks to demonstrate that the rationalisation of economic life characteristic of modern capitalism connects with *irrational* value commitments' (Giddens, 1971, p 131).

Bryan Turner (1996) argues that there is strong evidence to suggest that Weber's own life and sociology were influenced by his own commitment to religion. Turner suggests that Weber really did have a 'conviction that any genuine adherence to religious principles was ruled out by the processes of rationalisation and secularisation in modern society' (Turner, 1996, p 45). Indeed for Turner, on the one hand Weber's sociology of religion forms the key to his sociology as a whole. On the other we have a dark vision of religion as something that has gone and which forms the backdrop to Weber's seemingly pessimistic vision of capitalism. Indeed for Turner:

> *The Protestant Ethic and the Spirit of Capitalism* has often been taken to be an anti-materialist thesis demonstrating the autonomy of religious values from economic circumstances. In fact, these two essays provide a cultural history of the *failure* of

spiritual values to maintain their own religious authenticity and authority. (Turner, 1996, p 45)

Thus, for Turner, the spirit of capitalism actually represented the collapse of a genuine religious quest for personal salvation, rather than the triumph of Protestantism over secular practices. As Wolfgang Mommsen (1992) notes, when Weber presented the results of this study at the University of Vienna under the title 'A positive critique of the materialist view of history', he did so with highly ambivalent feelings – 'he never claimed that his *Protestant Ethic* thesis completely answered the question of how and why industrial capitalism arose' (Mommsen, 1992, p 57). One of the fundamentally important things about Weber's sociology is that it starts to address human motivation rather than wholly concentrating on social structure as we see in Marxism. This is a point that Alan Swingewood (2000) makes among others:

> The fundamental issue between Marxism and Weber's sociology lies ultimately in Weber's rejection of the Marxist philosophy of history, the view that capitalism necessarily develops through the workings of objective, economic laws determined by material forces which effectively render the subjective component – human action – irrelevant. (Swingewood, 2000, p 97)

For Swingewood, Weber recognises that change is change through human actions – human subjects are motivated in certain ways for differing reasons and it is this motivational structure of action which constitutes the spirit of capitalism and human beings are not just passive objects affected by impersonal forces. In addition there is also evidence to suggest, as Sayer (1991) argues, that Weber anticipated much of the essence of the work of latter writers including Foucault (1967) and Elias (1982), particularly if we think of the notion of leading an ethical way of life and the link this has with the construction of self and identity. As Sayer notes, the sect for Weber operated in much the same way as the panopticon, and the psychological internalisation of Puritan discipline which went hand in hand with the Protestant gaze and the notion of living a hardworking, simple, disciplined, and regulated, but ethical life. And of course there is the disciplining of the Puritan body.

In mentioning how Weber may have anticipated some of the thinking of more contemporary writers I want to switch the line of argumentation in this chapter to what Weber has contributed to sociological thinking and analysis rather than whether he was right or not. There are several elements that have been crucial for development of critical theory. First, there is no doubt that Weber's contribution to method is immense. His emphasis on understanding the meaning behind action shifts the focus of analysis away from the merely structural (although this is important) to the understanding of motivation. Understanding motivation is important for sociologist as we are unlikely to get any further with our endeavours if we can only explain *how* and not *why* social phenomena occur. Second, there is an undeniable link in Weber's social analysis between the concept of rationality and the creation of the self. This, as I have already mentioned, anticipated certainly the work of Foucault on the creation of Cartesian rational man, and also the notion of disciplinary society and technologies of the self. Weber's emphasis on the underlying ethic, the methodical self control and the disciplined body of the Puritan is arguably a precursor to Foucault's docile subject. Third, we start to see the development of a sociology of emotion when we think about the links between affectual, traditional, instrumental and value rational action. This is particularly the case if we look at the relationship between emotion and attachment to ways of life, to communities whether they be religious or secular, and the way in which emotional attachment is often rationalised as a value system develops. Fourth, Weber's view of capitalism introduces us to disenchantment with the world and the idea that rationality is not always a good thing. Rule books, written documents, calculation, law, administration and bureaucracy have done away with magic and wonder and positively provide the self with a sense of certainty, but as we know, nothing is certain. Finally for me, the greatest contribution Weber has made to critical theory is the insight that he provided into the obsessional basis of capitalist (il)logic, our tremendous obsession with material things, the consuming passions of the market place, and the manipulation of products and people as objects in the market place. This in many ways anticipated critiques of the culture industry, the sociology of consumption, of lifestyle and of course critiques of modernity and postmodernity.

So, we could view Weber in several ways. First, his pessimism, not just in the *Protestant Ethic* but also in his later writing may reflect the time that he lived in. After all, Weber did live long enough to see the terrible carnage of the First World War, the millions of people dead in trench warfare, the continuous use of technological industrial means to produce the weapons of war, in fact, a new type of war – total war. It is hard to see how anyone can be optimistic after this kind of experience. Second, we could argue that Weber was being quite realistic about the way in which our lives become dominated not so much by rationalisation, but by a culture of materialistic acquisition. And, finally, as Herbert Marcuse (1968) has suggested, it could be that Weber was issuing us with a fateful warning of the shape of things to come – 'and this you call reason?' In this next section I want to move on and look at Marcuse's critique of Weber to try and further our understanding of the relationship between reason, rationality and capitalism.

And This You Call Reason?

Herbert Marcuse (1968) offers one of the most interesting critiques of Weber's work. In *Negations*, Marcuse argues that industrialism and capitalism are problematic in Weber's work in two respects: first, the idea that they are the fate of the West and the decisive realisations of Western rationality, and second as the contemporary fate of Germany. It is the first problem I want to concentrate on in this section as it offers a critical dissection of the relationship between reason and capitalism through that all pervasive term *rationality*.

Reading Weber, Marcuse argues that rationality becomes the condition of profitability. This condition of profitability is orientated towards systematic calculation and capital accounting. The basis of this rationality is abstraction (Marcuse, 1968, p 205). That is, abstraction in the sense that everything is reduced to measure – quantities rather than qualities, and in this sense reason becomes technical, in as much as reason is reduced to the production and transformation of materials and people through the methodical scientific method. For Marcuse, the forms of capitalist rationality ascribed by Weber have disappeared and disintegrated. Marcuse gives the example of inner worldly asceticism which is no longer a motivating force in late capitalism. Indeed for Marcuse the disintegration of these forms have shone a very different light on the rationality of capitalistic industrialisation – in the light of *irrationality*. For Marcuse:

> In the unfolding of capitalist rationality, irrationality becomes reason: reason as frantic development of productivity. Conquest of nature, enlargement of the mass of goods (and their accessibility for broad strata of the population); irrational because higher productivity, domination of nature, and social wealth become destructive forces. (Marcuse, 1968, p 207)

For Marcuse, this destruction is both figurative, in as much as we see the destruction of 'so called higher cultural values', but also we see literal destruction in that the struggle for existence intensifies, particularly for Marcuse both within nation-states and internationally as the pent-up aggression is discharged. Marcuse is scathing in his critique of Weber, arguing that although Weber's value free concept of capitalist rationality is a critical concept – critical of pure science and reification, the critique stops there and accepts the inevitable, the inexorable and ignores any possible alternatives. The problem, argues Marcuse, lies in Weber's identification with the bourgeoisie and with bourgeoisie reason – the concept of reason remains tied to its origin. Max Weber's analysis of capitalism argues Marcuse, becomes an analysis of forms of domination. Industrialisation is the fate of the modern world and the main question is what is the most rational form of dominating industrialisation and hence society? How does domination figure in Weber's model?

Marcuse outlines succinctly Weber's thesis on reason and rationality. There are two conditions, or historical facts that formal rationality develops out of and these are the conditions for capitalism. First, we have *private enterprise*, and second *free labour*, that is a class who are forced to sell their labour or starve. These two forces enter into what we call formal reason. Capitalism expands as there is competitive struggle between those forced to sell their labour, entrepreneurs, and nation-states, and thus for Weber (according to Marcuse):

> The contemporary phase of capitalism is dominated by national power politics: capitalism is imperialism. But its administration remains formally rational, i.e. bureaucratic domination. It administers the control of men by things; rational, 'value free' technology is the separation of man from the means of production and his subordination to technical efficiency and necessity – all within the framework of private enterprise. (Marcuse, 1968, p 222)

For Marcuse, technical reason produces enslavement. It is the subordination of men to technology which becomes domination as formal (technical) rationality turns into political rationality. It is at this point argues Marcuse that Weber's analysis becomes self criticism. Weber is blinded by identifying technical reason with bourgeois reason which prevents him from seeing that it is not technical reason *per se* that enslaves us, but the reason of domination. In others words, technical reason can just as much be used to emancipate us as enslave us, depending on the way in which it is used. What Weber sees as fate, Marcuse sees as domination of man over man. The concept of technical reason is ideological; it is the domination of man and nature. It is a form of both social control and control over our natural environment – methodical, calculated, calculating control (Marcuse, 1968, p 224). Of course, it is ideological because someone somewhere decides how, why, and when technology is used, for what purposes, and to what ends. Who decides that the cutting edge of modern scientific calculability is invested in producing state of the art weapons of mass destruction – atom bombs, hydrogen bombs, cluster bombs? The reasoning behind this is political, value laden, ideological – technology can just as easily be used to make life better for people.

Marcuse also notes that things have changed, the private entrepreneur no longer answers to economic rationality but to his or herself, free labour is no longer enslaved by the threat of hunger – people enjoy a much better standard of living. The market is dominated by political and economic monopolies, but even so, since Marcuse's time of writing, monopolies themselves are subject to regulation. This critique was actually written in the 1930's although not published until 1968. Marcuse went on to write extensively about the evils of mass technology and forms of control in *One Dimensional Man* (1964) We have seen massive improvements in computing, communication and the internet that have extended the Western market into the global world. The machine is not neutral; it is guided by ruling and political interests. Indeed for Marcuse 'technical reason is the social ruling of a given society and can be changed in its very structure. As technical reason, it can become the technique of liberation' (Marcuse, 1968, p 225).

At about the same time that Marcuse was writing his critique of Weber and of formal rationality, his colleagues in the Frankfurt School were developing critical theory through a critique of culture. Max Horkheimer and Theodor Adorno (1994) were starting to develop their ideas on the relationship between Enlightenment ideals, formal rationality and what they were to term the 'Culture Industry'. The idea of the Culture Industry first appeared in *Dialectic of Enlightenment* (1947, 1994) and later in the paper by Adorno the *Culture Industry Reconsidered*. (1967, Trans 1975)

The Culture Industry

So, we must ask ourselves what is the result of this obsession with material things, of formal rationality and instrumental reason? The most scathing attack on the long term effects of instrumental reason and capitalism on culture are made by Horkheimer and Adorno (1994) in *Dialectic of Enlightenment* and Adorno in numerous other essays. Their basic thesis is that the culture industry produces and dictates mass consumption; cultural products are not a result of individual needs but are imposed on the individual from above through mass markets, advertising and the media. We have the mass standardised supermarket labels selling us cultural products whilst destroying the local, the historical and 'higher' forms of art and music. Music for example, is no longer 'lived', but simply a performance. Horkheimer and Adorno (1994) use the term 'culture industry' to differentiate their thinking from that of mass culture. The term mass culture suggests that culture actually emanates in some way from the masses, a bottom up approach if you like. The culture industry is far from this, it is top down, it imposes on, and manipulates the masses once integrated into capitalism – its goal is the production of goods that are profitable and consumable (Held, 1990, p 91).

For Horkheimer and Adorno any sociological theory that maintains that the dissolution of established religion, the end of pre-capitalism combined with technological and social differentiation and specialism has led to cultural chaos, is quite simply wrong:

'For culture now impresses the same stamp on everything. Films, radio and magazines make up a system which is uniform as a whole and in every part' (Horkheimer and Adorno, 1994, p 120). Horkheimer and Adorno in the opening paragraphs of the *Culture Industry* point to modern architecture, arguing that the vast concrete housing estates that seem as if they offer the occupants independent living and sanitary accommodation, actually make them more subservient to capitalism. As consumers and producers that are fitted into neat little units and well organised complexes, they simply become part of the culture industry rather than individuals. Controversially, Horkheimer and Adorno argue that films, movies, radio, no longer need claim to be art; they are industries, businesses that merely produce rubbish in a deliberate and calculated way. There is no truth in the claim that standards are based on consumers' needs, rather, for Horkheimer and Adorno they are based on manipulation and a 'retroactive' need in which the unity of system is placed at the centre of importance and steadily grows stronger. Again we can look back and see flashes of Marx and Weber in Horkheimer and Adorno's work and also certain symmetry with Marcuse – the culture industry is based on technology as business rather than art. Technology acquires power over society, but this is the power of those who hold economic power over society, and thus technology is a form of domination. Standardisation and mass production lead to a breakdown in the distinction between work and social system. Everyone and everything becomes co-dependent – economically interwoven – the film makers on the banks, the banks on the economy, the consumer on the film company and the film company on the electric company. The differentiation of films, magazines and radio does not depend on subject matter, but on labelling and classifying customers. Thus for Horkheimer and Adorno, the public is offered a hierarchical range of mass produced products of varying quality, thus advancing the rule of complete quantification. (Horkheimer and Adorno, 1994, p 123). People behave in accordance with their 'type' and must consume the products within the categories designated to them. The consumer becomes a number or a statistic within mass market research and ultimately a product of the propaganda of the culture industry. Horkheimer and Adorno give the example of cars and films. The difference between various forms of motor car is illusory, because in the end they are all the same, just different forms of the same product. Films too are formulaic, just a different arrangement of the number of stars, and the use of technology and labour. The important thing is (and the universal criteria of merit) the amount of 'conspicuous production' – of blatant cash investment. (Horkheimer and Adorno, 1994, p 125).

Pessimistically, Horkheimer and Adorno argue that real life is becoming indistinguishable from the movies. The film maker duplicates everyday life in an effort to create an illusion that the outside world is a continuation of the movie. This leaves no room for the imagination or any form of reflection by the audience. The movies become so formulaic that the viewer no longer has to guess the plot or think about what is happening. But is this really pessimistic? I feel it is true to say that more recently we have seen movies that reflect the paranoid nature of American society. Action hero's like Bruce Willis in *Die Hard*, Schwarzenegger, Sylvester Stallone – Rambo, Jean Claude Van Damme, all acting out and reworking to reverse the humiliation of Vietnam, and then the massive attack on the American psyche that was September 11th (See Clarke and Hoggett, 2004). Jason Cowley (2001) has noted how American culture is essentially an entertainment culture which is addicted to narratives of catastrophe in everything from film to computer games. Fiction becomes fact – Tom Clancy, the best selling author of fiction had already described the hijacking by Arab militants of civilian planes to use as weapons against the American people well before Sept 11th in his book the *Sum of All Fears*. The Culture industry is characterised by sameness, repetition and constantly cheats the consumer of what is promises. The destruction of the World Trade

Centre was a terrible event in world history, a terrible shock to the American psyche and brought terrible trauma to the ordinary people of New York. Stallone, Willis and Van Damme were not there to protect the ordinary person in the street, yet we have been brought up to believe in the omnipotent power of the action hero through constant repetition in films – we were cheated by the culture industry as the film no longer became an extension of real life.

For Horkheimer and Adorno, the stronger the position of the culture industry, the more it controls and disciplines the subject:

> In the culture industry the individual is an illusion not merely because of the standardisation of the means of production. He is tolerated only so long as his complete identification with the generality is unquestioned. Pseudo individuality is rife: from the standardised jazz improvisation to the exceptional film star whose hair curls over her eye to demonstrate her originality. What is individual is no more than the generality's power to stamp the accidental detail so firmly that it is accepted as such. (Horkheimer and Adorno, 1994, 155).

In other words people cease to be individuals and become part of the sameness that is the culture industry – they exist in a space where sameness and generality reign – people become objects to be manipulated. We are tricked into thinking that old material is new, but has merely been given a gloss over. It is all but standardised stuff which is endlessly repeated and plugged, such is the style (or lack of) of the culture industry. Horkheimer and Adorno end their original essay on the culture industry with a particularly gloomy observation. Personality means little anymore, it is signified by gleaming white teeth and freedom from odour and emotion – 'The triumph of advertising in the culture industry is that consumers feel compelled to buy and use products even though they see through them' (Horkheimer and Adorno, 1994, p 167).

The *Culture Industry* is a difficult essay to read and to follow. Adorno makes clearer some of the main arguments in his later paper *The Culture Industry Reconsidered* (Trans 1967). Adorno talks of the culture industry as something that fuses the old and familiar into something that appears to have a new quality. It consists of branches or structures that order themselves in to a system 'almost with no gap'. This is made possible by new technologies as well as economic and administrative concentration. If we go back to Weber for a minute then this is starting to sound very familiar – these are of course the tenets of formal instrumental rationality. The culture industry integrates its consumers from above, and indeed it seems justified for Weber to issue his fateful warning 'and this you call reason' – as Adorno argues 'the masses are not primary, but secondary; they are the object of calculation, an appendage of the machinery' (Adorno in Bronner and Kellner, 1989, p 129). Adorno reiterates that the expression *industry* should not be taken too literally – it is the actual *standardization* of the thing itself that is important and the processes of *rationalization* of distribution rather than production. The defence of the culture industry would maintain that its spirit (which for Adorno is an ideology) provides some kind of order in a world of chaos. It provides human beings with a standard by which to orientate themselves, but the opposite is the case for Adorno, in that what one imagines is preserved by the culture industry, is actually destroyed by it: 'The colour film demolishes the genial old tavern to a greater extent than bombs ever could: the film exterminates its imago. No homeland can survive being processed by films which celebrate it, and which thereby turn the unique character on which it thrives into an interchangeable sameness' (Bronner and Kellner, 1989, p 132).

The problem for Adorno is that the culture industry devalues what he calls high art in the process of standardisation and reproduction and blurs the long standing gap between high and low forms of art. The systematic ordering and rationalisation hinders and quells artistic talent both from the point of view of the artist and admirer who becomes consumer. The most sinister and thoroughly intrusive part of the culture industry is that it neither provides a guide for a blissful life or a new art of moral responsibility. What it does do however, is to encourage us to toe the line behind those who have power and to foster a consensus behind blind authority. In this sense the culture industry dis-empowers the individual who surrenders to the ideologically driven spirit of the machine – to dependence and servitude. The self referential nature of the culture industry causes an illusion that the world really is in the same kind of order that is suggested by the industry – life becomes like films and the individual is cheated out of his or her happiness in pursuit of this illusion. This is anti–Enlightenment, and anti–freedom, and, as Horkheimer and Adorno note, *mass deception*.

So, Adorno's critique of radio, film, astrology and music has been subsumed under the culture industry thesis. It should be noted that this is a critique of an over-administered, instrumental and standardised world, not a critique of popular culture *per se* which we noted for Adorno is only popular when it comes from the bottom up. Immediately we can see two problems with Horkheimer and Adorno's work. At the very base level they seem to assume that we are passive receptors or cultural dupes, and that we are unable to discern, or are undiscerning in our cultural choices, if in fact we make any choices at all. At another level, Adorno in particular seems to expounding some form of cultural snobbery in which only higher forms of culture, art, and music represent real culture; the rest is just mindless rubbish. But, as Simon Jarvis (1998) has noted 'If Adorno's theory of the culture industry presented us with dupes on the one hand and conspirators on the other it would indeed be trivial, because the trick would only need to be exposed to be brought to an end' (Jarvis, 1998, p 74). Seeing through one aspect of the culture industry is easy enough – we might be cynical about formulaic serial war films for example, but seeing through the culture industry as a whole is much harder as it is systematic illusion embedded in social relations. Again as Jarvis notes, participation in the culture industry is often based on a well-founded sense that consumers will be socially excluded if they fail to do so. Think of the images portrayed in magazines – the right style, the right shape, the right look. This exerts tremendous psychological pressure particularly in a sense of the creation of self in relation to others. The culture industry relies on avid rather than passive consumers who extend work time into leisure time. Again Jarvis illustrates:

> Under late capitalism it cost less effort to extend habits of mechanical activity into leisure time than it does to bring such mechanical activity to a halt. This goes both for intellectual and manual labour. For Adorno, the hobbyist's curiosity is positivism at play. The listener with an encyclopaedic recall of available recorded performances but with little understanding of music which can be heard on them is the leisure counterpart, as it were, of the professional biographer cataloguing textual variants with a labour out of all proportion to their conceivable interest. (Jarvis, 1998, p 75).

I am not sure if this is still not a form of cultural snobbery but it is a pertinent and timely warning of the encroachment of our working life into our leisure time and home life. Think particularly of the wide scale use of home computers. These are not only used to communicate (via e-mail), seek information (via the Web), play games and listen to music, but also as means of working from home. It is a two-sided coin, in that working from home may be more convenient for the employee, more cost effective for the employer – saving on lighting, heating and office space, but ultimately the home worker works longer hours extending the mechanical activity of work into leisure time.

Popular music argues Adorno, is like a multiple choice questionnaire, but with no right answer, and as long as the individual chooses, the culture industry exists and is sustained (see Held, 1980, p 100). According to Max Paddison (1996), Adorno's analysis of popular music is seen as the least convincing of his critique of Western twentieth century music. This is for much the same reasons as above, in that Adorno is perceived as ill-informed, prejudiced and dogmatic. His analysis divides music into two – serious and popular music. Whilst popular music is but a commodity, part of the structure of the culture industry, serious music is critical and self reflexive and thus becomes alienated from society as it refuses to take itself as a commodity object. But of course the term popular music is but a blanket term, covering the many types of music – usually the types that Adorno disliked. Paddison (1996) argues that Adorno's theory may indeed though contain some hidden potential which allows for a radical and critical popular music. The problem is though that it will immediately come upon the contradiction that is central to Adorno's argument – that a music that refuses to recognise itself as a commodity suffers the fate of alienation from society. (See Paddison, 1996 for an extremely clear exposition of Adorno's work on music).

Summary

In this chapter we have explored the relationship between meaning, human action, reason and wider society through the culture industry. The works of Weber are still pertinent today and have provided a fateful warning about the dangers of becoming overly obsessed with material things. Weber's sociology gives us an insight into types of social action and the underlying motive behind them. More importantly he was the first sociologist to study how a seemingly irrational idea or feeling becomes rationalised at a societal level. In his analysis of the peculiar specific form of Western capitalism, Weber in many ways anticipated the thinking of latter writers such as Foucault. There is an undeniable link in Weber's analysis of the link between rationality and the creation of the self particularly in his analysis of the *Protestant Ethic* and the self disciplinary measures undertaken by the Puritan. The greatest contribution Weber has made to critical sociological theory, as I have argued, is his insight into the obsessional basis of the logic of capitalism. Although Marcuse took Weber to task about his conceptions of rationality, Marcuse was able to see that Weber's ironic statements were tantamount to a fateful warning of one possible development of modern capitalism.

Marcuse of course introduces us to some of the central themes in the critical theory of the Frankfurt Institute for Social Research: the frantic development of production and control of man over nature, the critique of positivism and of science in general and the stealth like intrusion of irrationality into the capitalist social world. We start to see the domination of men by technology. The concept of technological reason is ideological and value based. After all technology can just as easily be used a form of emancipation rather than oppression. It is the use that technology is put to and by whom that makes the reasoning behind it ideological, and therefore a form of social control in which men dominate men and 'man' dominates nature. The work of the Frankfurt School becomes a massive critique of Enlightenment ideals, of the very notion of rationality and of popular culture. I have only touched on Adorno's huge literature here and of course the classic essay *The Culture Industry Reconsidered* to demonstrate the way in which theory addresses our everyday lives, and the way in which the application of a critical theory can show how culture is permeated by ideology and illusional dynamics that often have dramatic effects on the construction of self. Are we products of our own interests or are we simply pseudo individuals who have become manipulated by the constant ravages of the onslaught of capitalism in the mass culture market? Where do we draw the line between art for art's sake, and art merely as technological reason? I think that Adorno in particular goes some way to answering these questions in his writings on popular culture, but there are many gaps left open – not least that in Adorno's system of things the very radical nature of some forms of art, music, film will mean that they are always excluded from the mainstream, but perhaps that is where they want to be and stay. Therefore remaining critical and reflexive in opposition to standardisation and mass production – or, is this just another form of elitism?

In the following chapter I want to continue to look at the critical theory of the Frankfurt School and the idea that rationality is not always a good thing – indeed we may have witnessed the end of Enlightenment. The Enlightenment is far from freeing people and encouraging people to think for themselves. After Immanuel Kant (1784) Enlightenment is man's release from his self incurred tutelage. Tutelage is man's inability to make use of his understanding without direction from another. For Kant we should 'Have courage to use our own reason'; that is the motto of enlightenment. At the heart of Enlightenment thinking is the notion of freedom – freedom of speech, freedom of thought, freedom from tyrannical regimes, freedom from religious doctrines and perse-cution. In 1944 Max Horkheimer and Theodor Adorno introduced their seminal work *Dialectic of Enlightenment* with the following statement: 'In the most general sense of progressive thought, the Enlightenment has always aimed at liberating men from fear and establishing their sovereignty. Yet the fully enlightened earth radiates disaster triumphant' (Horkheimer and Adorno, 1994, p 3) The Enlightenment, rather than freeing people, has created totalitarian regimes through the principles of control, order and domination and this is nowhere better demonstrated, as we have seen in the culture indus-try which for Horkheimer and Adorno is a passive form of social control. For Horkheimer and Adorno, and indeed the whole of the Frankfurt School the central question in their social research was: 'Why is mankind, instead of entering into a truly humane condition, sinking into new forms of barbarism?' This is still a pertinent question today and Horkheimer and Adorno attempt to answer it through a critical welding of the work of Marx, Weber and Freud in what was really the first serious attempt to introduce psychoanalysis into social and political theory and thought.

Summary of Key Concepts and Terms

Rationality

Formal: Rationality is a matter of fact, it is about the most efficient means to a given ends and is based in accounting and calculation.

Substantive: Substantive rationality is a matter of value; it is about human wants, needs and desires and is based on ethical, aesthetic, religious and cultural beliefs.

Social Action

Reactive Action: Reacting directly to stimuli; for example putting up an umbrella if it starts raining.

(cont'd)

Social Action: An action is social when it takes into account the behaviour of others and is orientated towards this, so taking down my umbrella to avoid hitting someone is social.

Understanding the meaning in action: *Verstehen*: Two types:

Direct understanding: Taking things on face value. The direct observational understanding of the subjective meaning of an act.

Explanatory understanding: Looking at the motive behind the meaning that a social actor attaches to an action. Thus we gain insight into the *intended* meaning behind an action

Types of Social Action

Instrumentally Rational (*zweckrational*), that is, determined by the expectations as to the behaviour of objects in the environment and of other human beings; these expectations are used as 'conditions' or 'means' for the attainment of the actor's own rationally pursued and calculated ends.

Value-rational (*wertrational*), that is, determined by a conscious belief in the value for its own sake of some ethical, aesthetic, religious, or other forms of behaviour, independent of its prospects of success.

Affectual (especially emotional), that is, determined by the actor's specific affects and feeling states.

Traditional, that which is determined by ingrained habituation.

The Protestant Ethic

Religious work ethic which underpinned the spirit of capitalism

Worldly Asceticism: Psychological internalisation of a way of life in particular the Puritan ascetic which encouraged hard work, simple things, and shunned the material.

Predestination: The idea that your religious fate is predetermined by God and there is little you can do about this. You are either saved or damned.

Salvation Anxiety: Anxiety associated with predestination.

Work as a Calling: Takes religious practice out of the church and into the workplace. Working becomes a form of worship and to do well in one's calling is a sign of God's grace.

The Iron Cage: We become so obsessed with material things we are unable to let go. The pursuit, ownership and consumption of material goods and objects becomes an iron cage.

(cont'd)

The Culture Industry

The culture industry refers to the way in which the mass market, forces of production, advertising and the media dictate mass consumption and ultimately culture from above. It is top down, imposes on, and manipulates people towards its goal which is the production of goods that are profitable and consumable. The main characteristics are:

Standardization: The Standardization of goods with very little difference between products. For example, mass produced cars have slight differences in appearance and fittings to make them appeal to a certain type of customer. Standardization also leads to a breakdown in distinction between work and social system. Everyone and everything becomes co-dependent.

Rationalization: The rationalization of distribution. The public is offered a hierarchical range of products of varying quality. Differentiation is based on quantification and the labelling of customers. Culture becomes a business rather than art.

Sameness and Repetition: Nothing is new, just recycled as if it were new. There is a constant repetition in advertising. All standardised goods are endlessly repeated and plugged. This is particularly the case with music.

Mass Deception: The culture industry deceives the masses into thinking that they have a happy life and that the order of things is as it is, although in reality it has been produced by the culture industry itself. Life becomes like films, and the more we become part of the film the more we loose our sense of self identity and follow those who hold power.

Indicative Reading

Key Texts

Horkheimer, M. and Adorno, T. (1947, 1994). *Dialectic of Enlightenment*. London: Continuum. Esp: The Culture Industry pp 120–167.
Marcuse, H. (1968). *Negations*. London: Penguin.
Weber, M. (1921, 1978). *Economy and Society, Vol 1*. Berkeley: University of California Press.
Weber, M. (1930, 1992). *The Protestant Ethic and the Spirit of Capitalism*. London: Routledge.

Secondary Texts

Bendix, R. (1966). *Max Weber: An Intellectual Portrait*. London: Methuen.
Brubaker, R. (1991). *The Limits of Rationality: An Essay on the Social and Moral Thought of Max Weber*. London: Routledge.
Held, D. (1980, 1990). *Introduction to Critical Theory: Horkheimer to Habermas*. London: Polity.
Parkin, F. (1982). *Max Weber*. London: Tavistock.
Sayer, D. (1991). *Capitalism and Modernity: An Excursus on Marx and Weber*. London: Routledge.

3
The End of Enlightenment: Critical Theory, Modernity and Genocide

Introduction

No social theory book could claim to be complete without looking at modern genocide. The reason for this is not the sheer horror of the Holocaust, or the massacres in Rwanda, or even that we should not forget. The reason is that modern genocide is embedded in the structure of society, in the nature of capitalism and of modernity itself; that is, from the very structure of the nation state, the institutions of capitalism, bureaucracy, technical reason, charismatic leaders through the political in fascism and the ideology behind what Bauman (1991) describes as the 'gardening state'. In the last chapter we saw that for Horkheimer and Adorno (1994) the self referential nature of the culture industry makes an illusion that life really is the way that the industry portrays it, we live a life of films and supermarket labels, we fall into line behind leaders and those that have power, we are dominated in a far more subtle way than we think – this is anti-Enlightenment and mass deception. But what happens when this kind of analysis is applied to political ideologies, to fascism? How can we start to think about why people were motivated to follow leaders against their better judgement? What happens when Enlightenment ideals are turned in on themselves and used for the purpose of evil? This chapter will explore the nature of anti-Semitism, the Holocaust and Genocide through two differing perspectives, that of Horkheimer and Adorno and Bauman. Although the main theme is an examination of theoretical responses to genocide, the wider themes in this book follow – the creation of self in relation to others, the rationality of the modern world and the notion of the end of Enlightenment ideals, or perhaps even the end of an epoch – the end of modernity.

Dialectic of Enlightenment

The work of the early Frankfurt School has to be understood within the historical context of the formation of the school, in particular the Second World War in Europe and the impact of Nazism on Jewish intellectuals. The Institute for Social research (The Institute für Sozialforschung) was founded with the help of Felix Weil in 1923. Carl Grünberg was appointed the first director of the Institute and he made his inaugural speech in the Hall of Frankfurt University in June 1924. Grünberg's vision for the school was based in a deeply empirical form of social research grounded in economics and historical materialism. The institute was set on a course of study that combined Marxism, concrete historical studies and theoretical analysis. It is however the names of Max Horkheimer and Theodor Adorno which are most closely associated with the institute and with the idea of what we now call critical theory.

Max Horkheimer was appointed director of the institute in 1930. Within three years Horkheimer, together with many of his colleagues were forced to flee Germany as a result of the Nazi persecution of Jews and seek asylum in the United States. Horkheimer's vision for the institute was markedly different from his predecessor Grünberg. Social Philosophy became a leading point of discussion within the school as did an interest in Psychoanalytic thinking and the relationship between science, 'man' and nature. Marcuse became a member of the school in 1932 and following an association of several years, Adorno joined in 1938. Many of the School's most important, and certainly well known work was written in the period of exile between 1933 and 1950 including *Dialectic of Enlightenment* and *Studies in Prejudice*. (For a full Bibliography see Held 1990, Wiggershaus, 1994). Horkheimer and Adorno returned to Germany in the early 1950's and the institute was re-established in Frankfurt with Adorno as co-director. The writings of the school at the time must be understood within the historical context and background of the theorists in question; the mass persecution of Jewish peoples; social dislocation, war, fragmentation and a certain rage against what Hanna Arendt (1962) would later describe as the banality of evil.

Dialectic of Enlightenment is a powerful thesis which focuses on three broad areas that should be read as a series of essays with overlapping themes. First is the nature of enlightenment itself and the idea of enlightenment as myth, or more importantly how enlightenment reverts to mythology. What Horkheimer and Adorno are attempting to argue through an examination of Homer's *Odyssey*, is that enlightenment thinking is not a bad thing *per se*, but the Enlightenment presents us with an idea of reason which is based on mythology. Enlightenment thinking is simply not enlightened enough because it fails to reflect on its own relationship to tradition. This is a critique of positivistic notions of rationality that have become the dominant mode of cognition. The development of positivistic science has not only led to the domination of nature by man through the use of categorisation and biological discourses, but ultimately has led to the legitimisation of the domination of man by man. This is delineated through a discussion of Kant, Sade and Nietzsche. The second area, which I discussed in the previous chapter, is that of the culture industry, or the regression of enlightenment to ideology. This ideology expends itself in idolisation of given existence and of the power which controls technology (Horkheimer and Adorno, 1994, p xvi). The final thesis in *Dialectic* and the subject of this chapter is the way in which enlightenment reverts to the barbaric, to extermination and to genocide. In this way the Enlightenment as a series of ideas and a way of thinking can be seen as self destructive.

Elements of Anti-Semitism is where we see a real injection of something that many sociologists are critically wary of and often derisory, that of psychoanalytic theory drawn in the main from Freud's original writings on group psychology and the philosophical underpinnings from Freud's (1919) work *Das Unheimlich* on otherness and the notion of projection. The use of psychoanalysis is invaluable in two respects throughout this work. It addresses some of the very basic and primitive mechanisms underlying anti-Semitism and hate, and at the same time it allows for one of the central tenets of critical theory – that is, critical and sustained self reflection on the processes of, and reasons for research. I do not think Horkheimer and Adorno ever did this in *Dialectic of Enlightenment*, and it is something that is taken up at a much later date in Habermas' (1971b) *Knowledge and Human Interests*. What it does do though, is show very clearly the massive substantive irrationality that has accompanied the development of modernity and the emotional basis of political action and thinking. Some of the criticisms of this work are well known and I will discuss them at the end of the next section but what I want to do first is to outline the elements of anti-Semitism, including the psychological ideas that Horkheimer and Adorno use, and relate these back to some of Weber's ideas on modernity and identity before arguing that we can see a common thread developing right through to the work of Zygmunt Bauman at the end of the twentieth century. These common themes are typically Weberian with a psycho-social edge, and thus we get the idea of a critical theory that addresses both social structure and psychological affect.

Elements of Anti-Semitism

Elements of Anti-Semitism is a raging and polemic rant whose object is National Socialism, Nazism, fascism, whatever you want to call it; it is a considered and critical attack on racial ideology, hate crimes and German fascism. It pulls no punches and has arguably borne itself on the shockwaves of Auschwitz and the programme of human destruction in Nazi Germany. The Jews in Nazi Germany were viewed not as a minority group but as an opposing race that had to be exterminated to secure the future of National Socialism and the Aryan race. Horkheimer and Adorno describe the elements of anti-Semitism well, its blindness and murderous ethos: 'attacking or defending blindly, the persecutor and his victim belong to the same sphere of evil. Anti-Semitic behaviour is generated in situations where blinded men robbed of their subjectivity are set loose as subjects' (Horkheimer and Adorno, 1994, p 171). For Horkheimer and Adorno anti-Semitism is a deeply imprinted schema, it is a ritual of civilisation, indeed the very act of killing simply conforms to the way of life of the anti-Semite. There is, for Horkheimer and Adorno, a measure of truth in the idea that it is an outlet – anger is discharged on defenceless victims. Interestingly, they make the point that both the victims and persecutors in this type of dynamic are interchangeable. There is no such thing as a born anti-Semite, so gypsies, Jews, Protestants, Catholics may all take the place of the murderer as the norm.

For Horkheimer and Adorno bourgeois anti-Semitism has as its ethos an economic reason and this is the concealment of domination in production. In other words, power and ideology are concealed in the productive processes of modern society. Whereas in times gone by kings and rulers sat over the working classes scorning work themselves and dominating quite explicitly from the top down, for Horkheimer and Adorno: 'The new rulers simply took off the bright garb of the nobility and donned civilian clothing. They declared that work was not degrading, so as to control the others more rationally' (Horkheimer and Adorno, 1994, p 173). In reality the productive work of the capitalist is an ideology 'cloaking' the exploitation of man. The Jew becomes the scapegoat for the economic injustices of capitalism. There is thus an economic element to anti-Semitism. Horkheimer and Adorno note, the Jewish people travelled across Europe bringing with them the ways of capitalism and in doing so attracted all the hatred of those that had suffered under capitalism:

> The Jews remained objects, at the mercy of others, even when they insisted on their rights. Commerce was not their vocation but their fate. The Jews constituted the trauma of the knights of industry who had to pretend to be creative, while the claptrap of anti-Semitism announced a fact for which they secretly despised themselves; their anti-Semitism is self Hatred, the bad conscience of the parasite. (Horkheimer and Adorno, 1994, p 176).

National Socialism in Germany disposed of religious forms of anti-Semitism and concentrated on a biological notion of race purity. As I have previously outlined (Clarke, 2003) social engineering in Nazi Germany was the terrible culmination of race as a science, of social Darwinism, and of racial theories of inferiority and superiority between 'man' in the guise of the Aryan myth. The biologising of German society, the idea of racial superiority was an intrinsic part of Nazi ideology: the ideology that paved the road to Auschwitz and the systematic annihilation of Jews, Slavs, Gypsies, homosexuals and many other minorities in Europe. The nature of the Aryan myth was imbued with romanticism; with eroticism, with a strong emphasis on blood, soil, of bonding with fellow man and nature. The highly irrational romantic symbols that were used to generate myth contrast sharply with the highly rational, calculative, scientific methods of implementation of Hitler's plans for race purity and the notion of the *'Volksgemeinschaft'*, the racial or national community. Anti-Semitism in Germany was nihilistic with intent; the will to destroy the beliefs and values of others, the Jews, as a prelude to the creation of a new Reich. The Jewish community in Europe and in particular in Germany existed at the pleasure of 'kings, lords and barons' until the end of the nineteenth century (Gordon, 1984, p 97). The Jew transversed the boundaries of the emerging nation states, and in doing so they became rejected as outsiders, as not belonging to one nationalism. Anti-Semitism, dislike and suspicion were deepened and extenuated by Nazi propaganda and Hitler's paranoid hatred of Jews.

For Horkheimer and Adorno though this represented a dual edged sword. On the one hand you had the demise of religious anti-Semitism, but on the other the energy behind religious belief is channelled into rampant nationalism and a religious like attachment to the faith of the leader. Indeed for Horkheimer and Adorno:

> This is a dual benefit for the Fascists: uncontrolled longing is channelled into nationalistic rebellion, and the descendants of the evangelistic fanatics are turned – like Wagner's knight of the Holy Grail – into sworn members of blood brotherhoods and elite guards; religion as an institution is partly embodied in the system and partly converted into mass culture. (Horkheimer and Adorno, 1994, p 176).

Religious anti-Semitism wanes for Horkheimer and Adorno as people are no longer bothered about eternal salvation, or the salvation anxiety that I discussed in the last chapter. But, this religious anti-Semitism remains deep seated within; the anti-Semite religion has been subsumed, not abolished, as a cultural commodity. Horkheimer and Adorno look deeper than religious or economic motivations in the explanation of anti-Semitism. They look towards our biological pre-history arguing that the archetypal anti-Semite makes an appeal to an idiosyncrasy, to a distinct behaviour and mannerisms which evoke our archaic inheritance. Horkheimer and Adorno draw heavily on Freud's instinct theory, weaving together powerful primitive drives and projective mechanisms of defence to explain the pathological nature of anti-Semitism. Horkheimer and Adorno introduce us to the idea of mimesis. Mimesis is a powerful instinctual mechanism, a form of self protection in the natural world which has become perverted in the modern world. In our natural environment we mimic in order to camouflage and blend in. Quite simply this may mean freezing if we sense danger; it is part of our biological pre-history. The ego is no longer in control of itself as the body obeys fundamental biological reactions to stimuli: when men try to become like nature they harden themselves against it. Protection as fear is a form of mimicry.

The reflexes of stiffening and numbness in humans are archaic schemata of the urge to survive. (Horkheimer and Adorno, 1994, p 180).

After Freud's thesis on civilisation, Horkheimer and Adorno argue that civilisation, the modern world, has slowly and methodically prohibited instinctual behaviour: 'The angel with the fiery sword who drove man out of paradise and onto the path of technical progress is the very symbol of that progress' (Horkheimer and Adorno, 1994, p180). Initially this came about by the by the organisation of mimesis in the magical phase, through ceremony and rite. Religious practice outlaws the instinctual, rational practice banishes the display of emotions. People are taught behavioural norms in the school and workplace, children are no longer allowed to behave like children. Mimesis now takes a form in which society threatens nature; control equals self preservation and dominance over nature. We no longer make our 'self' like nature to survive but attempt to make nature like us: society continues threatening nature as the lasting organised compulsion which is reproduced in individuals as rational self preservation and rebounds on nature as social dominance over it. (Horkheimer and Adorno, 1994, p 181). In other words, the instinctual mechanism of mimesis becomes sublimated in the practice of the rational control of the modern environment. Horkheimer and Adorno note that we often see signs of repressed mimesis – all religious devotion and deflection has a feel of mimicry. Although the ego is formed in resistance to mimicry, science still represents the most sublimated form of mimicry. Mathematics and mathematical formula are simply a regression handled consciously. This is of course part of Horkheimer and Adorno's critique of science and positivism – science is repetition which has become rationalised as formula and refined in observed regularity, the product of which is stereotypy; scientific categories are the containers of stereotypy.

In the modern world mimesis has been consigned to oblivion. For Horkheimer and Adorno, those blinded by civilisation experience their own repressed and tabooed mimetic characteristics in others. Gestures, nuances, touching, feeling are experienced as embarrassing remnants from our pre-history that have survived in the rationalised environment of the modern world. It is at this point that Horkheimer and Adorno draw our attention to Freud's (1919) paper *The Uncanny* (Das Unheimlich) – 'what seems repellantly alien is in fact all too familiar'. It is worth revisiting Freud's paper as it has specific ramifications for understanding both fear and aggression towards the Other. In this monograph Freud investigates the subject of aesthetics. Aesthetics, Freud argues, generally concern themselves with questions of beauty, of that which is attractive, of the sublime, in other words, things, ideas and feelings of a positive nature. Freud however is little concerned with any theory of beauty in this instance, but a theory of the *quality* of feelings and particularly the quality of feelings that belong within the field of what we would call frightening: to what arouses dread and horror. (Freud, *SE, XVII*, p 219).

Freud follows a line of investigation that explores the linguistic usage of the term 'das unheimlich', and at the same time he considers the experiences and situations which arouse in people a sense of uncanniness. This leads Freud to the same conclusion: 'the uncanny is that class of frightening which leads back to what is known of old and long familiar' (*SE, XVII*, p 220). Thus we have a feeling, and crucially it is the *quality* of this feeling which is familiar, old and frightening. We are not always able to identify where this feeling comes from; this suggests that it emanates from something repressed, something in the unconscious mind, something triggered by certain symbols or events. Freud uses the example of the *Sandman* from *Eight Tales of Hoffman*. The sandman is equivalent to a type of 'bogeyman'. The 'bogeyman' is the kind of character which generates fear and keeps children in their beds at night. In a linguistic sense, the writer of the book creates something uncanny which plays on our unconscious fears and phantasies. In the same way religion has created gods and demons. These we feel we have surmounted, particularly with the spread of secularisation and the demise of religious practice. Note here, the very clear parallel with Horkheimer and Adorno's account of the perversion of mimesis. Despite living in a secular society, we still have uncanny feelings of super-natural powers that are frightening. Freud thus gives us two forms of the uncanny: first, feelings that are triggered by infantile complexes, and second, the uncanny which proceeds from actual experience, from animistic beliefs that have been surmounted. Freud draws our attention to themes in uncanni-ness that are prominent. In literature there is often a 'doubling' of characters, identical people who look alike, joined in some of telepathic union so that experiences and feelings become common. Freud also suggests that these char-acters represent or are marked by the fact that the subject identifies himself in some other. We start to see what Horkheimer and Adorno suggest when they talk about mimesis and false projection as Freud argues that the uncanny fulfils the condition of 'touching' the residues of our animistic mental activity and bringing them to expression.

How do we find a discharge for these frightening thoughts, thoughts that evoke a feeling of uncanniness, uneasiness, even repellence? Freud is clear, we project them on others. Projection is a mechanism of defence in which material is projected outwards as if it is something foreign to the self. In the properly psycho-analytic sense it is the operation whereby qualities, feelings, wishes or even 'objects', which the subject refuses to recognise or rejects in himself, are expelled from the self and located in another person or thing. (Laplanche and Pontalis, 1973, p 349). Projection for Freud is symptomatic of paranoia. Distorted feelings of persecution are expelled from the internal world onto some other. Internal perception is distorted and suppressed and in the case of persecution what should have been felt internally as love is perceived exter-nally as hate. Paranoia is a general Freudian term that covers systematic delu-sions, grandeur, persecution, jealousy; it is a mechanism of defence. Projection is part of a process of recovery in which thoughts and desires that have been suppressed internally are projected outward. Thus we only see the repressed elements of our mimetic behaviour in others, but this is surely a projection of our own longing to return to a pre-social state of nature, to act and behave in accordance with our repressed impulses. Horkheimer and Adorno give the example of a sense of smell:

> Of all the senses, that of smell – which is attracted without objectifying – bears clearest witness to the urge to lose oneself in and become the 'other'. As perception and perceived – both are united – smell is more expressive than the other senses. When we see we remain what we are, but when we smell we are taken over by otherness. (Horkheimer and Adorno, 1994, p 184)

Therefore, argue Horkheimer and Adorno, the sense of smell is considered a disgrace in civilisation, a sign of lesser beings and animals. The civilised person can only engage in actively smelling if it is rationalised in the form of the elimination of smell, such is the prohibition of this natural impulse. Anyone who sniffs in order to identify and eradicate bad smells may sniff to his hearts content because he has disinfected the impulse (which he enjoys craftily) with the permission of, and identification with authority. This all seems a very bizarre way to try and explain the psyche of the anti-Semite but as Horkheimer and Adorno note 'anti-Semites gather together to celebrate the moment when authority permits what is usually forbidden' (Horkheimer and Adorno, 1994, p 184). The whole purpose of the symbolism of fascist behaviour becomes apparent. To allow mimetic behaviour:

> The carefully thought out symbols (which are proper to every counterrevolutionary movement), the skulls and disguises, the barbaric drum beats, the monotonous repetition of words and gestures, are simply the organised imitation of magic practices, the mimesis of mimesis... Hitler can gesticulate like a clown, Mussolini strike false notes like a provincial tenor, Goebbels talk endlessly like a Jewish agent whom he wants murdered... (Horkheimer and Adorno, 1994, p 185)

The leader figure with his authoritarian stance, charisma, and near hysterical mannerisms acts as a representation of all that is forbidden in society – we have the mimesis of mimesis: a rebellion of all that is suppressed against domination turned both inward and outward to support domination. The anti-Semite needs the Jew because on one hand he see himself in opposition as someone good, caring and humane, but on the other this induces ill feelings and alienation – it matters little if the Jew actually possesses mimetic features, the Jew represents that which disturbs or disjoints the national society. The Jews are accused of behaving like animals, accused of participating in forbidden magic and ritual. This is phantasy and projection which forms part of the anti-Semitic dream and then is rationalised in the structures of National Socialism.

The Mimetic Impulse: False and Paranoid Projection

Anti-Semitism, for Horkheimer and Adorno is based on false projection. This is somewhat of a strange statement as there is no such mechanism as false projection per se. Projection is the psychological mechanism described by Freud (1919) in paper Das Unheimlich and used as an analytic and clinical tool throughout the psychoanalytic and academic community. It is little wonder then, that one of the very few references made by Horkheimer and Adorno in the chapter Elements of anti-Semitism is to Freud's Uncanny.

So, anti-Semitism is based in what Horkheimer and Adorno describe as false projection which is related to a repressed form of mimesis. In mimesis proper we see an imitation of the natural environment – a mechanism of defence which enables camouflage and protection; we make ourselves like nature in order that we may become one with nature. False projection, conversely, tries to make the environment like us – we try to control and rationalise nature projecting our own experiences and categories onto natural things and making that which not natural – natural, through a reification of scientific categories and constructions. Inner and outer worlds are confused and perceived as hostile:

> Impulses which the subject will not admit as his own even though they are most assuredly so, are attributed to the object – the prospective victim… The blind murderer has always seen his victim as persecutor against whom he must defend himself, and the strongest and wealthiest individuals have always felt their weakest neighbours to be an intolerable threat before they fell upon them to destroy them. (Horkheimer and Adorno, 1994, p 187)

Central to this argument then, is projection. The product of false projection is the stereotype, the transference of socially unpalatable thoughts from subject to object. This is also particularly alarming because Horkheimer and Adorno argue that the paranoiac cannot help or accept his own instincts. In doing so he or she attacks others, experiencing his or her own aggression as that of the 'other', a classic case of projection. The implication of this is twofold. First the Jew or 'other' reminds us of the peace and happiness that we cannot have. The persecuted minorities of Europe form a receptacle for those betrayed by modern society. We cannot have it so we will eliminate or destroy it in an envious attack. Second, the 'other' stands as a direct reminder, either real but often imaginary, of our repressed longings to return to a pre-social state of nature – to return to our mimetic existence. To satisfy these socially banished instinctual needs, we accuse outgroups of behaving like animals, because we long to behave like animals. This should not be taken too literally. What Horkheimer and Adorno mean by this is that we yearn to act on impulse, on our instincts, without the constraints of rationalised modern society. In this way, Horkheimer and Adorno argue, the Jew became the persecuted 'other'.

The product of false projection is the stereotype, a product of evil and of an ego which has sunk into its own depths lacking any form of self reflection. Reading Freudian theory Horkheimer and Adorno argue the ego projects, under pressure from the super-ego, the aggressive impulses of the id onto the outside world, but these are worked out as abstraction and identification with some form of supposed evil. Horkheimer and Adorno describe the anti-Semite:

> ...since he cannot allow himself the pleasure of following his own instincts, he attacks other individuals in envy or persecution just as the repressed beastialist hunts or torments an animal. (Horkheimer and Adorno, 1994, p 192).

For Horkheimer and Adorno, Fascism is a special case of paranoiac delusion in which we see a primitive suppression of animal instincts into scientific methods of controlling nature. Everything is objectified scientifically and held to be true despite the fact that 'facts' are judgements and formed in the human imagination which is open to the very unconscious feelings that the fascist seeks to get rid of. I think we need to think of Horkheimer and Adorno's thesis as a set of critiques: first as a critique of positivism, second as a critique of fascism, and finally as a critique of sociology (or theory) in which they move one step further and offer us a critical theory. The critique of positivism is a general theme in all of their work, but in *Dialectic of Enlightenment* it is particularly strong because it draws on the emphasis of science as the dominant mode of cognition in Nazi Germany (and the rest of the world). In one sense you can infer that all scientists are paranoid, projecting bizarre categories on nature in the form of the categorisation of the species as if these categories were natural. It is quite clear that all scientists plainly are not paranoid, but what they often forget is that scientific categories are social constructions. These constructions were made up and emanated from the mind and imagination of a scientist, but now appear as if they are natural, as if they have always existed. It is this overriding issue of the domination of nature, then the domination of people that concerns Horkheimer and Adorno – the idea that scientific rationality is not always a good thing and positivist methods are actually anti-Enlightenment. Rather than being free we are incarcerated within rigid frameworks of self and selfhood which are a projected imago constructed through the urge to dominate and control. Fascism encapsulated this rigidity within what Horkheimer and Adorno describe as the mad system which promotes a rage against the non identical. We have to be very careful indeed because as they demonstrate in their thesis on the culture industry, this becomes transposed into our everyday life and existence and has implications for the way in which we construct our identity and that of others. It is only with a critical sociological awareness that we can reflect and point to these systems of domination and control.

There is no doubt that Horkheimer and Adorno's ideas are problematic, but what they offer in terms of their explanation of anti-Semitism does provide, as I have previously argued (Clarke, 2002) a theoretical basis for the explanation of racism, hatred and exclusionary practices by using a critical fusion of both structural and psychological factors. It also serves as an introduction to the application and limitations of Freudian thought in an examination of the massive substantive irrationality that has accompanied the development of modern society. By placing an emphasis on affective forces they produce a more complete picture of the way in which psychological mechanisms support and perpetuate structural forms of racism. Jay (1994) notes that Horkheimer and Adorno go beyond a purely psychoanalytic account of para- noid false projection adding an epistemological dimension. Projection per se is not a problem; we all use it in our everyday lives. A healthy projection pre- serves the tension between subject and object. Reflection on the dialogue between subject and object creates understanding; it is (after Kant) the key to enlightenment. The 'morbid' aspect of anti-Semitism for Horkheimer and Adorno is not projection but lack of self reflection: when the subject is no longer able to return to the object what he has received from it, he becomes poorer rather than richer. He loses the reflection in both directions: since he no longer reflects the object, he ceases to reflect upon himself, and loses the ability to differentiate. (Horkheimer and Adorno, 1994, p 189).

Horkheimer and Adorno are often ignored because of their use of psycho- analysis which has only recently become acceptable within modern socio- logical analysis and still remains on the margins of the discipline. This is particularly true if we look at criticisms of their work on paranoia and pro- jection. Bahr (1994) is particularly scathing: To make projection understand- able as well as the manner in which it is deformed into false projection, a process regarded as part of the essence of false anti-Semitism, the authors employed a rather naively realistic physiological theory of perception. (Bahr, 1994, p 233). Bahr goes on to describe Horkheimer and Adorno's work as a far fetched theory pertaining to biological pre-history. In his criticism Bahr is noticeably uncritical. There is no doubt that some of the theoretical con- tributions made in *Dialectic of Enlightenment* are unclear and need developing. Bahr fails to notice some huge theoretical leaps; for example, it is not clear how the urge to control and dominate nature turns into the urge to control and dominate others. This tends to cloud some of the more useful components of the research. Bahr questions the link between the instinctual and its con- demnation in the modern world, ultimately challenging the institute's view of nature. Horkheimer and Adorno are clear about their position: 'The domina- tion of nature represents a particular type of relationship; nature has utility, in so far as it is instrumental to human purposes' (in Held, 1980, p 154).

The problem with Horkheimer and Adorno's work, as I have intimated, is that they do not find an easy passage between sociology and biology – two disciplines that have always been at odds with each other, or so we are led to believe. Rather than concentrating on the psychodynamic processes that connect society to the psyche and vice versa, they concentrate on biological instinct theory and notions of the unconscious mind that people find difficult to relate to. Had they pitched their explanation of anti-Semitism more in terms of what the human imagination is capable of constructing (either consciously or unconsciously) and destructing, then I think their work would be far more palatable for sociologists at least. In other words, how our imagination often can create difference through fear. This is mobilised as prejudice which leads to racism. At a societal level this has manifested itself in fascism and Nazism in a complex psychodynamic process of projection and introjection. In the next section of this chapter I will discuss the concept of the Stranger and Strangerdom, as I think that a by-product of Zygmunt Bauman's writings in this area is a sociology which we could describe as a sociology of the imagination which has specific ramifications for human rights and the way in which we perceive others.

The Universal Stranger

There is substantial literature on the concept of the stranger, with two key writers standing out. Georg Simmel (1950) portrays the stranger as the potential wanderer – 'the person that comes today and stays tomorrow' (Simmel, 1950, p 402). Zygmunt Bauman (1989, 1990) provides a sophisticated reworking of the concept of the stranger which has a particular quality, that of a psycho-social character, partly fictive, partly real, and partly a figment of our imagination – of our *phantasies* (see Clarke, 2002). Before I expand on Bauman's thesis I want to outline Simmel's essay, as it provides a fairly clear account that will help readers conceptualise the notion of strangerhood.

Simmel's stranger can be best described with one word – ambiguity. The stranger is a position that we find hard to put our finger on; it has something to do with a vague spatiality, of certain measures of nearness and distance. But at the same time, the stranger presents in some sense a unity for Simmel between 'wandering' and 'fixation'. The uncertainty associated with the potential for wandering leaves us in an ambiguous state of mind: is s/he one of us or one of them? The stranger has not belonged to the group from the start, but brings a certain something to it. The problem with this is that the qualities projected into the group by the stranger do not stem from the group itself, which fuels the anxiety of ambiguity.

Thus for Simmel, the stranger encompasses the nearness and remoteness of every human relationship: 'distance means that he, who is close by, is far, and strangeness means that he, who is also far, is actually near' (Simmel, 1950, p 402). Simmel gives an example from the sphere of economics where the trader appears as stranger. If an economy is self-sufficient then there is no 'middleman'. The trader is only required when products are imported from outside the group or economy, or, if members of a group go elsewhere to buy goods, they themselves then become the transient strangers. In economic terms then the trader is stranger, and the stranger stands out more when he settles in a particular spatial locality. The stranger may become geographically fixated for some time, but is never the owner of either the physical or symbolic space that s/he occupies. This for Simmel gives the stranger the characteristics of mobility which embrace nearness and distance within a closed group.

As the stranger is not committed to the group s/he occupies a place of objectivity, and as Simmel notes, is often subject to the most surprising openness and confidentiality's. This objectivity is structured around the spatial psychodynamics of distance and nearness, indifference and involvement. The stranger's objectivity for Simmel may be defined in terms of freedom, in that the individual is not bound by the prejudices of the group, or by commitment. This allows the stranger to step back and reflect on the social relations that s/he observes. The relationship between 'us' and the stranger is based in general rather than specific commonalties, on general features, rather than specific differences. Indeed for Simmel:

> The Stranger is close to us, insofar as we feel between him and ourselves common features of a national, social, occupational, or generally human, nature. He is far from us, insofar as these common features extend beyond him or us, and connect us only because they connect a great many people (Simmel, 1950, p 406).

Thus for Simmel a trace of strangeness exists in every human relationship, from the most intimate to the most fleeting and general encounter. This strangeness has a deeply psychical character. Zygmunt Bauman has re-iterated and built on Simmel's classic essay in a number of works including *Culture As Praxis* (1973), *Modernity and the Holocaust* (1989), *Thinking Sociologically* (1990), and *Modernity and Ambivalence* (1991) providing a sophisticated reworking of the concept within the context of the sociology of the Jewish Holocaust.

Bauman's starting point is a distinction between 'aliens' and 'strangers'. Unlike aliens, strangers are not *unfamiliar* people, but they cross, or break the dividing line of dualism, they are neither 'us' nor 'them'. There is a clear definition of the social and physical boundaries between 'us' and 'them', 'friends' and 'enemies'. Both are subject to the same structures and ideas, they define good and bad, true and false, they stand in polarity creating an illusion of order and symmetry. The stranger violates this structure and order; in Bauman's words 'they (the stranger) bring the "outside" "inside" and poison the comfort of order with the suspicion of chaos' (Bauman, 1991, p 56). The stranger is someone we know things about, who sits in 'our' world uninvited. The stranger has the characteristics of an enemy, but unlike the enemy, is not kept at a safe distance. Neither 'us' nor 'them', friend nor foe, the stranger undermines order by straddling the boundary, causing confusion and anxiety, and as such, becomes a target of hatred.

In *Culture as Praxis* (1973) Bauman explores the ways that cultures and societies deal with *in-between* phenomena: things that upset the neat divisions of cultural systems; things neither solid nor liquid; things that broach the divide between inside and outside; things that are unclassifiable. This is because classification and thought depend on oppositions and distinctions, not gradations between categories. Citing Edmund Leach (1964) he argues

> If each individual has to learn to construct his own environment in this way, it is crucially important that the basic discriminations should be clear-cut and unambiguous. There must be absolutely no doubt about the difference between *me* and *it*, or between *we* and *they* (Bauman, 1973, pp 123–4).

Thus, for Bauman those individuals and peoples deemed to straddle the boundary between me and not-me, between inside and outside of society, inspire dread because of the way that they seem to question the very substance of cultural boundaries and all other *necessary* certainties of social life (Bauman, 1973, p 123).

In constructing his portrait of the stranger, Bauman has drawn upon a variety of rich and evocative sources. These include the notion of stickiness as inherently repulsive, as explained so vividly by Jean-Paul Sartre (1993) in *Being and Nothingness*; the sociology of the 'stranger' of the early sociologists Robert Michels (1929) and of course Georg Simmel (the stranger as neither friend nor enemy, while serving certain important social functions because of his or her position as outsider, was also fear arousing, a threat to sociality because we could not fully know him or her); the phenomenologist Alfred Schutz's (1944) concept of the stranger as a threat to coherence, order and commonly held assumptions about identities, world views, reality and so on; and the work of anthropologists like Edmund Leach (1964), Evans-Pritchard (1965) and Mary Douglas (1966) on the cultural production of anomalies, ambiguity, pollution and dirt (the latter as 'things out of place'), which disturbed, and which were produced through the operation of classificatory systems, building up to entire societal orders (see Bauman, 1973, 1997a, 1997b).

The classic example of the stranger for Bauman is the Jew – *the universal stranger*. In this sense Bauman follows the traditional sociological explanation. Bauman argues that the Jew always stood at the border, as the inside/outside marker, of European society. This social positioning had sporadically disastrous consequences for Jews. Bauman has stressed in a number of works that modernity, with its quest for order, its levelling out of social differences and distinctions, is deeply implicated in nightmares like the Holocaust, where being a stranger meant not fitting into a utopian dream of purity. Ironically, this most vicious assault on Jewish strangers came after a period when assimilation had been so vigorously attempted, once the walls of the ghettoes had been taken down, and attempts had been made to integrate Jews fully into

European society. Part of Bauman's argument is that in modernity there was an exacerbation of boundary maintaining pressures. With the formation of the nation-state, everyone would be on the same plane within the national space, but this did not mean that boundaries between groups simply disappeared. Anti-Semitism, which had been around for two millennia, in fact intensified.

In a general critique of the modern nation-state's social engineering efforts, Bauman (1997b) has referred to two ways that modern states have attempted to deal with strangers: one he calls an *anthropophagic* process of 'annihilating ...strangers by *devouring* them and then metabolically transforming [them] into a tissue indistinguishable from one's own' (Bauman, 1997b, p 18). This, he argues, is driven by a paranoid fear of the danger of strangers; in modernity, the presence of strangers evokes fears about the breakdown of societal order, and the onset of chaos. If we think about this within the framework of critical theory we can see that processes of projection underlie these dynamics – the fear of disintegration and chaos inside fuels paranoid phantasies about disintegration in the external world. The alternative, and frequently complementary, state strategy was *anthropoemic*: 'vomiting' strangers, banishing them from the limits of the orderly world, barring them from communication with those inside, or, as a last resort, destroying them physically, as in the Holocaust. As we will explain later, both of these strategies have been utilised in attempts by the state to control and police Aborigines and their identities.

Although Bauman does not draw on the psychoanalytic ideas of critical theory, I feel that his 'stranger' represents a psycho-social character which is partly fictive, partly real and partly a figment of our imagination. 'The outsider who shows up in most places and periods in history is not only an actual figure', writes Zukier (1996, p 1117), 'but also a figment of society's imagination'. This insight is important as it bridges in some sense the gap between traditional sociology and what I would call the sociology of the imagination, that is, sociology that goes beyond the bounds of social structure, of function, of cause and effect and starts to address our inner world, a world of love and hate, of terror, fear, and human frailty. Implicit in Bauman's theories is not only recognition of the fragility of human existence, but recognition of the complexity of the inner world of the individual, and the inner world of society. He thus begins to push beyond the conventional sociological approach that sees the stranger as a 'social role category' (Stichweh, 1997, p 2).

The stranger is also a psychic entity, a construction in phantasy that symbolises our fears and anxieties. The stranger lives inside both our community and our own psyche – *a product of socio-historical forces, our own phantasy, of our imagination and of our projective identifications* (See Clarke and Moran, 2003). We attribute 'strangeness' to other groups and to real individuals. We are repulsed by what we see in them, as we see ourselves, our own fears and chaos, and are confronted by our phantasies – the contents of our unconscious mind. The way in which we perceive others and ultimately view others has specific implications for the basic human rights of the individuals concerned.

The stranger has been persecuted as Jew, as Gypsy, as Muslim, and, as indi-
gene in settler colonial societies. Bauman's concept of the Stranger is of course
crucial to his understanding of the relationship between modernity and the
Holocaust, the relationship between rationality and irrationality, and of
modern identity formation. I want to conclude this chapter by briefly out-
lining Bauman's views on the Jewish Holocaust and to argue that this
pessimistic vision of the relationship between modernity and rationality is in
some sense realistic and it is the job of critical theory to reflect on these realities and move forward to a position where we able to point to and identify
these areas and ideologies that make us slaves to reason.

Modernity, Reason and Genocide

In the previous chapter I noted that we are constantly reminded throughout
our lives to be reasonable, rational, and to constantly weigh things in a logical
way. The Holocaust seems to run contra to all these beliefs, but, is this really
the case? In *Modernity and the Holocaust* (1989) Zygmunt Bauman shows
us how rational planning, bureaucracy and standardisation actually make
genocide not only possible, but, as Bauman puts it, eminently reasonable.
Horkheimer and Adorno have already shown us how mass production and
standardisation have an effect on the way in which culture becomes a tool for
ideological indoctrination and domination. Bauman takes this one step further
by illustrating the way in which formal rationality justifies killing on a genocidal type scale.

Zygmunt Bauman rejects the notion that the 'Germaness' of the crime of the
Jewish Holocaust is unique by showing us how the genocidal project is
heavily rooted in the idea of progress and rationality, of the nation-state, of
social engineering, and the modern garden state (For an alternative view see
Goldhagen, 1996). Bauman's thesis as I have previously argued (Clarke 2003)
is in itself, anti-modernity. The rationality of the modern social world, and, in
particular, the rationalisation process is essentially bad for human beings. This
is certainly a view that Weber intimated, Marcuse described and Habermas
addressed in his numerous works. The instruments of rationality – the bureaucratic organisation, and structures of bureaucratic office work most efficiently,
and this is the goal of all bureaucracies, as part of a centralised power system –
a central command unit, if you like. Centralised power systems tend to be
totalitarian and terrorising, or at the very least oppressive and alienating. They
exercise various principles of social control, not least with the Nazi's, the idea
of social engineering.

There are two ways, for Bauman, to belittle the significance of the Holocaust
for Sociological analysis. The first, is to think of it as something that happened
to the Jews, as an event in Jewish history. The second, is to think of it as some
barbaric and loathsome event or practice that modernity will eventually over-
come (Bauman, 1989, p 1). No, says Bauman, far from overcoming barbarism,

modernity is inextricably linked. The Holocaust is deeply entrenched in the nature of modernity. First we have the rapid social change that modernity produced; the growth of the industrial landscape and industrial revolution led to rapid urbanisation which in turn produced mobility and social dislocation. The growth of forms of rampant nationalism espoused by fascism were on the increase, the nation state as a form of identification became much stronger. We only have to look at more recent examples of this in the former Yugoslavia to see how national identifications soon spiral into genocidal behaviours. Second, we have the triumph of science as a mode of cognition. Science and scientific enquiry heralded some of the most important breakthroughs in thinking in the 19th and 20th centuries. It also spawned more dubious forms of science in the form of eugenics and the development of race and scientifically legitimated racism. In this sense there was no need for Nazis to impose views on scientists and doctors, it was already there, part of scientific and moral philosophy of the time. The sheer scale of the destructive process would not have been possible if it were not for the scientific and technological advancements of modernity. Finally, the administrative procedures and practices of the nation state as exemplified by the bureaucratic organisation provided an efficient vehicle f or both the logistical intricacies of extermination, and also of moral absolvement of responsibility. Indeed for Bauman 'The most shattering of lessons deriving from the analysis of the 'twisted road to Auschwitz' is that – in the last resort – *the choice of physical extermination as the right means to the task of* Entfernung *was a product of routine bureaucratic procedures:* means-end calculus, budget balancing, universal rule application…(Bauman, 1989, p 17).

Bauman argues that at no point did the Holocaust come in any form of conflict with the principles of rationality and the rational world, indeed the 'final solution' did not clash with the means end rational pursuit of efficient goal implementation. That is not to say that the Holocaust was determined by bureaucracy or the culture of instrumental reason, rather Bauman is arguing that instrumental reason is not able to stop such phenomena, indeed the bureaucratic culture which objectifies and normalises society into a categorised, controlled and organised mass is the very atmosphere in which something like the Holocaust can be conceived, planned and implemented. In other words, the culture or 'spirit' of instrumental rationality not only made the Holocaust possible, but eminently 'reasonable' (Bauman, 1989, p 18).

Bauman uses the idea of the 'Gardening State' a metaphor to describe the modernist project of the twentieth century. This is a combination of designed and planned order, social engineering, and legislative reason that mark the transformation into an 'orderly society'.

Bauman (1991) argues that in Nazi Germany the ambitions of the state were firmly set on eradicating all the dangerous and uncontrollable elements of society through a joining of both the gardening and medical metaphor. Scientists were guided by the vision of a 'good 'society, one in which man dominated nature through the taming of the chaotic elements by the use of a systematic, rational scientific plan. Bauman argues, that it was the Jew that stood as the weed in the carefully designed garden of the future. There were other weeds as well, the mentally ill, the congenitally diseased and the bodily deformed. Some plants turned into weeds because reason dictated that the space they occupied should be someone else's garden. (Bauman, 1991, p 29)

Thus, for Bauman, modern genocide is different. It is genocide with a purpose, what Max Weber (1978) would describe as formal, purposeful rationality. Genocide becomes means ends, calculative, and therefore modern genocide, for Bauman, is an element of the gardening state, and of social engineering, which is meant to bring about 'a social order conforming to the design of a perfect society' (Bauman, 1989, p 91). The gardener' vision is that one can create a society, an ideal world, that is *objectively* (where science objectifies), better than the one that exists. In some sense for Bauman, this is the product of the civilising process gone wrong. Instead of outlawing violence and celebrating difference, modernity is characterised by a gardening culture.

Bauman argues that modern genocide is but one of the chores of the gardening state. If rational plans define gardens, then there will be weeds, and weeds have to be exterminated. As Bauman notes, Stalin and Hitler's victims were not killed to capture territory or material things, they were killed because they did not fit the design of a perfect society. Killing was not an act of destruction, but of creation, and this is wholly commensurable with the idea of the therapeutic imperative which I discuss in the following sections of this chapter. Indeed, for Bauman, modern genocide did not betray the spirit of modernity or depart from the trajectory of the civilising process. Modern genocides 'were the most consistent uninhibited expression of that spirit' (Bauman, 1989, p 93).

There are several ways in which Bauman can be misinterpreted. First, when Bauman argues that racism is a strictly modern product he does not mean that hatred, ethnic and group conflicts did not exist pre-modernity, rather that science defined race, and modern technology and state power made racism possible, and as such modernity not only made racism possible, but created a demand for it. Second, and following on from the first point, Bauman is not arguing that there is a direct causal relationship between modernity and the Holocaust, rather modern civilisation was a necessary condition in that it provided the administrative and technological tools and the ethos of scientific progress. Finally, Bauman draws our attention to the fact that he does not mean that we all live by 'Auschwitz principles' (Bauman, 1989, p 93). Just because the Holocaust is modern, does not mean, or he does not mean to imply that modernity is a Holocaust. The Holocaust is a by-product of the endless drive for control and design of the modern world, it is when the modernist dream is accompanied by absolute power, devoid of social controls and countervailing forces, that genocide follows.

The Problem with Genocide

The problem with Bauman's thesis in some sense is that all genocides are different and the Holocaust specific, you can hardly apply these same theories to the atrocities in Rwanda for example, where the killing was far from rational (or at least pertained to a different form of logic or rationality) and the means to achieve killing far from technological. Below are some examples which bring together common horrors from different atrocities.

> Urine and excreta poured down the prisoner's legs, and by nightfall the excrement, which had frozen to our limbs, gave off its stench.. We were really no longer human beings in the acceptable sense. Not even animals, but putrefying corpses moving on two legs. (Nazi death marches 1939–45, Niewyk, p 60)
>
> I cut their throats, cut off their hands, cut out their tongue, their hair. Scalped them... We almost wiped out the whole village, a whole community... Do you realise what it was like killing five hundred people in a matter of four or five hours? It was just like the gas chambers. (Vietnam, 1968, Bilton and Sim, p 130)
>
> Hundreds of women, children and old people had been packed into each freight car for sweltering journeys lasting three or more days... there was no food, no water and no fresh air. There was no toilet, just holes in the floor that piled high with excrement. An unknown number of people, particularly children and the aged died. (Banja Luka, 1993, Gutman, p 36)
>
> 20 people were hiding in the basement, when the forces broke in. They shot 18 people in the back of the head. A 10-year-old boy, was somehow only wounded in the left arm, and escaped by pretending to be dead, he managed to slip out a window, but he could not take his 2-year-old sister with him and she was burned alive when they torched the house. (Kosova, 1999, New York Times)

These testimonies come from four different situations and from different times. I think all these types of atrocities could and have happened in each individual conflict. So we have the forced displacement of peoples, and deportation of ethnic groups, whether by forced march or long disorientating rail journeys in horrific conditions, often into slave labour; we have the dehumanisation of ethnic groups, whether they are Jews, gypsies, Slavs or Muslims and persecution on political, racial ethnic grounds. We have the mass killing of civilians, men, women, and children. We have the wanton destruction of cities, towns and villages and the plunder of public and private properties; we have inhumane acts, killing, murder and torture that are carried out by professional soldiers. These contravene and violate the laws and customs of war. These examples according to the charter of the Nuremberg tribunal constitute war crimes; crimes against humanity or crimes against peace.

The problem is, how do we decide what constitutes a war crime. The victor in a war seldom gets punished for any atrocities committed by the state or allied forces. So, for example on February 14th 1945 three waves of bombers, two British, one American, some 1,300 heavy bombers dropped 3,300 tons of bombs on the city of Dresden. The incendiaries dropped on the old city started a firestorm where temperatures soared to high as 1,800 degrees Fahrenheit. Nobody has been able to ascertain how many died. The estimate ranges between 35,000 and 200,000 people. Bodies were burnt on 25 ft long grills to stop the spread of disease. There was no plausible military target, the worst devastation occurred in the cultural centre and a lot of the casualties were civilian refugees fleeing the fighting on the eastern front. In this campaign of the precision bombing of German cities it is estimated that half million people died, 1 million were seriously injured and 3 million homes were destroyed. The point I am trying to make is that according to the charter of the Nuremberg tribunal the 'wanton destruction of cities, towns, or villages, or devastation not justified by military necessity, is a war crime. A statue was erected some years ago of the mastermind behind the bombing of Dresden – Air Chief Marshall Sir Arthur Harris, or 'Bomber Harris' as he was known; a hero, rather than a war criminal. (See Garrett, S. 1993 and Hastings, M. 1993, for differing detailed accounts of allied bomber command)

I do not want to dwell on the rights and wrongs of the bombing of Dresden, but I think it is a very clear example of how difficult it is to actually prove that a war crime, or a crime against humanity has taken place, and how ambiguous international law is when you actually try and apply it to a concrete example, and how some atrocities just simply are not recognised as atrocities. This is no more better demonstrated than in the act of genocide. The General Assembly of the United Nations resolution 96, 1946 recognised genocide as a crime under international war, contrary to the spirit and aims of the United Nations and condemned by the civilised world. The 1948 Convention defines genocide thus: Genocide means any of the following acts committed with intent to destroy, in whole or in part, a national, ethnic or religious group, such as:

Killing members of the group
Causing serious bodily or mental harm to members of the group
Deliberately inflicting on the group conditions of life calculated to bring about its physical destruction in whole or in part
Imposing measures intended to prevent births within the group
Forcibly transferring children of the group to another group.
(For a full description of the 1948 Genocide convention see Roberts, A and Guelff, R. (1989) pp 157–68)
This became law in 1951.

It is of course the Nazi slaughter of Jewish people during the Second World War that immediately comes to mind when we talk or think of Genocide – the Shoah, the Holocaust. As Donald Niewyk (1997) notes ' The genocide of innocents by one of the world's most advanced nations mocks our optimism about human reason and progress' (Niewyk, 1997, p 1.) The destruction of European

Jewry led Horkheimer and Adorno (1994) to open *Dialectic of Enlightenment* with probably one of the most depressing introductions to a book: 'In the most general sense of progressive thought, the Enlightenment has always aimed at liberating men from fear and establishing their sovereignty. Yet the fully enlightened earth radiates disaster triumphant' (Horkheimer and Adorno, 1994, p 3). The Nazis took the notion of Social Darwinism and racism to its extreme limits introducing programmes of social engineering that have shocked the world. Most people have an image or a piece of text that conjures up the horror for them whether this be the camps, the forced deportations, the death marches, Nazi anti-Semitic propaganda or the ghettos. If this is not the case then Primo Levi's (1979) *If This is a Man* should give a fuller picture. I think the image that conveys the full dread of the Jewish Holocaust for me is a picture of Nazi doctor Fritz Klein standing in a trench full of bodies admiring his handy work. It is at this point that I have to stop intellectualising because I cannot even begin to understand how a person like Klein could have done what he did. A medical doctor, a person who has sworn an oath to stand by and implement a code of practice of the highest ethical position, quite easily reconciled his work in the death camps. Asked how he could reconcile his Hippocratic Oath as a doctor Klein replied:

> Of course I am a doctor and want to preserve life. And out of respect for human life, I would remove a gangrenous appendix from a diseased body. The Jew is the gangrenous appendix in the body of mankind. (Lifton, 1986, p 15)

If we are to return to intellectualising, then this is what is known as the *therapeutic imperative* – curing the social body of the German Volk of its ills, and of deadly racial diseases. A mixture of social Darwinism, race theory and eugenics in which the goal is to attain absolute control over the evolutionary process. An example of this would be the Nazi sterilisation campaign. I do not really want to dwell further on horrific examples but if one is to randomly open the indictment of the Nuremberg tribunal of the major war criminals then atrocities litter the pages:

> Pseudo-scientific experiments – sterilisation of women, study of the evolution of cancer of the womb, of typhus, heart injections, bone and muscular grafting... 1,500,000 persons exterminated at Maidanek, 4,000,000 at Auschwitz... In Ganov camp 200,000 peaceful citizens were exterminated. The most refined methods of cruelty were employed, such as disembowelling and the freezing of human beings in tubs of water. Mass shootings to the accompaniment of an orchestra... (http://www.yale.edu/lawweb/avalon/imt/proc/ount3.htm)

There is no doubt whatsoever that the extermination of European Jewry was genocide. The legal concept of genocide did not exist at the time, as Churchill said, it is a crime that has no name, and as a consequence the major war criminals were tried for crimes against the peace, against humanity and war crimes. The Genocide Convention was written specifically to encompass this crime against the Jewish people and it is very difficult to apply the concept elsewhere. The main problematic is proving the *intent* to destroy in *whole* or *part* a racial, ethnic or religious group. Many events have been referred to as genocidal but under international law it is very difficult to prove or secure a conviction.

The philosopher Jean-Paul Sartre (1968) has argued that the war waged in Vietnam by the United States of America was implicitly genocidal. Sartre's argument hinges in part on the actual nature of the warfare. By using techniques such as mass carpet bombing, defoliation and napalming great tracts of land, there is an intent to destroy in whole or in part groups of people. For Sartre, it was the Americans who committed the aggression in Vietnam, and as such they were the only people who could put an end to it: 'Declare you are beaten or we will bomb you back into the Stone Age' (Sartre, 1968, p 40)

Does this sound familiar? For Sartre, this is conditional genocide – give in or we will annihilate you. The genocidal intent is implicit rather than explicit. For Sartre, this is fed by the racism of American troops who were anti-black, anti-Asiatic and anti-Mexican, an attitude with deep historical roots which existed well before the Vietnamese conflict. The US government refused to ratify the Genocide Convention. This does not mean that in 1948 the US intended to exterminate people, rather, that the convention would conflict with the laws of several States which were founded on the anti-black racism of southern whites. Thus for Sartre, the Vietnam conflict meets all of Hitler's specifications. Hitler killed Jews because they were Jews.

> The armed forces of the United States kill men, women and children in Vietnam merely because they are Vietnamese... the spirit of genocide is in the minds of the soldiers. (Sartre, 1968, p 42)

Thus for Sartre, the United States of America is guilty of having preferred and still preferring a policy of war and aggression aimed at total genocide to a policy of peace:

> When a peasant falls in his rice paddy, mowed down by a machine gun, every one of us is hit. The Vietnamese fight for all men and the American forces against all... little by little the whole human race is being subjected to this genocidal blackmail piled on top of atomic blackmail, that is, to absolute, total war.... In this sense imperialist genocide can only become more complete. The group which the United States wants to intimidate and terrorise by way of the Vietnamese nation is the human group in its entirety. (Sartre, 1968, p 42)

This is Sartre's thesis. His words bear striking similarities to certain current events. The likelihood of a power like the United States being indicted for genocide, for any action, no matter how horrific, is zero. Of course, certain members of the US military services were prosecuted for the massacre at My Lai, most notably William Calley (guilty of the murder of 22 citizens) but later released after the intervention of Richard Nixon (See Bilton and Sim, 1992). The first actual conviction for Genocide by an international court occurred on September 2nd 1998 in Rwanda. As some may recall, approximately 800,000 Rwandans were killed in just 100 days. Most of those who died were Tutsi; those who perpetrated the crimes were in the majority Hutu. The international court found the Hutu mayor of the Rwandan village of Taba – Jean-Paul Akayesu guilty of genocide and crimes against humanity because there was intent to wipe out the Tutsi group in it's entirety. This is in contrast to the horrific killings by the Khmer Rouge of Cambodian peoples which was not technically genocide, rather a systematic killing by a government of its own people. Again the distinction between what constitutes genocide is blurred and this is particularly the case in the former Yugoslavia where the difference between genocide and ethnic cleansing is difficult to define let alone take action on. Individuals involved in atrocities in the former Yugoslavia and in particular Bosnia were charged with a combination of crimes including breaches of the Geneva Convention, crimes against humanity and genocide. The first European conviction for genocide was of Radislav Krstic in 2001 for the murder of 8,000 Bosnian Muslims in Srebenica in 1995. The court found the atrocities directed by this Bosnian Serb general were genocidal in that the killing of all male members of Srebrenica would result in the destruction of an ethnic group in its entirety.

These of course have been but a few examples. I have not mentioned the Armenians, the North American Indians, the Holocaust of black slavery, the USSR under Stalin, Burundi, East Timor, or even the Tasmanians. And then of course there is Kosova. I do not think the concept of genocide is helpful. It was specifically written in light of the Holocaust. It covers too many areas, and has become a catch all phrase. Many atrocities are crimes against humanity, but for some legal or technical loophole, they cannot be classified as genocide – the legality often overshadows the horror. I prefer the term 'crime against humanity' – all the examples I have talked about are crimes against humanity, and all the examples whilst having many factors in common have more that are different. The Holocaust is/was the Holocaust. What we need to be able to do is to recognise, as Sartre said that when a peasant falls in his rice paddy, mowed down by a machine gun, every one of us is hit. This is in some sense the problem with Bauman's thesis. It is not easily used to analyse other acts of what we might call genocide. For example the genocide in Rwanda bears little resemblance to the things that Bauman describes, there was no bureaucracy, no medical killing, no high technology, just murderous killing with machetes, about as low tech as you can get, but still with the same disastrous consequences, it seems that the critical psychoanalytic theory of Horkheimer and Adorno might be more appropriate as it deals with the powerful psychodynamics that exist between groups and individuals.

As the trial continues of Slobodan Milosevic in the Hague, who faces a total of sixty six counts of crimes against humanity, violating the laws and customs of war, and genocide, I want to leave the last words in this section to Zygmunt Bauman, a person who has done much to draw our attention to fundamental abuses of human rights, and of suffering. For Bauman, we all now live under conditions of 'universal strangerhood'. Pretending one does not look and listen, hear or see is but one short step to 'moral indifference, heartlessness, and disregard for the needs of others' (Bauman, 1990, p 70).

Summary

The big theme in this chapter has been an examination of two theoretical responses to modern genocide, but the other themes: the rationality of the modern world, the creation of self in relation to others and the constructions of Others, and the end of Enlightenment ideals are equally as important and are themes that run throughout this book and link the ideas of different theorists. This is particularly the case if we focus on Horkheimer and Adorno's work on anti-Semitism. It contains a critique of capitalism, positivism and scientific rationality on the one hand, on the other, it gives us a basis for the explanation of how we form our idea of self in relation to others, and our changing relationship to nature. It provides one of the first psycho-social accounts of racism by addressing both social structure and affect and this is one of the major threads we see developing in contemporary critical theory although the emphasis for many theorists has moved away from psychoanalysis to more eclectic psychological ideas – for example Bauman's stranger.

There are clear parallels in Horkheimer and Adorno's work with that of Freud's ideas of the Uncanny. Indeed this is one of the few specific references made in Elements of Anti-Semitism to Freud's work. We are drawn to some very clear issues in sociological analysis – the demise of religion or religious practice and the increasing secularisation of society. The increasing rationalisation of the social world in tandem with what some may term as the increasing civilisation of the Western world has taken us further away from our essence, that is our body, our natural self. We still see this in others but because of social taboos we find it repulsive as we become more sanitised and rational. For Horkheimer and Adorno the specific implication is that our animal instincts become sublimated into hierarchies of control of both man and nature which are symptomatic of the modern scientific world. Social constructions become natural categories, something we will see in the work of Foucault later on in this book. The basic problem for all of us is that we are no longer free, Enlightenment ideas and ideals have become perverted and we live in a world of ideological domination. I have provided a critique of Horkheimer and Adorno's work and have suggested that had they pitched their critical theory more in terms of what the human imagination is capable of constructing rather than concentrating on instinct theory, this would have been far more palatable for sociologists. I think the Bauman's notion of the stranger is far more persuasive in this respect and allows us to start thinking about more contemporary examples of social exclusion and othering in the form of asylum seekers and refuges and the popular conceptions of these groups which seem mainly the work of the imagination rather than any clear evidence.

Finally I have discussed the Holocaust and the concept of genocide to illustrate the way in which formal rationality and all its trappings can have terrible consequences when taken to its logical conclusion. But I have also attempted to demonstrate some of the limitations of theory by showing that while having many things in common, some modern genocides do not bear the mark of modernity at all – Rwanda is a prime example where the machete replaced the bureaucracy, medicalised killing and rational planning. Again I would reiterate that critical theory can only be successful if we pay attention to both social structure and the world of the irrational, of affect, and of human emotion. So it seems we have reached the end of Enlightenment. Horkheimer and Adorno's ideas are pessimistic at the core. Positivism dominates the modern world and in turn we are dominated. Modernity is marked by a distinct lack of self reflection, and a lack of freedom and formal rationality has penetrated far too deeply into our social spheres. We live in a world of social control. In the following chapter I want to address the work of Jurgen Habermas who shares many of the same concerns of his colleagues in the Frankfurt School but has a far more positive view of modernity as an incomplete project. Habermas is also significant because his body of work, and later commentators on his work form a very strong critique of some of the theorists that we will look at later in this book, particularly Michel Foucault and also the postmodernists who Habermas claims lack reflexivity and a sense of history.

Summary of Key Concepts and Terms

Mimesis

A powerful instinctual mechanism, a form of self protection in the natural world which has become perverted in the modern world.

Natural or Mimesis Proper. In our natural environment we mimic in order to camouflage and blend in; quite simply this may mean freezing if we sense danger. This is part of our biological pre-history. We make ourselves like nature.

Magical Mimesis: gradual prohibition of instinctual behaviour. Initially this came about by the by the organisation of mimesis in the magical phase, through ceremony and rite. For example, there is still an element of mimesis in the rituals of indigenous peoples – imitating animals, wearing bearskins.

Modern or Rational Mimesis People are taught behavioural norms in the school and workplace, children are no longer allowed to behave like children. Mimesis now takes a form in which society threatens nature; control equals self preservation and

(cont'd)

dominance over nature. We no longer make our 'self' like nature to survive but attempt to make nature like us. In other words, the instinctual mechanism of mimesis becomes sublimated in the practice of the rational control of the modern environment.

Projection: We project on the world experiences and qualities that are part of our-selves as if they are part of someone else. When the feeling involved is bad, the projection becomes paranoid

False Projection An attempt to change the environment, to make it like its 'self'. In a confusion of 'inner' and 'outer' worlds, the 'other' is no longer familiarised, but becomes dangerous, frightening and threatening. Intimate experiences are seen as hostile.

The Stranger A psycho-social character: The stranger is someone we know things about, who sits in 'our' world uninvited. The stranger has the characteristics of an enemy, but unlike the enemy, is not kept at a safe distance. The Stranger is neither 'us' nor 'them', friend or foe. The stranger undermines boundaries causing confusion and anxiety. This is Bauman's Stranger which we can contrast with the more positive Stranger of Simmel.

Modernity and the Holocaust

Modernity is marked by the following phenomena which facilitate genocidal type behaviours:

Rapid Social Change: Industrialisation, urbanisation, changes in political philo-sophy, dislocation, mobility and the growth of nationalism.

Science and Technology: The triumph of science as a mode of cognition; the sheer scale of the destructive process would not have been possible if it were not for the scientific and technological advancements of modernity.

Bureaucracy: The administrative procedures and practices of the nation state as exemplified by the bureaucratic organisation provided an efficient vehicle for both the logistical intricacies of extermination, and also the moral absolvement of responsibility.

Indicative Reading

Key Texts

Bauman, Z. (1989). *Modernity and the Holocaust*. Cambridge: Polity Press.
Bauman, Z. (1991). *Modernity and Ambivalence*. Cambridge: Polity Press.
Horkheimer, M. and Adorno, T. (1947, 1994). *Dialectic of Enlightenment*. London: Continuum.

Secondary Texts

Brown, C. (1985). *Fateful Months: essay on the Emergence of the Final Solution*. New York: Holmes & Meier.

Freud, S. (1919, 1961). 'The Uncanny', in *The Standard Edition of the Complete Psychological Works of Sigmund Freud vol. XVII (1917–1919)*. London: Hogarth Press, pp 219–252.

Goldhagen, D.J. (1996). *Hitler's Willing Executioners: Ordinary Germans and the Holocaust*. London: Abacus.

Gordon, S. (1984). *Hitler, Germans and the 'Jewish Question'*. Princetown: Princetown University Press.

Levi, P. (1979). *If This is a Man*. London: Abacus.

Lifton, R.J. (1988). *The Nazi Doctors: Medical Killing and the Psychology of Genocide*. London: Macmillan.

Niewyk, D. (1997). *The Holocaust*. New York: Houghton Mifflin.

Simmel, G. (1950). *The Sociology of Georg Simmel*. (ed. and trans.) Wolff, K. New York: The Free Press.

4

Jurgen Habermas: Self Reflection, Rationality and Communicative Action

Introduction

In the previous chapter I looked at the work of Horkheimer and Adorno and discussed their views on modernity and the end of Enlightenment. These views were pessimistic at the core. I feel for Horkheimer, Adorno and their colleagues that the Holocaust marked the end of Enlightenment. The bigger picture in *Dialectic* is the way in which scientific rationality and positivism have come to dominate the modern world. They are scathing in their critique of science, in the origins of the problems it studies, its social use and ultimately the purpose it serves. Scientific rationality is essentially paranoid, it is about controlling things, mastering nature, the desire to control outside, because you cannot control inside. In this chapter I want to briefly sketch some of the ideas of a contemporary member of the Frankfurt School – Jurgen Habermas. Habermas is described as a second generation member of the Frankfurt School, or a second generation critical theorist.

Habermas shares the same concerns as his colleagues before him but has a far more positive view of modernity as an incomplete project. He seeks to defend the Enlightenment project and to reconnect the idea of rational social arrangements with the idea of an emancipated and fulfilling human existence. Somewhere, somehow things have gone wrong and there are things that we can do to address these problems and get the project of modernity back on track. Habermas is particularly concerned about how we bring back into our lives the idea of a substantive rationality – in other words, how we bring back the ethical into our sense of what reason is about. Today, life is dominated by economic growth; by instrumental rationality. The rationalisation process has gone wrong, and for Habermas, as essentially a Kantian, this has led to the incomplete project of modernity. In what is probably one of his most important books *Knowledge and Human Interests* (1971b) Habermas develops a critique of positivism and a new theory of human knowledge. It is important to recognise that Habermas is continually refining and developing his ideas and is still writing today. What I want to do here is just outline some of the main strands of his thought as they directly relate to some of the later debates that I address in this book, particularly the work of Foucault and the work of postmodern theorists.

Knowledge and Human Interests: Reason, Rationality and Hermeneutics

The title of Habermas' book *Knowledge and Human Interests* describes precisely its contents. It is an attempt to analyse the connections between knowledge itself and the interests of the human species. It is also a critique of science as the dominant and only form of knowledge. As Held (1980) notes, Habermas investigates the way in which instrumental reason has quite literally dominated modern thought in modern times with the ascendance of positivism, and importantly the way in which the modern subject has all but lost his or her capacity to reflect on their activities (Held, 1980, p 254). We have seen in the previous chapter that for Horkheimer and Adorno the problem with anti-Semitism is not projection *per se*, but lack of self reflection. It is also Habermas' contention that systematic self reflection is the path to self knowledge; self knowledge helps us free ourselves from ideological domination. Self reflection therefore leads to emancipation.

If we are to understand Habermas then we need to briefly address Kant's division of reason. Although critical of Kant, a discussion of Kant's work forms the bedrock of Habermas' views on reason and knowledge. For Kant we have three broad divisions of reason: first there is Pure Reason which is about the establishment of 'truth', second we have Practical Reason – judgements about what is right and good, what is ethical, and finally, there is Aesthetic Reason – conclusions of beauty and pleasure. All these forms of judgement are dimensions of human reason. If we apply one form to an inappropriate area then things start to go wrong. The processes and institutions of modernity have developed pure reason – instrumental rationality at the expense of practical reasons, norms, values, rights and wrongs – we simply do not do enough practical reasoning. Habermas tries to establish Kant's practical reasoning by using hermeneutics – focussing on interpretation, looking at meaning, so success is not in prediction as in science, but in interpretation. Practical reason is about communication, setting norms and agreements and this is reflected in the way that we relate to other human beings. Habermas' interest in hermeneutics stems, as many people have noted, from the positivist dispute

in German sociology and the social sciences in general. His concern, particularly in *Knowledge and Human Interests* is epistemological – how can
we know, and how can we delineate the form or view of knowledge used by
critical theory from the dominant paradigm of the positivistic sciences?

Hermeneutics, the 'science' of interpretation, was devised by Schleiermacher
(1911) in the early nineteenth century largely around the codification of the
interpretation of text. This was developed by Wilhelm Dilthey into a method for
the interpretation of action. Action for Dilthey has both meaning and a narrative
structure, Dilthey argues:

> While the systematic human studies derive general laws and comprehensive pat-
> terns from the objective apprehension of the unique they still rest on understanding
> and interpretation... So, from the very beginning, we are facing a problem that
> distinguishes the human studies from the physical sciences (Dilthey, 1976, p 247)

From Dilthey we have the notion that understanding becomes a form of interpretation which is validated by the scrutinisation of the narrative structure of
action. This distinguishes the sociological method from that of the scientific
method. Dilthey however, fails to discuss the practical application of his
method. One action can be expressed as several movements; one movement
can be the result of several actions. Therefore there seems to be something
about action that eludes observation. We have seen just how important
hermeneutics were for some of the classic sociologists, particularly Max Weber
and the concept of *verstehen* which I outlined in chapter two. To reiterate,
Weber argues that if we are to understand the relationship between social
action, meaning and motivation, we have to delineate two types of understanding (*Verstehen*). First, we have the direct observational understanding of
our subjective meaning of an act, which for Weber includes verbal utterances.
What this means is that we basically understand on face value, what we see is
what we understand, and what we understand is based on observation.
So, confronted by someone with a smiling face and jovial manner we will
assume that certain facial expressions and utterances equate to happiness in
that particular individual. A second form of understanding is that of explanatory understanding where we look at the motive behind the meaning that a
social actor attaches to an action. In other words, what is the reason for
someone acting in a particular way, at a precise moment, in a certain context?
It is however, as both Outhwaite (1994) and How (2003) highlight, the work of
Hans-Georg Gadamer that Habermas looks to for hermeneutic inspiration,
and in particular the book *Truth and Method* (1989). How (2003) argues that for
much of interpretative sociology when we talk about *verstehen*, we are actually
talking about putting ourselves in someone else's shoes so that we objectively
imagine the world of another. This is often confused with empathy, where we
put ourselves in the position of another to feel what they feel, and therefore
empathise with their situation. We can of course put ourselves in the shoes of
another and feel no empathy whatsoever, particularly if we are to be objective.

For Gadamer, the problem with this method is it does not highlight the way in which the sociologist or researcher brings into the environment his or her own understanding. This has been the source of great debate for many years in anthropological research, in the debate between realism and relativism. In other words is there one reality that we can record effectively (realism) or multiple realities (relativism) that we can merely know something about?

In the *Interpretation of Cultures*, Clifford Geertz (1975) argues that we should follow Weber in the way in which we view other cultures, our analysis and method should not be based on science, searching for laws, but in the interpretation of meaning:

> The concept of culture I espouse, and whose utility the essays below attempt to demonstrate, is essentially a semiotic one. Believing, with Max Weber, that man is an animal suspended in webs of significance he himself has spun, I take culture to be these webs, and the analysis of it to be therefore not an experimental science in search of law but an interpretative one in search of meaning (Geertz, 1975:5)

Using the concepts of 'thin' and 'thick' description Geertz argues we can develop a hierarchy of meaning in action, which is the object of ethnography. Geertz uses the example of winks and twitches to differentiate between thick and thin description. Thin description is what the actual social actor is doing. So, in winking, he or she is rapidly contracting his or her eyelid and could also be construed as twitching. Thick description looks at the intended meaning in the action; the winker may be winking to extract a response from some other. If there is no intended meaning then the wink is not a wink but a twitch. Ethnography for Geertz is about thick description, the 'essential vocation of interpretative anthropology' is:

> Not to answer our deepest questions, but to make available to us answers that others, guarding other sheep in other valleys, have given, and thus to include them in the consultable record of what man has said (Geertz, 1975, p 26).

Geertz is clear that the limitation of interpretative ethnography is just that, it is interpretation, it is second or third hand and only the social actor who is part of a particular culture can give a first hand interpretation; can be certain of the intended meaning in action; can be sure that description is description, rather than fiction. Peter Winch refines this idea (1974, 2000) by proposing a method in which we can reach an empathetic understanding of the language(s) of subjects:

> It is because the use of language is so intimately, so inseparably, bound up with the other, non-linguistic, activities which men perform, that it is possible to speak of their non linguistic behaviour also as expressing discursive ideas (Winch, 2000:128)

In *Understanding a Primitive Society*, Winch (1974) identifies a paradoxical problem in the work of Evans-Pritchard (*Witchcraft, Oracles and Magic Among the Azande*: 1965), in that Evans-Pritchard is trying to work with a conception of reality which is not determined by its actual use in language. Winch notes that Evans-Pritchard views ritual and magical practices from a scientific perspective. And thus by implication, those who practice magic are making some form of error:

> There is more than one remark to the effect that 'obviously there are no witches'; and he writes of the difficulty he found, during his fieldwork with the Azande, in shaking off the 'unreason' on which Zande life is based and returning to a clear view of how things really are (Winch, 1974:79)

Science, according to Evans-Pritchard, has shown that there are no relations of cause and effect attached to magic and ritual. The Azande therefore, must be misguided in their use of magic and oracles. Winch disagrees, arguing that both science and ritual are valid within the language, meanings and values ascribed by society – they are ways of thinking that are provided by the society that we live in. For Winch reality is not what gives language sense. 'What is real and unreal shows itself in the sense that language has' (Winch, 1974, p 82). In other words, Winch is arguing that language is in some sense a realm in itself. The language user is located in a language community which has its own vocabulary of meaning, of norms and concepts of reality. We cannot transpose the language of science onto the language of Azande magic because it becomes meaningless. The two systems of language, as Thomas Kuhn (1970) would argue, are largely incommensurable with each other. The implication of Winch's thesis is twofold. First, if we take Winch's position, then the magic and ritual of the Azande represents a logical and coherent discourse of understanding and meaning within that society. Second, Winch's methods suggest that we can obtain an empathetic understanding through the language systems of individual subjects in a given society. This should enable us to avoid interpreting Other by reference to self, in other words we do not transpose our meanings and values on other cultures, we look at other societies from the perspective of the other. This is potentially problematic as Winch notes. Can we feasibly learn the language system of another culture in order to participate in that culture and how do we translate that back to the culture we are reporting to? How can one linguistically different community understand another without modifying language to make it comprehensible?

So, to return to Gadamer it would seem that we are not simply passive interpreters of our social world, but as How (2003) notes, for Gadamer our understanding has a *forestructure* that does not allow pure knowledge, rather our understanding of the world is shaped by our preconceptions and prejudices. We never see anything though conceptless eyes, rather we project on the world our own systems of understanding. This was why Max Horkheimer and Theodor Adorno, and later we shall see also Habermas thought psychoanalysis was so important for critical understanding of the social world. The process of understanding is never ending and circular; we constantly re-evaluate, re-invent and revise our conceptions and understanding of the social world, this is known as the hermeneutic circle. An endless interpretation of the bigger (and smaller) picture, this is, what it is to *be*. Outhwaite (1994) argues that the work of Habermas in the hermeneutic tradition builds on three elements or approaches – the work of Alfred Schutz (1932, 1972) in the phenomenological tradition, Winch (1974) as we have seen, in the linguistic tradition, and Gadamer in the Hermeneutic tradition. For Outhwaite each of these approaches goes beyond or transcends the other in their understanding of meaning in everyday life. (Outhwaite, 1994, p 26). So, what did Habermas get from hermeneutics? Clearly the emphasis on language was the basis for his later work and theory of communicative action. How (2003) elucidates:

> Habermas's engagement with hermeneutics was a critical one, but one from which he absorbed much. He was critical of its too accepting view of prejudice and tradition. He regarded both 'science' and 'reflection' as having the power to breach prejudice and tradition in a way that Gadamer did not allow. His view of the hermeneutic account of language was more conciliatory. He accepted much of its anti-positivist implications regarding the impossibility of presuppositionless (objective) knowledge. But more important for him, because language constitutes the common ground for our mutual understanding and is dialogic in character, it means through language we can establish further common ground. (How, 2003, p 123)

Habermas is critical in some sense of Gadamer's notion of prejudice. Prejudice comes from our past experience and traditions, but in the same way prejudice also upholds our traditions. It is a bit like Garfinkel's (1967) account of reflexivity in *Studies in Ethnomethodology* which I described in chapter two. We constantly suspend doubt about the way things are and accept them to be as they are because they have always been that way (tradition). This gives us a view of the world that is steeped in prejudice; our prejudices lead us to suspend doubt and preserve our naïve realism. This is not the case however for Habermas; reflection enables us to rethink what we have previously accepted, to question our current understanding and reformulate ideas. Again How (2003) gives a clear account of this issue:

> Habermas is arguing that Gadamer does not recognise the truth of his own argument. If tradition, like understanding, is dialogic, then its natural back and forth movement should allow reflection to offer the hope of emancipation. It is only Gadamer's conservatism that refuses to see that reflection can break up assumptions that have been inculcated by tradition. A prejudice that has been made transparent by our self reflection on it can no longer function as a simple reinforcement of tradition. (How, 2003, p 126).

So, from this we can see that idea of reflection and particularly self reflection is key to Habermas' project for understanding the relationship between knowledge and human activity. Ultimately self reflection can free us from the constraints of ideology and other forces that we have not been able to recognise as having a substantial effect on our lives. The key to this is to think about hermeneutics in terms of reflection which is why Habermas turns to psychoanalysis. I will discuss this later in this chapter but first I want to turn to something that grounds all human knowledge for Habermas – our cognitive interests.

Cognitive Interests

All knowledge for Habermas is founded on cognitive interests. These interests are the basic interests of the human species and are the underlying modes through which reality is disclosed and acted upon. They delineate a general orientation which yields a viewpoint – from which reality is constructed. Cognitive strategies are determined by the conditions and problems governing the reproduction of the human species. (Held, 1980, p 296) Habermas' theory is often dense and difficult to unravel but, if we imagine that different forms of knowledge have different types of interest (cognitive) in-built in them, and that these types of interest overlap, then this is a challenge to the objectifying positivistic science. Indeed this is more than a challenge, but an attempt to integrate science into a more general theory of knowledge and action in which science far from merely objectifying and recording in an empirico analytic sense, also has an interest in control. Something that Horkheimer and Adorno highlighted at length in *Dialectic of Enlightenment*. How (2003) reminds us that when Habermas uses the term 'interest', he does not mean that knowledge directly serves the interest of a particular group in society, rather that knowledge is orientated in a certain way to produce different kinds of truth. (How, 2003 p 51). In other words it is a question of epistemology – how we know about things. So for Habermas:

> There are three categories of processes of inquiry for which a specific connection between logical-methodological rules and knowledge-constitutive interests can be demonstrated. This demonstration is the task of a critical philosophy of science that escapes the snares of positivism. The approach of the empirical-analytic sciences incorporates a *technical* cognitive interest; that of the historical-hermeneutic sciences incorporates a *practical* one; and the approach of critically orientated sciences incorporates the *emancipatory* cognitive interest. (Habermas, 1971b, p 308)

We can therefore delineate three forms of *cognitive interest* and relate them to a form of *knowledge* and a *social dimension*:

Technical Cognitive Interest: Empirical-analytic knowledge which is characteristic of positivistic sciences. These sciences prejudge the meaning of possible statements and establish rules for the construction of theory and the testing of that theory. For Habermas, 'theories comprise of hypothetico-deductive connections of propositions which permit the deduction of lawlike hypothesis with empirical content. The latter can be interpreted as statements about the covariance of observable events' (Habermas, 1971b, p 308). In other words, we have the classic scientific model of cause and effect based on objective observation in which a hypothesis is tested and a lawlike observation noted.

This implies however an interest in control and certainly the control of nature. Habermas does not dismiss this form of knowledge but attempts to clarify the limitations of it – this is the cognitive interest in technical control of objectified processes. The social dimension is the world of work.

Practical Cognitive Interest: Historical-hermeneutic knowledge characterised by the interpretative sciences, for example hermeneutics, the humanities literature and any discipline concerned with understanding meaning. Access to facts for Habermas is gained not through observation but through the understanding of meaning – 'the verification of lawlike hypothesis in the empirico-analytic sciences has it counterpart here in the interpretation of texts. Thus the rules of hermeneutics determine the possible meaning of the validity of statements of the cultural sciences. (Habermas, 1971b, p 309). Habermas notes, that hermeneutic knowledge is always mediated by the interpreter's pre-understanding. Knowledge is located at the juncture between text and interpreter and the outlook is governed by an interest in preserving and expanding the intersubjectivity of action orientated understanding. So the practical interest has as its social dimension interaction, communication, and language but fails to tackle cause and effect.

Emancipatory Cognitive interest: Is the knowledge generated by Critical Theory. In essence this interest seeks to combine in a reflexive manner the two other interests whilst filling the gaps that the others miss out. 'It is concerned with going beyond this goal [nomological knowledge] to determine when theoretical statements grasp invariant regularities of social action as such and when they express ideological frozen relations of dependence that can be in principle transformed' (Habermas, 1971b, p 310). In other words critical theory seeks to provide undistorted communication through critical self reflection. This will free us from both our internal and external compulsions. The social dimension of the emancipatory interest is power relations whether both through authority or control. The interest seeks to point to this and free us from the constraints of ideology. So, all three interests can be simplified thus:

Cognitive Interest	Social Dimension	Type of Knowledge
Technical	Work	Empirical-Analytic Prediction/Control
Practical	Interaction Language/Communication	Historical-Hermeneutic Understanding
Emancipatory	Power Relations Authority/Control	Critical Theory Undistorted Communication

The distinction between technical and practical interests is crucial. Medicine for example is able to offer a technical solution to ill health, whereas changing your lifestyle may offer a practical one. Although logically separate, these interests are interrelated and interact with each other. The third is essential for the second if we are to establish consensual norms. One of the reasons that we cannot achieve a proper substantive rationality is some groups are more powerful than others; norms are imposed by external forces. Hence the third emancipatory interest which helps point towards systems of domination and ideology. Ideology in effect applies the wrong sort of knowledge for a particular domain; we need the third interest as it is based on open and free communication and inquiry. How (2003) notes that there is a certain ambiguity in the status that Habermas gives these interests. As we have seen Habermas is quite plainly criticising the unreflective nature of the positivistic sciences and the way in which knowledge is viewed. In other words knowledge is always created for a reason, and in the case of the positivistic sciences, for technical control. The big question is where do these interests come from? Held (1980) argues:

> While accepting the need to understand knowledge as a result of the constituting activity of the cognizing subject, Habermas rejects the Kantian approach of locating such activity in an a historical, transcendental subject. Rather, starting with an essential tenet of historical materialism – that history, social reality and nature (as known) are all a product of the constituting labour of the human species – Habermas understands knowledge in the light of the problems man encounters in his efforts to 'produce his existence and reproduce his species being'. (Held, 1980, p 255).

In other words knowledge is produced or constituted within the context of the historical and material conditions in which the human species has developed. So, for example the human species has had an interest in creating and producing a certain type of knowledge that enables technological control of nature, in terms of survival, and of communication in terms of reproduction. This is why the third interest, the emancipatory interest is so important; without the sustained self reflection attached to it, we simply would not recognise the interest attached to knowledge: The technical and practical cognitive interests can be comprehended as knowledge-constitutive interests only in connection with the emancipatory cognitive interest of rational reflection' (Habermas, 1971b, p 198). The emancipatory interest in some sense rescues reason through self reflection simply by arguing that if we are aware of the interests attached to knowledge then we can make rational and reasoned judgements (through self reflection) and therefore act in a rational way. Habermas describes the cognitive interests as quasi-transcendental. In other words they are neither instinctual animal behaviour nor entirely empirical rational contemplation – neither biological or psychological constraints nor limitations of knowledge. Dews (1999) argues that the phrase quasi-transcendental points to a fact for Habermas that these interests, the possibility of knowing, is grounded in the life of the human species, and yet have *a priori* status for us – they make knowledge possible rather than constrain it (Dews, 1999, p 8). So, for Habermas all human knowledge is guided by interests and only a self reflective person can have such interests; self reflection itself is an expression of an interest – the emancipatory interest, which in turn enables us to use explanation and understanding to free ourselves from the clutches of power relations and ideology. For Habermas the only form of knowledge which expresses this interest, indeed all three interests, is psychoanalysis.

Psychoanalysis and the Self Reflection Model

The self reflection model for Habermas is at the heart of Enlightenment thinking and embedded in Western tradition. The basic idea is self knowledge through self reflection. Self reflection brings to consciousness the elements of the self formative process. Structures of distortion can be revealed and isolated. Indeed for Habermas: through self reflection, individuals can become aware of forces which have exerted a hitherto unacknowledged influence over them. It is psychoanalysis that Habermas turns to as a basis or model for a critical social science which incorporates the emancipatory interest. As Held (1980) notes, it is the type of psychoanalysis developed by Freud (Held presumably recognises that there are now many schools of psychoanalytic thought) that Habermas turns to as it represents the only example of a science incorporating methodical self reflection. (Held, 1980, p 319). Held notes that Freud was mistaken with nature of his own discipline when he ascribed it the status of a natural science. There has been a huge debate surrounding the epistemological and scientific nature of psychoanalysis. The dismissal of psychoanalysis as a science, as Ian Craib (1998) notes, 'is the usual ground for the philosophical dismissal of Freud', and this dismissal is based on positivistic notions of science. Freud proposed a new theory and practice. The practice – 'the talking cure' is very much based on an interpretative and hermeneutic understanding of the human psyche. Freud however claimed throughout his life that psychoanalysis was very much a science, and in doing so, left himself open to constant criticism from medical, philosophical and sociological traditions. The debate on whether psychoanalysis is a science, as expressed in the views of Popper (1983), Gellner (1985) and particularly Grunbaum (1984) exploded in 1993 when the *New York Review of Books* published Frederick Crew's (1993) essay *The Unknown Freud*. It was a damming report on psychoanalysis and Freud's theory in which Crews describes psychoanalysis as an explanatory worthless hobbyhorse. The problem with taking this as a definitive is that it detracts from what Freud does give us in terms of interpretation, and it detracts from other less scientific interpretations of Freud's work in terms of its hermeneutic and philosophical quality. Arguably then, what Freud developed was a systematic hermeneutic method for analysing the human condition. Psychoanalysis becomes a theory of human nature, that can be used both as a tool of investigation (as an academic subject) and as a technical practice (the talking cure).

For Habermas, it is very much the idea of psychoanalysis as a hermeneutic interpretative science based on self reflection that lends itself as model for the mapping of cognitive interests. Freud provided a model that reflected on its presuppositions and after all, that is what critical theory is all about – critical sustained self reflection on our methods and practices. Habermas argues that initially psychoanalysis appears only as a special form of interpretation, but on closer inspection we can see that psychoanalysis involves a much deeper form of hermeneutics, in other words a depth hermeneutics that addresses both conscious forces (as Dilthey's hermeneutics did) and unconscious or unknown memories that make up historical life:

> Psychoanalytic interpretation is concerned with those connections of symbols in which a subject deceives itself about itself. The depth *hermeneutics* that Freud contraposes to Dilthey's philological hermeneutics deals with texts indicating self deceptions of the author. Beside the manifest content (and the associated indirect but intended communications), such texts document the latent content of a portion of the authors orientations that has become inaccessible to him and alienated from him, yet belongs to him nevertheless. (Habermas, 1971b, p 218).

Habermas is pointing to the method and role that psychoanalysis can play in uncovering distortions and meanings in everyday language, in linguistic expressions and text. Of course for Freud the royal road to the unconscious was through dream analysis and as Habermas notes, for Freud the dream was the 'normal' model of pathological conditions. The dreamer awakes, but does not understand his or her own creation – the dream. Psychoanalysis goes beyond the hermeneutic because not only does it try to grasp the meaning of distorted text, but also the meaning of the text distortion itself. Transposing this to society we can start to see a method for uncovering distorted communication and ideology. The emancipatory cognitive interest aims at the pursuit of reflection – 'in the power of self-reflection, knowledge and interest are one' (Habermas, 1971b, p 314). The problem for Habermas is the way in which the sciences apply their methods without reflecting on the knowledge constitutive interest. This has led to the ideologically infused nature of Nazi bio-medical science, and for Habermas, Stalinism and Soviet Marxist genetics. Thus we have a three level methodology that incorporates all three interests able to point too, and identify distortion in communication. Psychoanalysis is the only knowledge system that has all three levels:

Empirico-analytic: Knowledge of the development and structure of mind – id, ego, superego

Historico-hermeneutic: dialogue and communication between patient and analyst, mutual understanding, (for example) interpretation of dreams.

Critical: Frees the individual from internal compulsions, works at achieving freedom.

Therefore for Habermas freedom equals knowledge of the real processes underlying human consciousness and motivation. What makes us 'unfree' is that we are driven by both internal and external forces that we are not aware of. Internal forces are covered by repression; external forces are masked by ideology. Self reflection can free us from both these internal and external constraints. In doing this, Habermas is trying to introduce us to a way in which a substantive rationality unclouded by ideology can be introduced back into the project of modernity. There have of course been some major criticisms of Habermas' work many of which he addresses in an additional postscript to *Knowledge and Human Interests*. As David Held (1980) notes, Habermas' formulation of the emancipatory interest can be ambiguous. So, the basic conditions of human existence are defined as work, language and domination, which are the basis for the cognitive orientations and are given equal standing. Yet in other places Habermas views work and language as *the* fundamental conditions of human existence which are distorted by domination. The emancipatory interest develops to transcend these distortions. (Held, 1980, p 319). In addition to the continuing general critique of psychoanalysis epistemologically which I have already highlighted, Outhwaite (1994) draws our attention to the sceptical response Habermas has received for using psychoanalysis as a model for a critical science. Outhwaite argues that this in some sense has been a misunderstanding of Habermas' work in which critical theorists were being portrayed as social psychoanalysts in a therapeutic role in relation to society. This is quite plainly not was Habermas was saying argues Outhwaite (Outhwaite, 1994, p 34). Despite this, Outhwaite argues that Habermas does offer a somewhat idealised version of the analytic situation, stressing aspects of self-reflection and enlightenment above all else. Outhwaite further criticises a point that Habermas has systematically addressed; his notion of the technical-instrumental interest attached to empirical science. Outhwaite argues that Habermas' view of the sciences is very much based on a Comtean model of positivism – of prediction and control, and therefore power. There has however been a change in the way that science is viewed, particularly after, and influenced by the publication of Kuhn's (1970) *The Structure of Scientific Revolutions*. There has been an acknowledgement of the role of interpretation in science and the role of practical choice in the work of scientists. (Outhwaite, 1994, p 36). Interestingly Dews (1999) points out that emancipation from oppressive regimes and power structures is not a process which is essential for the continuation of social life – ' Hierarchical, violent and restrictive societies can endure for centuries, whereas a degree of control over nature and a minimum level of intersubjective agreement are indeed necessary for social life' (Dews, 1999, p 9). This does not fit in well with Habermas' cognitive structure.

Despite these criticisms Outhwaite reminds us that even if Habermas had stopped writing in the 1960's he would have provided us with a huge contribution to philosophy, social theory and sociology. *Knowledge and Human Interests* itself and its 'positive implications amount to an enormous promissory note to fill out, some time, just what a critical social science would look like. (Outhwaite, 1994, p 37). Habermas, however, did not stop writing and although many view *Knowledge and Human Interests* as his crowning glory, he builds on these ideas in another major book *The Theory of Communicative Action* (1981, 1987) in what sociologists term his linguistic turn. In this book Habermas has solved his search for a substantive rationality as he claims that it is lodged in our species character as communicative language users. This re-asserts the Enlightenment view that systematic self reflection on human nature (communication) is ultimately liberating, in what Habermas calls the 'ideal speech situation'

System and lifeworld

Habermas distinguishes between system and lifeworld to differentiate between the world of communication and the world of work and the meaning of action for social actors. Introduced in *Towards a Rational Society* (1971) Habermas draws on the work of Huxley to differentiate between two cultural realms – literature and the natural sciences. 'Huxley juxtaposes the social lifeworld and the wordless universe of facts' – of science. We therefore have the world of literature, a world of love and hate, madness and despair, of communication – this is the social life world and on the other hand we have the world of the system, of science, of bureaucracy, something that Habermas would later call the system world. For Habermas (1981, 1987) a 'distinction between a *social integration* of society, which takes effect in action orientations, and a *systemic integration*, which reaches through and beyond action orientations, calls for a corresponding differentiation in the concept of society itself' (Habermas, 1981, p 117). Hence we have system and lifeworld. Habermas' notion of the lifeworld emanates from phenomenology and draws on the work of Mead (1962), Schutz (1932, 1972), Berger and Luckmann (1967) and Durkheim (1964) to name but a few authors. The lifeworld for Habermas is our world of interaction, the province of reality that the average adult takes for granted; it is not a private world as such, but a world of intersubjectivity, a world of cultural transmission. Indeed for Habermas:

> The social integration of the lifeworld ensures that newly arising situations are connected up with existing conditions in the world in the dimension of social space: it takes care of co-ordinating actions by the way of legitimately regulated interpersonal

relations and stabilises the identity of groups to an extent sufficient for everyday practice. (Habermas, 1981, p 140).

Socialisation in the lifeworld therefore ensures continuity of tradition and coherence of knowledge in everyday life. The lifeworld is then in some sense a world of norms and values which become differentiated into subsystems that encourage integration on a societal level whilst upholding cultural assumptions and values. Outhwaite (1994) argues that Habermas' lifeworld embodies: cultural reproduction (continuity of tradition, coherence and rationality of knowledge), social integration (stabilisation of group identities, solidarity), and socialisation (transmission of generalised competencies for action, harmonisation of individual biographies with collective forms of life). (Outhwaite, 1994, p 87). The most important thing for Habermas is that this lifeworld is our world of interaction, of communication and communicative action where people really do make a difference – constant change counters tradition and assumed knowledge. It is almost as if Habermas is suggesting that it is a safe place to tweak and experiment with ideas and knowledge without going too far – communicative reason provides a brake for the over zealous. I will discuss the notion of communicative action later on in this chapter but basically Habermas argues that human beings have built into to their essence as language users the ability to reach a rational consensus through dialogue. When social actors engage in argumentation, they reinterpret culture and reach a rational consensus through the force of a better argument. Therein lies for Habermas a notion of freedom and greater emancipation in language. Drawing partly on the work of Talcott Parsons (1949 *The Structure of Social Action*), Habermas argues that the system comprises not surprisingly of the large institutionalised aspects of society: the polity, economy and the state. Although the system world has evolved from the lifeworld in the way in which society is a product of human interaction, the system has become decoupled from the lifeworld, it is in some sense external to it, but often intrudes upon it. They have become differentiated from each other and within themselves. Habermas' view is quite complex, but it seems that he is arguing that this uncoupling of worlds have both good and bad characteristics. In the modern world differentiation and rationalisation allow the individual to see how different aspects of society work and to recognise that it is of their own creation (some overtones of Freud here no doubt). But negatively Habermas also talks of the colonisation of the lifeworld by the system:

> Neither the secularisation of worldviews nor the structural differentiation of society has unavoidable pathological side effects per se. It is not the differentiation and the independent development of cultural value spheres that lead to the cultural impoverishment of everyday communicative practice, but an elitist splitting off of expert cultures from the context of communicative action in daily life. (Habermas, 1981, p 330)

Habermas goes on to argue that the penetration of forms of economic and administrative rationality means the lifeworld becomes dominated by money and power. We start to loose the communicative discourse in which we reach a language based consensus. The system therefore starts to dominate the lifeworld in a way that blinds people to any alternatives; people cannot see anything other than their dependency on the market where action is strategic rather than communicative. Essentially Habermas is arguing that we relate to other human beings in two ways, first we relate to others simply as human beings, and second, we relate to others as objects to be manipulated. So we have two spheres in which there is a sharp distinction between work and interaction. In our lifeworld, our world of interaction, we relate to other people as whole people, as a communicative species, we use communicative action. In our system world we relate to other people as badge holders; we use them to gain access. This is typical of the world of work. So, you may for example have regular contact with your university tutors, not because you like them, but because you want to get your degree. This is means end, purposeful action, what Habermas describes as strategic action – efficiency rather than niceness. So, work is instrumental, whereas interaction is marked by habit, emotion and values:

Life world	System World
Interaction – Habit, Emotion, Values	Work – Instrumental, Rationalised
Communicative Action	Strategic Action

So the world of work has been rationalised into a system and we have the enormous apparatus of the state and public life; bureaucracies, multi-national firms, formal systems of law, all which have described in classical sociology by Max Weber and Karl Marx. The modern world is typified by system and life worlds with the system steadily encroaching on the latter. We have domination by administrative organisation and the use of science as a legitimisation for this domination. Habermas however remains committed to a project of emancipation, and this project must have at its heart an alternative account of rationality – a substantive rationality.

Communicative Action and the Ideal Speech Situation

For Habermas, somewhere lodged in our essence as a communicative species is a model of communicative rationality that we can call on to challenge authority, domination and ideology and reach some form of consensual agreement that is the result of the mutual understanding of participants in speech. Again, Habermas' theory is extremely dense and all that I want to attempt here is to provide a brief sketch, an overview of Habermas' (1981) theory of communicative action. Drawing on the work of Austin (1962), Searle (1969) and Chomsky (1965) on linguistic competence and speech acts, Habermas develops what he calls universal pragmatics. Universal pragmatics as Outhwaite (1994) notes are distinguished from linguistics by a focus on utterances rather than sentences. Outhwaite argues paraphrasing Habermas 'The task of universal pragmatics is to identify and reconstruct universal conditions of possible understanding' (Outhwaite, 1994, p 40). For Habermas every utterance contains a number of speech acts. A locutionary speech act involves *saying* something, illocutionary speech act *does* something in the process of saying and a perlocutionary speech act produces a certain *effect*. Thus a speech act – the employment of a sentence in an utterance under certain conditions means that we actually do things by saying things. For example if I say to a colleague 'good morning' I am saying something (locutionary); in saying something I am offering a greeting (illocutionary) and showing how friendly I am, but, if I were to utter the phrase 'Bore da' – Welsh for good morning, this will have an effect (perlocutionary), not least why is he talking in Welsh, is he trying to be clever, is there something strategic about this? For Habermas, perlocutionary effects are intended but not always specific. Again Outhwaite gives a very good example – By saying 'I promise to return the book' (locutionary) I am issuing a promise (illocutionary) and therefore doing something by saying something I produce an effect (perlocutionary) – I offer reassurance to a possibly suspicious lender that I will return the book. (Outhwaite, 1994, p 46). Thus for Habermas we can reveal a truly communicative use of language to attain goals common to the human species where all participants in speech pursue their illocutionary aims. Contra to this we have the perlocutory use of speech which often has a strategic, non explicit purpose. In order to reach a rational consensual agreement action needs to be communicative.

The purpose of Habermas for this investigation into the underlying modes of language use is to uncover the way in which human beings maintain their existence and cooperate through the medium of language. In other words how we reach the complex position of a consensus or the possibility of agreement in communication. The theoretical model that expresses a pure type of communicative action and rationality is what Habermas refers to as the 'ideal speech situation':

In this regard, I tried to delineate the general pragmatic presuppositions of argumentation as specifications of an ideal speech situation. This proposal may be unsatisfactory in its details; but I still view as correct my intention to reconstruct the general symmetry conditions that every competent speaker must presuppose are sufficiently satisfied insofar as he intends to enter into argumentation at all. (Habermas, 1981, vol. 1, p 25)

Thus Habermas describes three aspects of argumentative speech in the ideal speech situation. First, participants in argumentative communication have to presuppose that their communication is free from all force, except the force of a better argument. Argumentation in this form can be described as a reflective continuation of reaching an understanding. Second, as argumentation is a procedure, we need a set of rules that enable a co-operative division of labour to point to problematic validity claims that we can test with reason. Finally, argumentation has as its aim to produce cogent arguments from which validity claims can be rejected or redeemed. So, to translate this into more understandable terms we could say that the ideal speech situation is just that – ideal. It is a situation with the following characteristics:

- There is a mutual understanding between participants
- Everyone has an equal chance to select and employ speech acts
- There is a recognition of the legitimacy of each to participate in the dialogue as an autonomous and equal partner
- The resulting consensus is due to the force of a better argument

So, in other words, everyone has an equal opportunity for discussion which is free from domination, either internal or external and therefore everyone has the same chance of influencing the outcome. There is, therefore, built into our nature as language users, some form of a model of democracy. In discussion we constantly challenge each other on the basis of four validity claims and reach a consensus in discourse. The Validity claims are:

Validity Claim	Functions of Speech	Domain of Reality	Mode of Communication
Truth	Representation of Facts	The External World of Nature	Cognitive: Objectivating Attitude
Rightness	Establishment of Legitimate Interpersonal Relations	Our World of Society	Interactive: Conformative Attitude
Truthfulness	Disclosure of Speakers Subjectivity	My world of Internal Nature	Expressive: Expressive Attitude
Comprehensibility		Language	

Every speech act involves these four validity claims and different ones come to the fore at different times. For Habermas all successful forms of communication have a rational foundation and this foundation is a series of validity claims that has a cognitive character. In order for us to act communicatively we must challenge, vindicate or redeem the validity claim in the light of our speech acts. Communicative interaction can only be sustained in light of the validity claims which we implicitly raise in the act of an utterance. They are basically the things that make the utterance convincing or believable in everyday conversation, and we constantly challenge on the basis of them – that it is understood (comprehensibility), that it is true (truth), that it is right (rightness), and that it is sincere and a real expression of the utterer's feelings or intentions (truthfulness). In mundane social interaction these claims are taken for granted, but if some consensus is brought into dispute, then the utterer could vindicate or dismiss on the basis of the validity claims. This is something that implicitly happens every time we enter into dialogue with another person. So, if we take the simple utterance: It's raining.

I hereby wish	Truthfulness
To Assert	Rightness
That it is raining	Truth

The whole lot is comprehensible but we might challenge this if it is uttered in Russian.

These validity claims then are essentially claims to truth that we raise in everyday communication. Claims are made on the basis of both fact and value, in other words its raining may well be a fact, but to say the rain is refreshing is certainly a matter of value. But we might want to defend our claim on the basis of certain value judgements in which we could subjectively reach a conclusion or consensus – rain is only refreshing when it tends to be hot. Of course there are far reaching implications in everyday life in terms of Habermas' model. If we could sit down and reach a rational consensus, we might abort wars, armed conflicts and the unnecessary loss of human life. Habermas' model could be applied to organisational dynamics to help large scale organisations manage conflict in the workplace and increase harmony and worker satisfaction. This of course would mean the encroachment of lifeworld onto system where strategic action is replaced by communicative action. As we will see in the criticisms of Habermas' model, it is without a doubt that communicative practices based on values and norms already exist within the system just as Weber's faceless bureaucracy is anything but faceless. The question we need to ask is that if discussion replaces disagreement through rational consensus via argumentation, why are we still in conflict with each other?

One of the main problems with Habermas' work and one that he is often criticised for is the sheer abstraction of his theory which is often so theoretically dense that it is difficult to understand and even more difficult to apply to everyday life. I think this really is less of a problem in one way because we can quite clearly see how the notions of life and system world apply to organisations, work and social life. What I feel is more worrying is that the nature of Habermas' writing, because of its density is open to all kinds of misinterpretation. It is not easy to understand and therefore open to misinterpretation, something that is slightly disturbing when Habermas is writing about communication, consensus and agreement. There are however, some far more detailed criticisms. David Held (1980) argues that the conditions of the ideal speech situation fail to cover a number of phenomena. These range from different cultural traditions and how might understand them to the distribution of material resources, as Held notes, these 'are obviously important determinants of the possibility of discourse' (Held, 1980, p 396). Held goes on to argue that the idea that all speech is directed or orientated to some idea of genuine consensus is hard, if not difficult to sustain. The rules for understanding vary across different social settings; if we take one set of rules for one situation and apply them to another they simply do not work. As Held notes, conditions of understanding are closely linked to practical purposes and the interests of participants – 'it appears that understanding is always the understanding of something for particular purposes. Why we should take discourse as the model of communicative action and why we should employ criteria from it for the assessment of other spheres of ordinary language communication, remains obscure' (Held, 1980, p 396). I think that one of the most important points that Held highlights is that Habermas is essentially telling us that within the ideal speech situation we are able to step outside our everyday beliefs and commitments in a form of communication where the constraints of action are suspended. For Habermas, as a thinker who has been greatly influenced by psychoanalysis this seems somewhat of a contradiction not least to his own thinking – 'This implies a capacity for complete transformation in psychic states and interests – a capacity that would lead one to expect that people could adopt wholly new concerns and attitudes in systematic argument' (Held, 1980, p 397).

In a similar vein, William Outhwaite (1994) questions whether there really is such a thing as communicative action where action is orientated *to* understanding and *by* understanding. Indeed, Outhwaite argues ' that there is a substantial body of theory which sees all social action as, in Habermasian terms, strategic, treating normatively regulated and communicative action as at best marginal deviations from the strategic principle of the pursuit of rational self interest' (Outhwaite, 1994, p 110). In other words, in our everyday lives we tend to act and communicate in a strategic way to get what we want; we act in our own rational self interest. Outhwaite notes, that the one issue that has raised more criticism than any other is Habermas' differentiation between system and lifeworlds, the incoherence of the concept and the way in which system and life are too clearly delineated when it is apparent that both overlap considerably. How (2003) draws our attention to the 'purity' of Habermas' distinction between the system and lifeworld:

> Habermas tends to find all the good things in life in the lifeworld and all the bad things he attributes to the system. The lifeworld offers us the chance, albeit only theoretically, of perfect communication, of achieving a consensus through the ideal speech situation, whereas the system offers us only the chance of being colonised by its imperatives, of being subjected to its power. The choice seems too stark. (How, 2003, p 133)

As How notes, in trying to develop a benchmark, a universal norm that we should all aspire to, Habermas tends to view the lifeworld as devoid of power, somewhere we can reach a true consensus. Power imposes itself from the external world and distorts communication. How argues, and theoretically I agree with him, that power comes from a number of sources and is tied into people's lives in some very subtle ways; for example, the power of the unconscious mind as espoused by psychoanalysis which shapes all kinds of conscious thoughts and actions without us knowing about it – this power is not always negative, and if we are to believe Freud, has made civilisation possible. How also notes the Foucauldian critique of power and the death of the subject which I want to turn to in the following chapters where power is part of the subject and not imposed from external forces. Quite clearly there are some deep philosophical and theoretical problems with Habermas' work and these are discussed at length in Honneth and Joas' (1991) book *Communicative Action*, but now I want to focus on some of the practical problems.

The ideal speech situation is threatened by a number of factors. First there is power and fear. Some people are more powerful than others; they are better at commanding situations and are more prone to dominate conversation. Conversely, some people are too scared to talk and challenge. They find social and communicative situations difficult and feel intimidated by those who hold power, or appear to. The ideal speech situation becomes less than ideal. Second, there is unequal access to information, so people are privy to certain types of information while others are excluded – you can only talk and discuss on the basis of what you know – again the ideal speech situation is less than ideal. Finally, we could think about the unequal ability to articulate; some people are simply better at talking, articulating ideas and are trained to argue – think of sociologists, this is what we do for a living. The ideal speech situation again is less than ideal, or should we say that it is an ideal! There are quite clearly then wider issues here that revolve around social class, education and culture that make the idea of an ideal speech situation seem quite impossible. Some of these criticisms of Habermas seem unnecessarily harsh, and often distract from the fact that Habermas is actually trying throughout his theory to do something good, to find some basis of a way of knowing, communicating and acting that will make the world a better place for people. It is more likely that we can use the ideal speech situation as a yardstick rather than something set in stone. In other words how close are we to reaching a rational consensus? As How (2003) notes, Habermas offers through the uncovering of the grounds for rational communication an academic challenge to the nihilistic and very pessimistic view that reason has disappeared. Again, Outhwaite (1994) notes that like many of the creative theorists Habermas does not offer ready made solutions, 'but possible ways of developing what he calls the grammar of our ways of life' (Outhwaite, 1994, p 120).

Summary

I have discussed in detail two of Habermas' major works – *Knowledge and Human Interests* and *Communicative Action* because I feel that they underpin most of Habermas' thinking which he has constantly refined in answer to his critics. Habermas, for me, practices what he preaches in a constant dialogue. Habermas' output has been vast (see Habermas, 1971a and 1971b, 1974, 1976, 1987, 1989, 1992, 2003 for examples) which I cannot possibly discuss in this brief overview. The subject of Habermas' thought in addition to that which I have already discussed includes the nature of modernity, the application of law and in his very latest writings he focuses on the latest developments in bio-technology and genetic intervention. 'Modernity – an Unfinished Project', the title of speech given by Habermas on his acceptance of the Adorno prize in 1980 broadcast a clear message to poststructualist and postmodern thinkers such as Lyotard that Modernity indeed what not at its end, but merely an unfinished project. For Habermas 'This theme, disputed and multifaceted as it is, never lost its hold on me' (Habermas, 1987, xx). This lecture, together with a number of others was published as the *Philosophical Discourse of Modernity* in 1987 (trans 1987) in which Habermas engages critically with Derrida and Foucault amongst others:

> No matter whether Adorno paradoxically reclaims truth-validity, or Foucault refuses to draw consequences from manifest contradictions; no matter whether Heidegger and Derrida evade the obligation to provide grounds by fleeing into the esoteric or by fusing the logical with the rhetorical: There always emerges a symbiosis of incompatibles, an almagam that resists 'normal' scientific analysis at its core. Things are only shifted to a different place if we change the frame of reference and no longer treat the same discourse as philosophy or science, but as a piece of literature. That the self referential critique of reason is located everywhere and nowhere, so to speak, in discourses without a place, renders it almost immune to competing interpretations. (Habermas, 1987, p 336)

These themes I will take up in the following chapters when I address the work of Foucault, Lyotard, Baudrillard and others. But for the meantime Habermas has solved that search for a substantive rationality that so evaded Weber and this substantive rationality is lodged in our very essence, in our *species character* as language users. Habermas goes on to apply the theoretical foundations he establishes in *The Theory of Communicative Action* to law and the public sphere in his 1992 book *Between Facts and Norms*. In it Habermas develops his own views on the nature of law and links them with the formation of the state and deliberative democracy (see Outhwaite, 1994, Hoggett and Thompson, 2001). More recently Habermas has turned to questions of ethics in genetics and biotechnological research. In *The Future of Human Nature* (2003), Habermas is concerned with advances in biotechnological development that enable on the one hand the prevention of disease through genetic intervention, but on the other pose huge ethical issues as human beings start to play God. Again, at the heart of this book in some sense is the idea that has played on Habermas' mind throughout his entire career – the notion of freedom and equality and the things that undermine this freedom.

So, we can say Habermas is far more positive about the project of modernity which he views as an incomplete project. He defends the Enlightenment project and reconnects the idea of rationality to social arrangements, in particular the way in which we can bring a positive form of substantive rationality into our lives and how we can free ourselves from ideologies that have been behind some of the worst events in the last couple of hundred years. We have seen his answer to ideology in the self reflection model and the use of psychoanalysis before going on to examine the search for a substantive rationality in our nature as language users. This again re-asserts the Enlightenment view that systematic reflection on human nature, through communication, is ultimately liberating. But of course cynics would argue that this is just a recipe for endless talk, it is not about consensus but influence, it is about taken for granted points and finally people are often cruel and deceptive in the their use of language. Habermas is significant because his body of work and later commentators on his work form a very strong critique of some of the theorists that I will look at later in this book, particularly Michel Foucault and also the postmodernists who Habermas claims lack reflexivity and a sense of history. His views are obviously contra to the position of Lyotard who opposes all stories of progress as illusory, whilst Habermas remains committed to the project of modernity and its promise of enlightenment.

Summary of Key Concepts and Terms

Cognitive Interests: All knowledge is founded on cognitive interests. These interests are the basic interests of the human species. They are the underlying modes through which reality is disclosed and acted upon. They are the basic interests of the human species and basic to the survival of the species.

(cont'd)

Technical Cognitive Interest: Empirical-analytic knowledge which is characteristic of positivistic sciences. These sciences prejudge the meaning of possible statements and establish rules for the construction of theory and the testing of that theory. The social dimension is work.

Practical Cognitive Interest: Historical-hermeneutic knowledge characterised by the interpretative sciences, for example hermeneutics, the humanities literature and any discipline concerned with understanding meaning. The social dimension is interaction, language and communication.

Emancipatory Cognitive Interest: Is the knowledge generated by Critical Theory. In essence this interest seeks to combine in a reflexive manner the two other interests whilst filling the gaps that the others miss out. The social dimension is power relations typified by power and control.

System and Lifeworld

System world is characterised by the world of work which is rationalised in a system of instrumental communication and action. It is comprised of the large institutionalised aspects of society: polity, economy and state. Action is strategic.

The Lifeworld is a world of interaction, habit, emotion and value. It is the site of intersubjectivity and the transmission of cultural values that we take for granted. Socialisation in the lifeworld ensures continuity of tradition and coherence of knowledge in everyday life. Action is communicative.

Ideal Speech Situation

Where we are able to reach a rational consensus through the force of a better argument. Characteristically there is a mutual understanding between participants. Everyone has the chance to select and employ speech acts. There is a recognition of the legitimacy of each to participate as equals.. We reach consensual agreement through the force of a better argument. It implies that built into our very nature as language users is a model of democracy.

Validity Claims

In order for us to act communicatively we challenge, vindicate or redeem a validity claim. Validity claims have cognitive character and we implicitly raise in them in the act of an utterance. They make the utterance convincing, or believable in everyday conversation and we constantly challenge it on the basis of them. The validity claims are:

Truth which functions in speech to represent facts

Rightness which functions in speech to establish legitimate interpersonal relations

Truthfulness which functions in speech to disclose the speakers subjectivity

Indicative Reading

Key Texts

Habermas, J. (1971). *Knowledge and Human Interests*. London: Heinemann.
Habermas, J. (1981, 1984). *The Theory of Communicative Action Vol 1: Reason and the Rationalization of Society*. London: Heinemann.
Habermas, J. (1985). *The Philosophical Discourse of Modernity*. London: Polity Press.
Habermas, J. (1987). *The Theory of Communicative Action Vol 2: The Critique of Functionalist Reason*. London: Heinemann.

Secondary Texts

Held, D. (1980, 1990). *Introduction to Critical Theory: Horkheimer to Habermas*. London: Polity.
Honneth, A. and Joas, H. (eds) (1991). *Communicative Action*. London: Polity.
How, A. (2003). *Critical Theory*. London: Palgrave.
Outhwaite, W. (1994). *Habermas: A Critical Introduction*. London: Polity.
Weber, M. (1921, 1978). *Economy and Society, Vol 1*. Berkeley: University of California Press.
Winch, P. (2000). *The Idea of a Social Science and its Relation to Philosophy*. (2nd ed.). London: Routledge.

5

Michel Foucault: Reason and Unreason – From 'The Ship of Fools' to Disciplinary Society

Introduction

Michel Foucault's work has almost produced a culture industry in its own right, and although strictly not sociology in the sense that Foucault would deny this himself, his work has had a profound influence on sociological thinking since his death in 1984. Foucault's radically different reframing of the history of madness, of deviancy and sexuality are the focus of this chapter. Foucault takes us on a critical voyage from the 'ship of fools', a strange 'drunken' boat that glides along the calm waters of the Rhineland and Flemish canals, a time when madmen had an easy wandering existence, to a very different existence – to disciplinary society (Foucault, 1995, p 7). In doing so, Foucault questions the very notion of what it means to be mad, to be a delinquent, and in his later work, the way in which expert systems have tried to construct sexuality.

Continuing the theme of identity construction and its relationship to rationality, this chapter explores after Foucault, the processes and historical circumstances that give rise to the modern person, to the creation of rational man and the objectification of the Other. Key themes in this chapter are the processes of normalisation and objectification of the subject, expert discourses and their relationship to power and knowledge, and the idea that we live in a disciplinary society, whether this has been self discipline or governmentality – or government as the *conduct* of our *conduct*. There is an emphasis on the critique of expert discourses, in particular psychiatry, criminology and psychoanalysis. There are similarities, or at least convergences between the work of Foucault, Weber and the Frankfurt School particularly when we think about the notion of rationality. Put simply, on the one hand Weber was concerned about the domination of means-ends formal rationality and rationalisation of the social world as a process. Foucault, on the other hand, was more interested in specifics, key events in history which can be read through the lens of the power/knowledge relationship Foucault provides us with a social history of rationality. Again in Foucault's work there is the idea that rationality is not always a good thing.

It is of course impossible to pigeonhole Foucault's work in one discipline, something he refused to do himself choosing the eclectic title of Professor of the History of Systems of Thought on taking up his chair at the Collegè de France in 1970. There is a distinct originality in Foucault's writings which put them part way between philosophy and history but in neither camp. For sociologists and critical theorists it is his social history of the creation of ways of thinking about key aspects of human existence that has become important and the way in which the individual is inextricably bound up in the relations between power and knowledge. In the afterward to *Power/Knowledge* (1980) Colin Gordon argues that what Foucault 'may have to offer is a set of possible tools, tools for the identification of the conditions of possibility which operate through the obviousness and enigmas of our present, tools perhaps also for the eventual modification of those conditions' (Gordon in Foucault, 1980, p 258). I want to structure this chapter around three key texts: *Madness and Civilisation* (1967, 1995), *Discipline and Punish* (1975, 1977) and *The History of Sexuality* (1977, 1984a, b) to pick out the key themes in Foucault's work and relate them to the creation of self, the rationality of the modern world and the end of Enlightenment. Finally I will return to some of the criticisms of Foucault, and in particular his engagement with Jurgen Habermas.

Reason and Insanity

In his first major book *Madness and Civilisation* (1961 (in French), 1967, 1995) Foucault plots a social history of the development of the concept of reason and madness in the classical age, to insanity and sanity in our modern age. In doing so he maps a voyage in relation to madness which moves from disorder and excess to a medical and dysfunctional model of insanity in our modern age. The main themes of the book revolve around notions of unreason and reason, integration and exclusion, power and knowledge and the creation of Cartesian rational man. This is underpinned as Dreyfus and Rabinow (1982) note by Foucault tracing the growth of 'scientific positivism as an overlay for the real explanation of the power to cure that lay behind objectivity' (Dreyfus and Rabinow, 1982, p 11). Scientific knowledge for Foucault, far from being objective is a discourse from which the powerful dominate. Foucault is effectively showing us in *Madness and Civilisation* that there is a discourse on madness in western civilisation that has four distinct stages. In medieval times the madman was considered almost holy, in the Renaissance, the madman was not feared but had a different form of high reason. At the end of the seventeenth century madness started to become more clearly delineated from sanity and we saw the start of confinement, of hospitals. The mad were not excluded but confined. Towards the end of the eighteenth century the asylum was developed together with psychiatric discourse which further separated reason from unreason. Finally, argues Foucault, all nineteenth century psychiatry converges on Freud, on psychoanalysis. (Foucault, 1995, p 277).

Foucault starts his examination of the development of madness by noting that by the end of the Middle Ages, leprosy had all but disappeared from the Western world. Throughout the Middle Ages leprosariums had proliferated throughout the cities of Europe but they were suddenly laid bare. For example Foucault notes that 'In Stuttgart a magistrate's report of 1589 indicates that for fifty years already there had been no lepers in the house provided for them' (Foucault, 1995, p 6). For Foucault, what remained in these empty houses of confinement were the values and images attached to the highly symbolic figure of the leper. So, while leprosy disappeared the structures that excluded the leper remained intact and were to be used many years later to house and socially exclude the poor, mad and deranged. It is perhaps the 'ship of fools' that provides the most striking reference in Foucault's analysis:

> Something new appears in the imaginary landscape of the Renaissance; soon it will occupy a privileged place there: the Ship of Fools, a strange 'drunken boat' that glides along the calm rivers of the Rhineland and the Flemish canals. (Foucault, 1995, p 7).

The mad were loaded onto boats and sent in search of their own sanity, excluded from the social body, they became on one hand a cultural figure of major concern (Dreyfus & Rabinow, 1982), on the other, there was a certain ambivalence, as if the mad person simply had a higher or different form of reason. Indeed for Foucault, the mad led an easy wandering existence. The expulsion of the mad by ship also had a highly symbolic or ritualistic function. Not only were the mad to go in search of their sanity but the passage itself through water was almost a process of purification. The madman, the folly, the fool did indeed live a very different existence in the Renaissance period when madness replaced death as a fixation, madness becomes a living death, or as Foucault describes it 'the déjà-là of death' (Foucault, 1995, p 16). Although the mad were expelled they were not confined, the ship of fools sails through a landscape of delights, there is a certain wisdom of fools, but for Foucault something else appears on the horizon in the classical age:

> The classical experience of madness is born. The great threat that dawned on the horizon of the fifteenth century subsides... Oblivion falls upon the world navigated by the free slaves of the Ship of Fools. Madness will no longer proceed from a point within the world to a point beyond, on its strange voyage; it will never again be that

fugitive and absolute limit. Behold it moored now, made fast among things and men. Retained and maintained. No longer a ship but a hospital. (Foucault, 1995, p 35).

For Foucault, this marks a transformation from a strange liberation of the mad to confinement. The seventeenth century saw a change from the Renaissance to the classical age and with it a shift in the way that madness was thought of, and most importantly for Foucault this was marked by confinement, by the appearance of the madhouse. This marks the shift that pathologises madness – unreason becomes a disease. Foucault's basic argument is then, that as leprosy was eradicated in Western Europe through confinement and exclusion, the actual buildings and structures of exclusion lay dormant in the western culture. These actual buildings remained and these structures of exclusion returned in the seventeenth and eighteenth centuries to house poor criminals and those deemed as deranged, in the shape of the houses of confinement, as the madhouse. According to Foucault ' By a strange act of force, the classical age was to reduce to silence the madness whose voices the Renaissance had just liberated, but whose violence it had already tamed. (Foucault, 1995, p 38). Foucault talks of the Great Confinement, arguing that it is common knowledge that the seventeenth century created enormous houses of confinement, but, he suggests that it is less commonly known that a substantial number of Parisians were confined. In his now famous claim, Foucault argues that one in every one hundred Parisians were confined in a relatively short period of time, about three months, and one date stands as a landmark – 1656, which saw the creation of the Hôpital Général in Paris. These hospitals were not medical institutions as we would recognise them, rather they were a mixture of a workhouse and a prison:

> From the very start, one thing is clear: the Hôpital Général is not a medical establishment. It is rather a sort of semijudicial structure, an administrative entity which, along with the already constituted powers, and outside of the courts, decides, judges, and executes. 'The directors having for these purposes stakes, irons, prisons and dungeons…' (Foucault, 1995, p 40).

The houses of confinement had nothing to do with any medical concept, they housed the poor, the unemployed, the criminal, the mad, but had everything to do with order, supervision and social control. Foucault is clear that the house of confinement was a house of correction. Gutting (1994) argues that on one level confinement was an economic policy designed to deal with poverty, begging and unemployment, to get the idle off the streets and into work in a controlled environment. Crucially, Gutting argues that Foucault 'is not interested in the event of confinement for its own sake, but in the attitudes toward and perceptions of madness connected with it' (Gutting, 1994, p 54). Indeed for Foucault:

> Confinement was an institutional creation peculiar to the seventeenth century. It acquired from the first an importance that left it no rapport with imprisonment as practised in the Middle Ages. As an economic measure and a social precaution, it

had the value of inventiveness. But in the history of unreason, it marked a decisive event: the moment when madness was perceived on the social horizon of poverty, of incapacity for work, of inability to integrate with the group; the moment when madness began to rank among the problems of the city. The new meanings assigned to poverty, the importance given to the obligation to work, and all the ethical values that are linked to labor, ultimately determined the experience of madness and inflected its course. (Foucault, 1995, p 65)

Therefore for Foucault a social sensibility was born. Confinement is a manifestation of this sensibility in which society chose to banish. Order no longer confronted disorder as it was locked away in the confines of the workhouse, the madhouse, the hospital. Madness was torn away from its imaginary freedom and ' in less than a half-century, it had been sequestered (hidden away) and, in the fortress of confinement, bound to Reason, to the rules of morality and to their monotonous nights' (Foucault, 1995, p 65). There is therefore implicit in Foucault's argument that the treatment of madness in the classical age represents not exactly a regression, but a situation in which the mad became part of a larger mass who where interned for other reasons, mostly moral and economic, the mad actually became less of an object of medical attention. Classical madness, as Gutting (1994) notes is regarded as a disorder of the will and tied in with unreason. The madman was not treated as a human being but as an animal. Foucault details the practices of incarceration, of chaining people on leads, being kept in cells that are akin to dog kennels and being fed food through bars. 'The animality that rages in madness dispossesses man of what is specifically human in him; not in order to deliver him to other powers, but simply to establish him at the zero degree of his own nature. For classicism, madness in its ultimate form is man in immediate relation to his animality, without other reference, without recourse' (Foucault, 1995, p 74). Foucault goes on to argue that this is why madness was less than ever linked to medicine, because unchained animality could only be mastered by *discipline* and *brutalising*. This is not to say that the medical examination of madness did not take place in the classical age, far from it argues Foucault:

> The therapeutics of madness did not function in the hospital, whose chief concern was to sever or to 'correct'. And yet in the non-hospital domain, treatment continued to develop throughout the classical period: long cures for madness were elaborated whose aim was not so much to care for the soul as to cure the entire individual, his nervous fibre as well as the course of his imagination. The madman's body was regarded as the visible and solid presence of his disease. (Foucault, 1995, p 159).

These were of course physical therapeutics, because as Foucault points out, psychology did not exist, but the physical therapeutic was meant to scour the body and soul. For Foucault, psychology was born, not as the truth of madness, but as a sign that madness was now detached from its truth which is unreason. So, in the classical age, we could say the rational man was created by locking away all the people who did not fit the picture of rationality and morality of the time. In the eighteenth century the houses of confinement began to become the focus of concern and social anxiety. Unreason started to be associated with contagion and disease. This created a fear, what Foucault describes as the *Great Fear*. People were in dread of a mysterious disease spreading from the houses of confinement; they spoke of prison fevers, scurvy, left in the wake of the transportation of prisoners and foul air. In some sense, this was for Foucault the dread of leprosy re-emerging and confronting the inhabitants of cities in the eighteenth century. After all many of the houses of confinement were built on the site of old leper houses, and their new occupants had picked up the contagion. For Foucault, the evil that men had attempted to exclude reappeared as a certain kind of rottenness which combined the corruption of morals and the decomposition of the flesh (Foucault, 1995, p 202). Fears of contagion were expressed through the idea of the permeable nature of the walls of the house of confinement, of vapours and liquids seeping out:

> These wards are a dreadful place where all crimes together ferment and spread around them, as by fermentation, a contagious atmosphere which those who live there breathe and seems to become attached to them. These burning vapours then rise, spread through the air, and finally fall upon the neighbourhood, impregnating bodies and contaminating souls. (Foucault, 1995, p 203)

People were forever aware of their own potential madness, of becoming confined. So this was a double fear in the sense that people were horrified by the disease and perversity seeping out of the asylum on one hand, on the other, locked away in our own minds are thoughts and feelings that do not quite align with the popular moral image of rationality. So we have actual walls – the walls of the house of confinement, the madhouse, the asylum, which create walls inside us in the shape of rationality and in turn we fear our own potential madness. In some sense you could argue that the whole discourse of psychiatry grew in relation to the fear of the disease spreading from the houses of confinement as the doctors entered to control it. At the end of the eighteenth century we saw the separation of the mad from criminals and the poor with the birth of the Asylum. Psychiatric reforms practiced by William Tuke and Philippe Pinel liberated the insane from their chains. Foucault tells us of Pinel's liberation of the insane at Bicêtre where the insane were removed from their chains in the dungeons – 'Citizen, I am convinced that these madmen are so intractable only because they have been deprived of air and liberty' (Foucault, 1995, p 242). The insane were removed and as Merquior (1991) notes, placed under a benign educational regime, which Foucault was convinced was done only in order to better capture their minds.

Although the mad were free of the physical constraints imposed by confinement, they were now subjected in the asylum to systematic control, endless routines and the idea of self restraint. As Smart (2002) notes, the aim of the regime in the asylum was to enforce and internalise particular moral values and codes of conduct. As Dreyfus and Rabinow (1982) argue, the strategy of Quakers like Tuke was to make the inmate responsible for his own illness which required a therapeutic intervention based on reward and punishment. The objectified subject would be described in greater detail later by Foucault in *Discipline and Punish*, but the principle remains the same. The subject is constantly observed and made aware of the error of his ways. The mad are made to see their transgressions and brought back to the rational norms of society by restraint, retraining and discipline of the body and mind. (Dreyfus and Rabinow, 1982, p 9). As Smart notes:

> Through the twin technologies of surveillance and judgement the figure of the 'keeper', and later the 'psychiatrist', emerged between guards and patients. This figure of authority, a bearer of reason rather than physical repression intervened in madness with observation and language, in a context where 'unreason's defeat was inscribed in advance' (Smart, 2002, p 25).

It is perhaps the most significant development for Foucault, that when the doctor enters the asylum, we have the birth of the doctor-patient relationship and the expert discourses of psychiatry. This in turns leads Foucault to Freud. The physician, argues Foucault, plays no part in the life of confinement but becomes a central figure in the asylum. He is the gate keeper; the point of entry. He signs the certificate of admission and diagnoses the disorder. As Merquior (1991) notes, the asylum and the practice of psychiatry amount to no less than a gigantic moral imprisonment where the asylum mirrors the authoritarian structure of bourgeois society (Merquior, 1991, p 24). Foucault shows us how expert discourses develop systems of knowledge that sustain power relations and domination in society. It is through the personage of the doctor that madness becomes insanity, and thus an objectification for investigation in medical discourse. For Foucault, the more that positivism imposed itself on medicine, the more obscure psychiatry became, and the more miraculous the psychiatrist's power. The psychiatrist himself could not account for the success of his own cure and for Foucault it was only with the advent of Freud's work that we saw this real emphasis on the importance of doctor-patient relationship over silence and observation:

> ...all nineteenth century psychiatry converges on Freud, the first man to accept in all its seriousness the reality of the physician-patient couple, the first to consent not to look away nor to investigate elsewhere, the first not to attempt to hide it in psychiatric theory that more or less harmonized with the rest of medical knowledge; the first to follow its consequences with absolute rigor. Freud demystified all the other

asylum structures: he abolished silence and observation, he eliminated madness's recognition of itself in the mirror of its own spectacle, he silenced the instances of condemnation. (Foucault, 1995, p 277)

On the other hand for Foucault, Freud was also guilty of exploiting the structure of the medical personage, amplifying the magical powers of the analyst: a judge who punishes and rewards in a judgement that does not even condescend to language (Foucault, 1995, p 278). So, although Freud liberated the mad from the asylum it was still under the authoritarian stance of the patient-doctor relationship, a relationship of power and domination. For Foucault, although psychoanalysis can unravel some forms of madness it remains a stranger to unreason: 'it can neither liberate or transcribe, nor most certainly explain, what is essential in this enterprise' (Foucault, 1995, p 278).

There are of course several criticisms of Foucault's work on madness, not least that it is based in very specific studies and historical events that do not lend themselves to wider application. As Smart (2002) notes, Foucault's work has seen polarities in response from dismissive criticism to uncritical admiration. The criticism is often levelled at the historical inaccuracy of Foucault's work, and is often predicated, as Smart puts it, on the incorporation of Foucault's ideas within traditional history (Smart, 2002, p 63). But, Foucault was not a traditional historian, and it was precisely the traditional way of conceiving and looking at madness that Foucault sought to undermine and expose. In particular, the popular conception that Enlightenment ideas and humanitarianism meant the population had a better life – quite the opposite says Foucault, the mad became more repressed, contained and incarcerated as the centuries moved on. Merquior (1991) argues that at the time of writing *Madness and Civilisation* 'in the young Foucault the 'anti-historian' was not yet in full existence. In its place, there was just a *counter*-historian, that is to say, a historian challenging prevailing interpretations of a given strand of our past: madness' (Merquior, 1991, p 26). There are however quite clearly problems with Foucault's history which Merquior covers in some detail quoting very specific examples, and here it is worth detailing a couple of them. There is a problem with Foucault's contrast between the Medieval/ Renaissance period and modern times. Quoting Sedgwick's (1982) *Psycho Politics*, Merquior notes that long before the great confinement many mad or insane people were interned and treated for their madness. There were hospitals which had special accommodation for the mentally ill – 'There was a nationwide chain of charitable asylums, from the fifteenth century, in, of all places, Spain – not exactly a society devoted to embracing modern rationalism' (Merquior, 1991, p 27). Merquior goes on, arguing that many of the crude techniques such as dieting, fasting, bleeding, which Foucault attributes to the Age of Reason were actually rife in pre-rationalist Europe, (Merquior, 1991, p 27). The list of criticisms goes on for several pages with detailed examples of where Foucault has got his facts wrong. This is supported by Gutting's (1994) writings on Foucault

Among the Historians. Citing Roy Porter (1990) Gutting notes that Foucault
was way off the mark in his analysis of large scale confinement. The vast
majority of people were not confined in institutions and in particular in Britain
in the eighteenth century, where the mad still roamed free under the eye of
the parish. It was not until the nineteenth century that confinement became a
widespread phenomenon (Gutting, 1994, p 52). All these criticisms, as Gutting
notes, are in some sense based on a specific view of what constitutes history,
and none of the criticisms really undermine the interpretive power of
Foucault's idealist history, or its fruitfulness (Gutting, 1994, p 66). It is clear
though that Foucault has drawn our attention to a number of themes in
Madness and Civilisation.

First, there is the growing tension in modern society and the separation of
reason from unreason. We have the birth of rational 'man'. In this sense the
work of Foucault helps us understand one of the major themes of this book,
the tension between the rational and irrational and the way in which rationality steadily encroaches on our private life, and indeed on the way in which our
identity is construction both by, and in relation to others. Second, Foucault
draws our attention to the structures and institutions of modern society that
facilitate exclusion, and indeed practice social exclusion. It seems that again
Enlightenment ideals have gone wrong, rather than developing a form of
humanitarianism we punish the mad and exclude them from the social body.
There is this complex link between modernity and reason that gives rise to
practices that punish the sick and incarcerate the poor, and this leads on to the
third theme in *Madness and Civilisation*, that of organised social control. This is
very much the focus of *Discipline and Punish* which I now want to look at in
some detail.

Disciplinary Society and Social Control

If *Madness and Civilisation* charts Western attitudes toward madness over the
centuries then *Discipline and Punish* takes an equally novel historical view of
the penal system and the way in which organisations have developed to
administer hierarchies of social control that permeate far beyond the prison
into wider society. In examining the nature of discipline and punishment
Foucault highlights the subtle changes in the application of power from the
Sovereign king and the spectacle of the scaffold to disciplinary society with
objects of surveillance we have all become used to – CCTV, speed cameras and
the data trail left by our credit and utility cards. In doing so, Foucault also highlights the relationship between power and knowledge, and again, as in *Madness
and Civilisation*, the emergence of expert systems where discursive practices discipline both body and mind. All organisations start to take on the characteristics of the prison – hospitals, schools, universities, all have a form of
organisation which makes it possible not just too simply organise an individual's use of time, but to control it. To paraphrase Dreyfus and Rabinow (1982),

'Foucault presents the genealogy of the modern individual as a docile and mute body by showing the interplay of a disciplinary technology and a normative social science. Foucault's book is not a litany of progress. Rather it is a sombre recounting of the growth of disciplinary technology...' (Dreyfus and Rabinow, 1982, p 143).

In *Discipline and Punish* Foucault takes us on a journey from sovereign torture to normalising detention. His starting point is the rather gruesome spectacle of the scaffold in which the regicide Damiens is executed in a horrible and very public way. Foucault describes the botched execution of Damiens in great detail. An extract from the punishment schedule gives the reader an idea of the scene:

> On 2 March 1757 Damiens the regicide was condemned to make the *amende honorable* before the main door of the Church of Paris', where he was to be 'taken and conveyed in a cart, wearing nothing but a shirt, holding a torch of burning wax weighing two pounds'; then, 'in said cart, to the Place de Grève, where, on a scaffold that will be erected there, the flesh will be torn from his breasts, arms, thighs and calves with red-hot pincers, his right hand, holding the knife with which he committed the said parricide, burnt with sulphur, and, on those places where the flesh will be torn away, poured molten lead, boiling oil, burning resin, wax and sulphur melted together and then his body drawn and quartered by four horses and his limbs and body consumed by fire, reduced to ashes and his ashes thrown to the winds' (Foucault, 1977, p 3).

Foucault continues in great detail to explain and describe the execution of Damiens as a public spectacle before quite abruptly listing the rules for the House of young prisoners in Paris just eighty years later.

> ....The prisoners day will begin at six in the morning in winter and at five in summer. They will work for nine hours a day throughout the year. Two hours a day will be devoted to instruction. Work and the day will end at nine o'clock in winter and at eight in summer. (Foucault, 1977, p 6).

Listing the prisoner's day from six in the morning to seven thirty at night Foucault takes us on a journey of transition from a public execution to a timetable in less than one hundred years. In many ways this first part of the book sums up the whole of *Discipline and Punish* – the move from one form of penal style to another. Again, the development of the penitentiary is bound up in the objectification of the other, this time rather than the madman, we have the criminal – the deviant. The starting point in *Discipline and Punish* is as we have seen the Sovereign spectacle, public torture at its most gruesome. The spectacle of the scaffold is almost a microcosm of medieval society with a simple hierarchy – God, King, and People – a hierarchy in which punishment represents God's will. For Foucault the public execution, the spectacle of the scaffold, must be understood not only as judicial, but also as a form of political ritual 'it belongs, even in minor cases, to the ceremonies by which power is manifested' (Foucault, 1977, p 47). Any crime, not only involves breaking some law, and possibly affecting a victim, but also it is a personal attack on the sovereign because the law of the land is the personal will of the sovereign. The right to punish is part of the same idea that allows the sovereign to make war on his enemies:

> The public execution, then, has a juridico-political function. It is a ceremonial by which a momentarily injured sovereignty is reconstituted. It restores the sovereign by manifesting it at its most spectacular. The public execution, however hasty and everyday, belongs to a whole series of great rituals in which power is eclipsed and restored (Foucault, 1977, p 48).

The aim of this is not so much to establish or re-establish a balance but to demonstrate absolute power in which the criminal is beaten down, almost vaporised as ashes are thrown to the wind; this is spectacle, as Foucault puts it, not of measure, but of imbalance and excess. The problem with this excess is that often the spectacle had to display more excess every time in order to convey the feeling of absolute power. The spectacle of the scaffold gradually turned into an unruly affair. People started to object, some criminals became folk heroes, and the crowd would often try and prevent execution where they felt it was unjust. Foucault notes, that in these executions which ought to show the terrorising power of the sovereign, an atmosphere of carnival developed in which all the rules were inverted, the authority mocked and criminals transformed into heroes (Foucault, 1977, p 61). We thus saw a period of humanist reform in the eighteenth century which condemned the excesses of violence and called for an end to torture – 'Let penalties be regulated and proportioned to the offences, let the death sentence be passed only on those convicted of murder, and let the tortures that revolt humanity be abolished' (Foucault, 1977, p 73). Reformers called for the abolition of the spectacle of atrocity which centred on revenge and violence. Instead of taking revenge a criminal justice system should punish and reform.

New forms of punishment should reflect and redress the wrong done to society. Complex rules and tables of crimes were drawn up. The offender should be transformed into a useful member of society. Foucault notes that the reformers developed a series of prescriptions based on a theory of judicial representations – the punishment should not be arbitrary, but fit the crime; the crime should be made less attractive by making the penalty feared; one must use temporal modulation – the penalty transforms and modifies... the role of duration of punishment should fit the crime; the punishment should not only be directed at the guilty person, but at all potential offenders; there is a learned economy of publicity, making an example is now based on a lesson, the representation of a moral discourse – the punishments must be a school rather than a festival and finally this will make possible in society the inversion of the traditional discourse of crime; in other words the criminal will no longer be a hero (Foucault, 1977, pp 104–112). This whole discourse revolved around the notion of the criminal and created the discourse of the deviant. The criminal was no longer a person to be ritually slaughtered and eradicated from society, rather he or she became removed from society, transformed, changed, no longer a folk hero but someone who had morally transgressed, a soul to be corrected. And as such for Foucault, just as we saw in *Madness and Civilisation*, confinement and detention developed in, and as a response to, a rational discourse, this time of criminality.

Thus, in the modern age, we saw the birth of the prison, the penitentiary as a transforming apparatus based on the ethos of its predecessors the Enlightenment reformers. Foucault cites the early Dutch and Flemish models based on a transforming apparatus of work and timetables; the *Maison de Force* at Ghent organised penal labour around economic imperatives, the reason being that criminality was seen to stem from idleness. Foucault argues that the English models of detention (Gloucester) added another element on top of work – correction and isolation; in other words, reforming incarceration. Then there is the famous penitentiary in Philadelphia – the Walnut street prison which opened in 1790:

> There was compulsory work in the workshops; prisoners were kept constantly occupied; the prison was financed by this work, but the prisoners were also rewarded... life was partitioned, therefore according to an absolutely strict timetable, under constant supervision; each moment of the day was devoted to a particular type of activity, and brought with it its own obligations and prohibitions... (Foucault, 1977, p 124).

The prisoners were no longer visible to the public and therefore there could be no outcries of mis-justice. The punishment and correction were a matter between prisoner and those who supervise him.

Discipline: The Means of Correct Training

As Barry Smart (2002) has noted, it is evident from Foucault's writings that the disciplinary technology that emerged in the Age of Reason did not emanate simply from the prison but was a product and practice of monasteries, armies and workshops. Think again about Weber's argument in the Protestant Ethic: 'For when aestheticism was carried out of the monastic cells into everyday life, and began to dominate worldly morality, it did its part in building the tremendous cosmos of the modern economic order' (Weber, 1992, p 181). As Dreyfus and Rabinow (1982) argue, the prison is only one example among others of the organisation of the technology of discipline, surveillance and punishment – 'discipline is a technique, not an institution' (Dreyfus and Rabinow, 1982, p 153). Joseph Rouse (In Gutting, 1994) notes that the most important transformation that Foucault described in *Discipline and Punish* was the scale and continuity of power. (Rouse, 1994, p 94). Indeed, for Merquior (1991): 'The web of discipline aims at generalizing the *homo docilis* required by 'rational', efficient, 'technical' society: an obedient, hardworking, conscience-ridden, useful creature, pliable to all modern tactics of production and warfare' (Merquior, 1991, p 94). Discipline is a technique that coerces docile bodies. Foucault offers us a set of instruments through which power keeps hold on the social body.

First, we have *Hierarchical Observation*; surveillance becomes an integral part of production and control. Architecturally, factories, hospitals, schools, and remember this is before CCTV, are designed to enable the constant surveillance of the workforce, the inmate or the patient. Think of the layout of the hospital ward, the sister can see the kidney in bed number nine. This is not for the patient's well being, but to achieve order in the hospital and to increase efficiency. As Foucault points out, the thick heavy walls of confinement were replaced with passages and transparencies – the calculation of openings which allowed better observation. The school building became the very apparatus for observation, internal windows for example not only let in more light but increased visibility, the visibility of the inmate, patient, schoolboy, deviant:

> The perfect disciplinary apparatus would make it possible for a single gaze to see everything constantly. A central point would be both the source of light illuminating everything, and a locus of convergence for everything that must be known: a perfect eye that nothing would escape and a centre towards which all gazes would be turned. (Foucault, 1977, p 173)

Foucault argues that while hierarchised surveillance was not one of great inventions of the eighteenth century, the importance of the mechanism became inscribed in the way in which it operated. Disciplinary power became an integrated system linked from the inside to the economy in a network of relations from top to bottom, from bottom to top – supervisors constantly supervised – power was infused into the social body permanently and discreetly, in silence. As Smart (2002) notes ' It is important to remember here that power exercised through hierarchical surveillance is not a possession or property, rather it has the character of a machine or apparatus through which power is produced and individuals are distributed in a permanent and continuous field' (Smart, 2002, p 86). In order for this system to work, there had to be standard and Foucault describes this is as the *normalising judgement* – the continuous comparison between good and bad citizens, between right and wrong. The normalising judgement covers minor and local areas of life not embraced by the legal system. Foucault refers to the normalising judgement as a sort of micro-penality:

> The work-shop, the school, the army were subject to a whole micro-penality of time (latenesses, absences, interruptions of tasks), of activity (inattention, negligence, lack

of zeal), of behaviour (impoliteness, disobedience), of speech (idle chatter, inso-lence), of the body ('incorrect' attitudes, irregular gestures, lack of cleanliness) and of sexuality (impurity, indecency). At the same time, by way of punishment, a whole series of subtle procedures was used, from light physical punishment to minor deprivations and petty humiliations. It was a question both of making the slightest departures from correct behaviour subject to punishment, and of giving a punitive function to the apparently indifferent elements of the disciplinary appara-tus; so that, if necessary, everything might serve to punish the slightest thing; each subject finds himself caught in a punishable, punishing universality. (Foucault, 1977, p 178)

Thus we have the idea of society bringing itself back to the 'norm' by the subtle yet intrusive application of power into our everyday lives. This again is quite clearly linked with the notion of rationality and rational 'man'. The nor-malising judgement steers us back to the norm while identifying people who do not fit the perfect picture of rationality. Our habit, our lifestyle, one could say even our identities are constructed by application of corrective power and surveillance that permeates the whole of society and of course for Foucault this is nowhere better demonstrated than in the examination. 'The success of disciplinary power derives no doubt from the use of simple instruments; hierarchical observation, normalizing judgement and their combination in a procedure that is specific to it, the *examination*' (Foucault, 1977, p 170). The examination is for Foucault, the *normalising gaze*; it is the ultimate co-joining between *power* and *knowledge* which makes it possible to qualify, classify and punish. It is the ultimate site of the objectification of the Other. The exam lies at the heart of discipline and as a ritual it renders the subject-object completely visible. The exam goes beyond the examination *per se*, and is used in all forms of social institutions. You are examined in hospitals, in armies, in universities, in schools; you pass an examination order to drive a car. If you fail then you measured in terms of deviance from the 'norm'. Again Smart succinctly sums up Foucault's thesis:

Through the mechanism of the examination individuals are located in a field of vis-ibility, subjected to a mechanism of objectification, and thereby to the exercise of power. Disciplinary power, in contrast to the spectacular public ceremonials of sovereign power, itself remains invisible whilst those subject to it are rendered visible. (Smart, 2002, p 87)

Constant visibility has been an important way in which discipline has been exercised over individuals in prisons, schools and factories – 'we are entering an age of the infinite examination and of compulsory objectification' (Foucault, 1977, p 189). Foucault notes that a second phenomenon arises from examina-tion – paperwork, mounds of documentation and files. A 'power of writing' develops as an essential part of the disciplinary nature of power relations. Everyone has a file, a medical record, a set of dental notes, a school record.

The register in school, argues Foucault, enables one to know the habits of children. These documents are serialised and correlated, compared with each other forming trails of data which eventually find their way to centralised bodies. The examination, argues Foucault, with the help of documentation, turns the individual into a 'case'. The case becomes an object of study by a branch of knowledge and a hold for a branch of power. The examination, for Foucault, 'is at the centre of the procedures that constitute the individual as effect and object of power' (p 192). In disciplinary society the dynamic of individualisation is reversed. In a society marked by sovereign power, to be noted as an individual, you must have some form of power and riches. In disciplinary regimes individualisation is descending; as power becomes more anonymous and more functional, the objects of powers become more individualised. As Dreyfus and Rabinow (1982) note, the very self definition of the human, or social sciences is linked to the spread of disciplinary technologies, in that they produced their own rules for observation of evidence. In other words they developed expert discourses and practices within the particular institutions of power – hospitals, prisons, universities. 'All the sciences, analyses or practices employing the root 'psycho-' have their origin in this historical reversal of individualisation. The moment that saw the transition from historico-ritual mechanisms for the formation of individuality to the scientifico-disciplinary mechanisms, when the normal took over from the ancestral, and measurement from status' (Foucault, 1977, p 193). Thus for Foucault we saw the shift from the memorable man to the calculable man. The epitome of the disciplinary drive for Foucault is the Panopticon.

The All Seeing Eye

The notion of panopticism is probably one of Foucault's most widely used ideas in sociology and related disciplines and this is because of the simplicity of an idea that has wide ranging social and political ramifications. Foucault begins his analysis of panopticism by describing the measures taken when the plague appeared in a town. He does this to demonstrate some of the very basic principles of panopticism – the spatial partitioning of the town; confinement to houses; ceaseless inspections; observation posts and sentinels; and everyday everyone is counted. This surveillance for Foucault is based on a system of permanent registrations – *the plague is met by order*. We then move on to the prison – Bentham's Panopticon:

> ...at the periphery, an annular building; at the centre, a tower; this tower is pierced with wide windows that open onto the inner side of the ring; the peripheric building is divided into cells, each of which extends the whole width of the building; they have two windows, one on the inside, corresponding to the windows of the tower; the other, on the outside, allows the light to cross the cell from one end to the other. All that is needed, then, is to place a supervisor in a central tower and shut up in each cell a madman, a patient, a condemned man, a worker or a schoolboy... They

are like so many cages, so many small theatres, in which each actor is alone, perfectly individualized and constantly visible. (Foucault, 1977, p 200)

Thus for Foucault, the panoptic effect reverses the principle of the dungeon, it disposes of the deprivation of light, and the idea that you hide the prisoner retaining only the function of incarceration – visibility becomes a trap. Each inmate is confined to cell, only the supervisor, or inspector can see him, he cannot communicate with fellow inmates – 'he is seen, but he does not see; he is the object of information, never a subject in communication' (Foucault, 1977, p 200). For Foucault, this highly visible invisibility ensures there is no communication with fellow inmates and therefore no likelihood of further criminal dealing, or mass escape. If the inmate is a patient, there is no possibility of contagion, if they are madmen, then no risk of violence, if they are school children, then there is no hope of copying. Order is maintained through the gaze, no noise, no chatter, no wasting time, in the office, the workshop or the factory. Crucially for Foucault, the major effect of the Panopticon is to: '*Induce in the inmate a state of conscious and permanent visibility that assures the automatic functioning of power*' (p 201). This is achieved by making the prisoner think and feel that he is the object of constant surveillance, of the eye of power. The tower in the centre houses the inspector, but the inmate cannot see in, his view is concealed by Venetian blinds or mirrored glass in later models. The inspector may or may not be present. The Panopticon is a machine for disassociating seeing and being, it automatises power. Gradually the inmate internalises the inspector, the inspector is everywhere and nowhere, and it is, for all intents and purposes, the psychological internalisation of power. It is of course a method of conditioning; Foucault describes the Panopticon as a laboratory, in which we can see experimentation in behaviour modification and the means to correct people.

The Panopticon, as Dreyfus and Rabinow (1982) note, brings together power, knowledge, control (of the body, and of space, and time) in an integrated technology of discipline. Although the Panopticon was never actually built, the idea and ideas that surround it, make up disciplinarity, and the techniques permeate the whole of disciplinary society, from the speed camera to the arrangement of timetables, rooms, examinations, students' records in the university, in the temporal, spatial and the observational organisation of our lives. For Foucault, panopticism is the general principle of a new political anatomy whose object is not sovereignty, but relations of discipline. Think of the gathering of official statistics, the monitoring of populations; these are all part of disciplinary society. The objectification of people led to the notion of a population. Government is impossible without a statistical population which can be quantified, categorised, normalised and therefore governed – this is the essence of what Foucault refers to as governmentality. We have a huge gathering of knowledge through political economy and discourses of psychiatry, welfare, criminal justice in a society where power and knowledge are inextricably linked. Discourses of criminology create the deviant, but the prison, the penitentiary has not really worked; again for Foucault it has a political function. Criminology produces a whole class of deviants which justify all kinds of social control – the development of a professional police for instance. The delinquent is important because it makes us put up with generalised surveillance, which is there to 'keep an eye on you'. The question is: Is that eye there to protect and look after our interests, or is it there to judge and control us?

Many of the same criticisms can be levelled at *Discipline and Punish* that were directed toward *Madness and Civilisation*, that of specificity, historical inaccuracy and generalisations. I think that Smart (2002) vocalises some of the misunderstandings that surround Foucault's work in a fairly lucid way. Foucault's concept of discipline implies that modern societies are disciplined societies. Not so, argues Smart: 'The concept of the disciplinary society refers <u>not</u> to the realization of a programme for a disciplined and orderly society but to the diffusion of disciplinary mechanisms throughout the social body' (Smart, 2002 p 91). In other words, it refers to the way in which processes of discipline form a general air of domination. This domination is not suggested by Foucault to have some logical goal or end; in fact the very notion of resistance in Foucault's concept of power means that often a programme of social action will have a very different outcome to the desired effect. Indeed one of the most important factors in the domination of 'man', certainly in Foucault's work, is the area of sexuality which I want to now turn to in penultimate section of this chapter.

The Social Construction of Sexuality

The History of Sexuality (3 Volumes: *The Will to Knowledge* (1976), *The Use of Pleasure* (1984), *The Care of the Self* (1984)) contains at its heart three main themes: a rejection of the 'Repressive Hypothesis', the idea of the 'confession' and the notion of 'Bio-power'. Importantly Foucault was one of, but not the first person, to draw attention to the social construction of sexuality. Rather than taking it as a natural given, the idea of sexuality becomes a discursive practice – sexuality was constructed argues Foucault through discourse (see also Wilton, 2004). Foucault starts his examination of sexuality by questioning the role of repression, or the power of repression in the Victorian era. In some sense he is not calling into question the historical existence of repression; rather he is questioning the role that the Repressive Hypothesis has in terms of explanatory power when examining the relationship between power and sex. The Repressive Hypothesis is fairly simple. We have moved from a pre-Victorian era of openness about our bodies and frankness where sexual activities had little need of secrecy to an era of increasing repression and hypocrisy largely influenced by the Victorian bourgeoisie.

> Codes regulating the coarse, the obscene, and the indecent were quite lax compared to those of the nineteenth century. It was a time of direct gestures, shameless discourse, and open transgressions, when anatomies were shown and intermingled at

will, and knowing children hung about amid the laughter of adults: it was a period when bodies 'made a display of themselves' (Foucault, 1976, p 3)

By the time of the Victorian era, the mid nineteenth century, things had altered dramatically. Sexuality was confined to the home. The nuclear family took care of it and subsumed it into the function of reproduction. Sex became something that was not talked about – the subject was silenced. The married couple became the norm and the locus of sexuality was the 'parents' bedroom. 'repression operated as a sentence to disappear, but also as an injunction to silence, an affirmation of non-existence, and, by implication, an admission that there was nothing to say about such things, nothing to see and nothing to know' (Foucault, 1976,. p 4). Concessions were made on the periphery, but really were not concessions at all; sexual deviance was outcast to the brothel and the mental hospital where they could be policed. The Repressive Hypothesis holds also that sex was repressed because it countered the logic of capitalism, it was incompatible with the ethic of work, and thus ultimately capitalism – 'at a time when labor capacity was being systematically exploited, how could this capacity be allowed to dissipate itself in pleasurable pursuits' (Foucault, 1976, p 6). Foucault argues that there is another reason that makes it gratifying for us to define the relationship between power and sex in terms of repression. By the very fact we talk about sex, we make a transgression, we put ourselves outside the reach of power and established law:

> What sustains our eagerness to speak of sex in terms of repression is doubtless this opportunity to speak out against the powers that be, to utter truths and promise bliss, to link together enlightenment, liberation and manifold pleasures; to pronounce a discourse that combines the fervour of knowledge, the determination to change the laws, and the longing for the garden of earthly delights (Foucault, 1976, p 7).

So, this is the Repressive Hypothesis, the idea that modern industrial societies have ushered in a new age of increased sexual repression and the locus of sex is the nuclear family. For Foucault, this simply is not the case. Importantly, what we have to consider is not the amount of repression per se, but the form of power that was exercised. What we actually saw, argues Foucault, is the social construction of sexuality in the modern age: Whole new discourses about perversion, homosexuality and deviance that simply did not exist before they were invented. Indeed, for Foucault we saw a 'discursive explosion' in the eighteenth and nineteenth centuries around what constituted a legitimate alliance between people. At the same time we saw the construction of perversions and peripheral sexualities – the nineteenth-century homosexual became a personage (p 43). The psychological and psychiatric/medical category of homosexual was constituted from the moment it was characterised (in 1870), not as a type of sexual relations, but as a certain quality of sexual sensibility. The psychiatrists were busy at work, identifying various forms of minor perverts and giving them strange names. For Foucault, the medical or psychiatric examination functions as a mechanism with two sides – pleasure and power. First there is the pleasure that comes from the monitoring and outing; exercising a power that searches out and exposes. On the other hand there is the pleasure that comes from evading this power:

> The power that lets itself be invaded by the pleasure it is pursing; and opposite it, power asserting itself in the pleasure of showing off, scandalizing, or resisting. Capture and seduction, confrontation and mutual reinforcement: parents and children, adults and adolescents, educators and students, doctors and patients, the psychiatrist with his hysteric and perverts, all have played the game continuously since the nineteenth century. These attractions, these evasions, these circular incitements have traced around bodies and sexes, not boundaries not to be crossed, but *perpetual spirals of power and pleasure*. (Foucault, 1977, p 45)

We therefore start to see a veritable explosion of discourses around sexuality which were increasingly articulated in scientific terms – *scientia sexualis* – procedures that are geared towards telling the truth about sex which are geared to a form of knowledge-power. (Foucault, 1977, p 58). The central concept in the scientific study and increasing administration of sexuality was the confession. Although originating in the Christian confessional, the confession itself became one of the West's foremost ways of producing truth. For Foucault, the confession now plays a part in all our everyday lives – we have become a confessing society. We confess to our teachers, our friends, our doctor, in public, in private, we even pay to confess. Although the form of confession may have changed over the years, it is for Foucault, still the general standard by which a true discourse on sex is produced. The confession has lost much of its ritualistic elements, and no longer located merely within the church or the torturer's dungeon. It has spread to wider society and exists in the relationship between doctors and patients, parents and children, delinquents and experts, and of course for Foucault, in the very practice of psychoanalysis. Through technologies of the self there is the idea that with the help of experts we can know the truth about our sense of being, of self and identity. It is in this way that the scientific discourse on sexuality developed within the framework of the confessional in which the subject became the object of study – a case history. Just as disciplinary technologies exercised their power over the unruly working classes, Bio-power and technologies of the self were applied to the bourgeoisie.

Bio-power, the exercise of power of life and bodies was thus born. Foucault identifies four specific power-knowledge mechanisms centring on sex that emerged in the eighteenth and nineteenth century: first, the *hysterisation of women's bodies* whereby the feminine was analysed, quantified and qualified. *Second, a pedagogisation of children's sex* in which there is an assertion that all children indulge in sexual activity, but at the same time this is unnatural, immoral and dangerous and doctors, parents and psychiatrists would have to take care of this dangerous potential. Third, we have the *socialisation of pro-*

creative behaviour. The couple became the locus of sensibility, and responsibility for the social body. Finally, there has been a *psychiatrisation of perverse pleasure*. A clinical assessment is made of all anomalies and either normalised or patho-logised with respect to all behaviour, and appropriate corrective technology sought for those that err. Foucault asks us what this is all about – Is it a struggle against sexuality? An effort to gain control over sexuality? An effort to regulate sexuality? No, says Foucault, it is the very production of sexuality itself. Sexuality should not be seen as a natural given, rather, it is a social construction. Sexuality is produced through discourse. Sexuality was invented then, as a tool for the infusion of Bio-power into the social body. As Dreyfus and Rabinow note, for Foucault: 'Through the deployment of sexuality, bio power spread its net down to the smallest twitches of the body and the most minute stirrings of the soul... the body, knowledge, discourse and power – were brought into a common localization' (Dreyfus and Rabinow, 1982, p 169). As Barry Smart (2002) has noted, Foucault's work addresses the way in which through the application of power and objectification human beings are made subjects.

The concluding two volumes of the *History of Sexuality – The Use of Pleasure* and *The Care of the Self*, offer case studies from another period. Foucault, rather than analysing modern times looks back to antiquity to examine the way in which sexual activities and the pleasures associated with them become the object of moral concern. In looking at the Greek and Greco-Roman culture, Foucault seeks to reveal the technologies of self that would be later incor-porated into Christianity, and then the psychiatric and scientific discourses around sexuality. He argues that early Christian teachings demonstrated a link to some of the principles of pagan philosophy, in particular the association of sexual activity and evil and the condemnation of same sex relations. It is far more likely argues Foucault, that in Greek or Greco-Roman times there was far more emphasis in terms of moral considerations on practices of the self rather than rules about what was, or was not permitted in terms of sexual activity. There was no equivalent of sexuality in these times; the nearest term argues Foucault is *aphrodisia*, but the point for Foucault is, that although moderation was encouraged through the regulation of aphrodisia, it was achieved through self discipline rather than legislative justice. Foucault notes that there was a shift in emphasis in ancient Greek times from relationships with boys to relationships with men and women. There was also a shift in emphasis on the mistrust of the uses of pleasure which becomes the focus of *The Care of the Self*:

A whole corpus of moral reflection on sexual activity and its pleasures seems to mark, in the first centuries of the era, a certain strengthening of austerity themes. Physicians worry about the effects of sexual practice, unhesitatingly recommend abstention, and declare a preference for virginity over the use of pleasure. Philosophers condemn any sexual relation that might take place outside of marriage and prescribe a strict fidelity between spouses, admitting no exceptions. Further-more, a certain doctrinal disqualification seems to bear on the love for boys. (Foucault, 1984, p 235).

For Foucault, although there may be some analogy to be drawn from the first centuries in terms of sexual austerity, the real change came with the onset of Christianity as it transformed the way in which people related to their own sexual activity establishing a relationship between sex and subjectivity. Through Christianity and then more secular scientific ideas, people were constantly examining themselves, trying to find the truth about their own sexual being – 'from a different way of constituting oneself as the ethical subject of one's sexual behaviour' – subjectivity and confession ran hand in hand.

Power, Knowledge, and Critique

If we try conceptualising Foucault's notion of power, then what he is asking is how power is exercised and what the effects of the exercise of power are. Power for Foucault exists in a relational way. Power is not an institution *per se*, but a complex set of techniques. Power is invested in, and transmitted by the subject – hence the notion of Bio-power. Power, for Foucault, in a very Nietzschean sense, is everywhere. Where there is power there is resistance, the individual is a product of power and a transmitter of power. Power produces knowledge, or at least the apparatuses of knowledge, and knowledge becomes power; the two are bound together. The problem is, how can we do anything about that which we are a product of and what would a politics of resistance, for example, look like? Would its just turn into another set of normalising regimes in which a different subject is objectified? Many of the criticisms of Foucault are well known and covered by an immense secondary literature (see for example: Dean (1999), Burchell, Gordon and Miller (1991), Kritzman (1988), Gutting (1994), Hoy (1986), and Dreyfus and Rabinow (1982)). I have addressed some of the problems of Foucault's method, in particular his view of history. In this short section I want to return to thoughts of Jurgen Habermas and his position contra Foucault over the question of power and the nature of modernity. In *The Philosophical Discourse of Modernity* (1985), Habermas critiques Foucault's notion of power and knowledge his idea of the subject, and his notion of modernity:

> Foucault wants to show that beneath this was concealed a brutal change in the practices of power, " an adaptation and a refinement of the machinery that assumes responsibility for the places under surveillance, their everyday behaviour, their identity, their activity, their apparently unimportant gestures". Foucault can illustrate this thesis with impressive cases; nevertheless, the thesis is false in its generality (Habermas, 1985, p 288)

False, argues Habermas, because Foucault effectively conflates the notion of panopticism for example with the whole structure of society and modernisation. He filters out the internal aspects of the development of law, and thus jumps from sovereign legal power to administrative power. Foucault pays no attention whatsoever to penal law 'Otherwise, he would have had to submit the unmistakeable gains in liberality and legal security, and the expansion of civil rights guarantee even in this area, to an exact interpretation in terms of the theory of power' (Habermas, 1985, p 290). Habermas argues that Foucault presents us with a distorted picture in which he filters out important aspects of penal practice and reform, particularly in terms of legal regulation. Habermas argues that in schools, prisons, clinics, there do exist special power relations, but they have by no means been left untouched by the advancement of legal rights. There are several readings of the debate between Foucault and Habermas (see Kelly (1998), Ashenden & Owen (1999), Gutting (1994)) but I think the most readable and clear account is Steven Best's (1995) *The Politics of Historical Vision*. In it, Best provide a summary of the Habermasian critique of Foucault's work. First he notes, that Habermas views Foucault as a postmodernist. This runs counter to Habermas' thesis that modernity is an unfinished project. Best notes, that although Habermas is highly critical of postmodernists, he shows Foucault the most respect and certainly in the *Philosophical Discourse of Modernity* Habermas demonstrates a very thoughtful reading of Foucault's work. Nevertheless, Habermas is critical, understanding postmodern theory as anti-modern rather than postmodern. For Habermas, Foucault effects a number of reductions that Best describes thus:

> First, following structuralism, Foucault reduces the problem of the meaning of social practices as interpreted by conscious agents to that of explaining the conditions of possibility of discourse by the archaeologist. Subsequently, Foucault cannot account for his own interpretive standpoint... Second, following Nietzsche, Foucault reduces truth-validity claims to mere power effects. Third, following positivism, Foucault reduces the problem of justifying critique to establishing pseudo-value-free historical explanations and thus conflates foundations with 'foundationalism' (Best, 1995, p 184)

Thus with these claims, for Foucault all truth claims are illusory and all discourse equals power, and therefore the same must be true of Foucault's own discourse. In this sense he undermines the very notion of critical theory. If Foucault fails to recognise some of the gains made by the instrument of law and just looks to the effect of domination, then similarly he sees the construction of modern sexualities as nothing more than normalised subjects, in doing so for Habermas, Foucault fails to recognise that the 'eroticization and internalization of subjective nature also meant a gain in freedom and expressive possibilities' (Habermas, 1985, p 292). Best goes on to point out that at the root of Habermas and Foucault's opposed views of modernity are their different assumptions about the essence of discourse. On the one hand Foucault would argue discourse is constituted by truth claims that legitimate forms of power, the discourse of the mad, the clinically ill, etc, and therefore through discourse groups and individuals struggle for power over one another. On the other hand, Habermas would argue, that although Foucault is right to a certain degree, in so far as having to acknowledge these forms of conflict, as we have seen in the last chapter, language for Habermas is fundamentally orientated toward achieving a communicative rationality and understanding. Ultimately though, Foucault's work reflects his own politics. After Habermas, Merquior (1991) notes that 'demystifying culture only makes sense if we preserve a standard of truth capable of telling theory from ideology, knowledge from mystification' (Merquior, 1991, p 148)

Summary

So, are there any parallels with the work of the Frankfurt School – Horkheimer, Adorno, Habermas and even Weber before them? In some sense I detect a very Habermasian admiration for Foucault's works. Habermas engages with Foucault's ideas around Modernity and power in an earnest and constructive way. There is no doubt that they are both concerned with the notion of rationality, but in really quite a different way. We saw in chapter two how deeply concerned Weber was about the increasing rationality of the modern world, but even more so, he was concerned with the rationalisation process and deeply pessimistic about the fate of Western civilisation. Similarly Horkheimer and Adorno follow Weber in seeing formal rationality taking a stranglehold in modern society, and particular being used for very cruel things. Something that stands out in Foucault's analysis of madness, that what we see as progressive in the treatment of mental illness can actually be more barbaric than previous centuries. We assume that the lot of the madman was not good in medieval times, but Foucault draws to our attention that being confined to a hospital and becoming an object of the discourse of psychiatry can be equally as cruel. The difference between Foucault and the Frankfurt School to simplify matters is that the Frankfurt School look at a bigger picture of rationality, Foucault looks at specific instances – the mad, the imprisoned, the sexual deviant, to reveal different forms of rationality which have different effects and relationships to one another. You could argue that Horkheimer and Adorno are similar in their views of the nature of modernity to Foucault. Horkheimer and Adorno see the Holocaust as proof of the end of Enlightenment and civilisation, rationality gone wrong, or more of a case of rationality being put to use in the execution of evil, but in this sense Habermas would argue that Foucault is more anti-modernist, rather than a postmodernist.

So, what has Foucault shown us? First, as Barry Smart (2002) has noted. Foucault asks us 'at what price' have people defined, or have been defined as criminal, deviant, mad. Does this represent progress? Certainly for the Sociologist *Madness and Civilisation* turns on its head popular conceptions of how the mad were treated and defined over the ages. Second, there is a deep suspicion in Foucault's work of experts and expert discourses. Similarly in *Discipline and Punish* we can question whether the panoptic principle is there to transform, or for our own good, or is it really just another form of social control where the CCTV camera on the one hand keeps an eye out for us, protecting out material goods, but on the other keeps an eye on us, a diffuse and subtle application of power which makes us toe-the-line, bringing us back to the norm of someone's version of rationality. Third, if we put all these things together then there are huge implications for the construction of self. The *History of Sexuality* effectively charts the social construction of sexuality and perversion: Who do we derive our sense of identity from? Are we the passive carriers of Bio-power? If we have a choice, how do we make that choice, and how much of it is made for us? These are questions that arise from Foucault's examinations of what are really commonly held beliefs about the nature of identity and the modern subject.

In the next chapter I want to explore the notion(s) of postmodernity and postmodernism continuing the examination of the key themes of this book, that of the creation of self in relation to others, the rationality of the modern world, and as Foucault has once again demonstrated, the idea that rationality is not always a good thing. In the postmodern turn I want to examine the idea of the defragmented and decentred self, the idea that we have gone as far as we can, and life is just a series of simulations and simulacra. This will be primarily through the work of Jean Baudrillard and Jean François Lyotard. Also I want to examine postmodern ways of thinking and seeing which may entail a return to some of the theorists that we have already met.

Summary of Key Concepts and Terms

Four Stages of the History of Madness: In medieval times the madman was considered almost holy; during the Renaissance, the madman was not feared but had a different form of high reason; at the end of the seventeenth century madness started to become more clearly delineated from sanity and we saw the start of confinement, of hospitals. The mad were not excluded but confined. Towards the end of the eighteenth century the asylum was developed together with psychiatric discourse which further separated reason from unreason.

The Great Confinement: The age of the confinement of the mad rather than exclusion. Foucault cites 1656 as a significant date as it saw the creation of the Hôspital Général in Paris. These hospitals were not medical institutions as we would recognise them, rather they were a mixture between a workhouse and a prison

(cont'd)

The Great Fear. People were in dread of a mysterious disease spreading from the houses of confinement. They spoke of prison fevers, scurvy left in the wake of the transportation of prisoners, foul air. People were forever aware of their own potential madness, of becoming confined. So this was a double fear in the sense that people were horrified by the disease and perversity seeping out of the asylum on one hand, on the other, locked away in our own minds are thoughts and feelings that do not quite align with the popular moral image of rationality.

Panopticism: Based in the idea of the panoptican whereby the prison inspector is internalised; the notion that techniques of surveillance induce in the wider population a sense of permanent and conscious visibility which ensures the subtle application of power in disciplinary society. Think of speed cameras. We never know whether there is a film in them so we slow down.

Disciplinary Society. Discipline is a technique that coerces docile bodies. Foucault offers us a set of instruments through which power keeps hold on the social body. 1) Hierarchical Observation 2) Normalising Judgements. These are combined in the technique of Examination, what Foucault describes as the Normalizing Gaze – the co-joining power and knowledge.

The Repressive Hypothesis: The idea that people in the Eighteenth and Nineteenth century repressed their sexuality. Far from it argues Foucault. This era saw a whole new discourse on sexuality – in fact, the creation of sexuality, or the social construction of sexuality.

The Confession. The notion we live in a confessing society, confession plays a part in our everyday lives and forms part of what Foucault call technologies of the self. Truth is extracted about sex for example, in the confession and this becomes part of an expert discourse.

Bio Power. Borne out of the confession, Bio-power is the exercise of power over life and bodies, drawing us back to the norm within the discourse of sexuality. Power is both invested in, and transmitted by the subject. Power is not an institution but a set of techniques or practices. Through constant self examination we become both the object of, and transmitter of power.

Indicative Reading

Key Texts

Foucault, M. (1961, 1967, 1995). *Madness and Civilisation: A History of Insanity in the Age of Reason.* London: Routledge.
Foucault, M. (1975, 1977). *Discipline and Punish: The Birth of the Prison*. London: Penguin.
Foucault, M. (1976). *The History of Sexuality Vol 1: The Will to Knowledge*. London: Penguin.
Foucault, M. (1984). *The History of Sexuality Vol 2: The Use of Pleasure*. London: Penguin.
Foucault, M. (1984). *The History of Sexuality Vol 3: The Care of the Self*. London: Penguin.

Secondary Texts

Dreyfus, H. and Rabinow, P. (1982). *Michel Foucault: Beyond Structuralism and Hermeneutics*. London: Havester Wheatsheaf.
Gutting, G. (ed.). *The Cambridge Companion to Foucault*. Cambridge: Cambridge University Press.
Habermas, J. (1985). *The Philosophical Discourse of Modernity*. London: Polity Press.
Merquior, J.G. (1991). *Foucault*. London: Fontana Press.
Smart, B. (2002). *Michel Foucault*. London: Routledge.

6

Post Modernism, Post Modernity and Hyperreality

Since the world is on a delusional course, we must adopt a delusional standpoint towards the world (Baudrillard, 1993)

Introduction

So, what is Post-Modernism and what relationship does it have to postmodernity? Are these epochs in time, ways of thinking, feeling, seeing the world? Are they theories or practices, or both? How can we have a notion of postmodernity when surely today is modern? How can we have post where we are now, this must be the future? This chapter tries to make sense of the postmodern debate asking what are the differences between postmodernism and postmodernity? Are we in a new epoch of time with different cultural and political signs and economies? And if so, what are implications for the constructions of the self and has our old favourite rationality been thrown out of the window?

This chapter explores the work of Jean François Lyotard, Jean Baudrillard and David Harvey, looking at the way in which consumption, fragmentation and the notion of the decentred self have come to the fore in cultural and sociological thinking. Have we really taken on postmodern ways of thinking? Rejecting the metanarrative and universal truths about society, postmodern thinkers instead see a society, or culture, based on the mode of consumption, rather than production, in which identity is drawn from a series of simulations and simulacra. We are seduced by images of hyperreality which hold us in their grip through obscene fascination. The chapter addresses the theme of consumer society and builds on Adorno's work on the culture industry which we examined earlier in this book. There is also the continued debate as to whether modernity is an unfinished project, as Habermas has shown us, or indeed whether we are indeed in a new epoch. Even Foucault's post-modern ideas of power are challenged by Baudrillard (1987) who famously wrote *Forget Foucault*. Do we really live in this type of society though? Or, possibly a less exaggerated form of it in which post-modern theory is really just a warning to us, as Adorno's culture industry suggests, a warning that we should be more self reflexive, lest we end up in the meaningless world of Baudrillard's simulacra.

What is Post-Modernism – Postmodernism – Postmodernity?

So, how do we conceptualise postmodernism at its most basic, and what is the difference between postmodernism and postmodernity? First we could say, and we have to bear mind the complexity of the idea, that postmodernism is a reference to a cultural trend in art and architecture. Postmodernity however, is a new phase or epoch in history, and the cultural referents we refer to as postmodernism are simply symptoms of that historic shift (See Harvey, *The Condition of Postmodernity*, 1989). If we look at architecture for example, then Charles Jencks (1977, 1991) cites the dynamiting of the *Pruitt-Igoe* housing development in St Louis as heralding the symbolic end of modernism and the passage to the postmodern at 3.32 pm on the 15th July 1972. This prize wining development, a version of Le Corbusier's vision of modern living, was deemed uninhabitable for the low income families that resided there. Modern architecture was influenced by our old friend rationality. The design of buildings was functional, scientific and rational. We saw the development of huge concrete blocks of flats, utilising every spare inch of space and growing out of the ground like towering symbolic icons of progress in the 50's and 60's . The problem was however, that the planners took very little account of the needs of human beings and the idea of sociability and community. As a design for social progress, these structures were a complete failure, they soon became uninhabitable. Postmodern architecture is more of a pastiche of styles and building methods using new and more traditional materials, and indeed for Jencks (1991) the postmodern movement was and is 'a wider social protest against modernisation, against the destruction of local culture by the combined forces of rationalisation, bureaucracy, large scale development…' (Jencks, 1991, p 26). The same could be said of a parallel trend in art as well. High modernism was represented by abstraction, unintelligible to ordinary person, but then we saw the development of pop art, Andy Warhol is a good example. Jencks also cites James Rosenquist's eighty six feet long depiction of an *F111* fighter plane, a clear protest against the Vietnam War. Postmodern art was about provoking a response in a pastiche that people could understand. The same was happening in social and political theory, a change from the overarching world view to a multiplicity of perspectives.

Best and Kellner (1997) note that we live in the time of the 'posts'. We have post structuralism, post fordism, post industrial society and of course postmodernism. All suggest new epochs and 'an apocalyptic sense of rupture' (Best and Kellner, 1997, p 3). Charles Jencks (1991) argues that at the end of the twentieth century at least, postmodernism has become more than a social condition, or a cultural movement; it has become a world view – 'post-modernism means the end of a single world view and, by extension, 'a war on totality', a resistance to single explanations, a respect for difference, and a celebration of the regional, local and particular' (Jencks, 1992, p 11). Scott Lash (1990) contends that postmodernism is not a condition, or a type of society, rather it is confined to the realm of culture – 'Postmodernism is then, for me, strictly cultural. It is indeed a sort of cultural paradigm' (Lash, 1990, p 4). David Lyon (1999) argues that the concept of postmodernity is a valuable 'problematic, insofar as it alerts us to many key questions regarding contemporary society and social change – 'I see it as a concept that invites participation in a debate over the nature and direction of present-day societies, in a globalized context, rather than one describing an already existing state of affairs' (Lyon, 1999, p 108). Zygmunt Bauman (1993) argues that while the postmodern perspective on life offers more wisdom, the actual modern setting makes acting on that wisdom more difficult. We become increasingly aware that there are no solutions to certain problems in social life and we must learn to live with ambiguity:

> The postmodern mind does not expect anymore to find the all-embracing, total and ultimate formula of life without ambiguity, risk, danger and error, and is deeply suspicious of any voice that promises otherwise. The postmodern mind is aware that each local, specialized and focussed treatment, effective or not when measured by its ostensive target, spoils as much as, if not more than, it repairs. The postmodern mind is reconciled to the idea that the messiness of the human predicament is here to stay. This is, in the broadest of outlines, what can be called postmodern wisdom. (Bauman, 1993, p 245).

Thus we start to get a feeling that postmodernism is more a state of mind, than anything else, something that David Harvey (1989) describes as 'profound shift in the structure of feeling' (Harvey, 1989, p 65). For Baudrillard (1983) we live in an exhausted world of simulations where the mass media no longer represents the world we live in, but defines it. On quite a different and more positive note Lyotard (1984) defines postmodernism as an incredulity toward metanarratives. This view has specific implications for Feminism. As Best and Kellner (1991) note, the postmodern emphasis on heterogeneity, difference, micropolitics and plurality can help prevent the occlusion of significant differences between men and women, thus articulating the specific needs of women (Best and Kellner, 1991 p 210). The postmodern turn does away with grand narrative of patriarchal society and can be used to challenge dominant ideologies around sexuality (see Foucault, 1976). Indeed we have seen an articulation of a postmodern feminist psychoanalysis by authors such as Jane Flax

(1990), a synthesis of postmodern and feminist theory by Nancy Fraser and Linda Nicholson (1988) and the incorporation of postmodern gender theory and psychoanalysis in the work of Lynne Layton (1998). Before I go on to look at the work of Jean Francois Lyotard in some detail I want to outline what I feel are some of the main tenets of postmodernism in social and political thought in the light of the examples above.

First, there is shift in emphasis from realism to relativism; that is, there are many realities, local knowledge is important and we cannot rely on any universal truths. In particular, any political system that claims some universal formula for emancipation, of universal truth or knowledge is treated with utmost suspicion. Second, postmodernism provides a critique of history, of the teleological unfolding of events and logic. In other words, it counters the idea of the rationalisation process that we have looked at in some detail, and for example, we can see this in the work of Foucault in the previous chapter where the history of madness does not square with the popular image of the treatment of the mad as increasingly getting better and more humane over the ages. Third, certainly in social theory there is very much an emphasis on the fragmented and decentred nature of the self. The self is made up of a multiplicity of things and is no longer lodged in tradition, ideas of community and of the nuclear family. Far from being a bad thing, certainly for Lyotard, the fragmented self is positive and indeed fragmentation should be cultivated. Finally, there is emphasis on the interconnection between power and discourse. We have seen this demonstrated in Foucault's work, and it is something that Lyotard also discusses at length. In order to demonstrate some of the shifts between modern and postmodern paradigms, I have adapted Jencks' (1991, p 34) diagram below. Care must be taken however, as Jencks notes, these are not binary oppositions, rather the postmodern represents a shift, or hybridisation of the modern.

Modern	hybridised to	Postmodern
	In Politics	
Nation-states		regions/supranational bodies
Totalitarian		democratic
Consensus		contested consensus
Class friction		eco politics, new agendas
	In Economics	
Fordism		post-fordism
Monopoly capital		regulated socialised capitalism
Centralised		decentralised
	In Society	
High growth		steady state
Industrial		post-industrial
Class structured		many clustered

Jencks, goes on to list a numbers of spheres of change, but the above gives a taste of a shift of emphasis to local knowledge, diversity and the cultivation of difference. In the next section of this chapter I want to look at what is often regarded as the seminal text on the postmodern condition as well as examining some of Lyotard's other influential works.

The Postmodern Condition

Jean François Lyotard more than any other author is linked with the idea of postmodernism. As Best and Kellner (1991) note, 'Lyotard is celebrated as the postmodern theorist *par excellence*' (Best and Kellner, 1991, p 146). Lyotard, they argue, has in some sense emerged as the champion of difference, attacking grand or metanarratives as totalising and terrorising regimes that stifle plurality. Lyotard's early writing is against a backdrop of Marxism, but also of the Nietzschean influence in French intellectual life. As Stuart Sim (1996) notes 'He is part of a generation which was heavily infected by the doctrines of Marxism, and in fact until very recently it was hardly possible not to be in dialogue with Marxism if one were a French intellectual or academic' (Sim, 1996, p xvii). One only has to think of the influence of Jean-Paul Sartre in post war years and his own philosophical struggle between Marxism and Existentialism (See Farrell Fox, 2003). But while structuralists like Althusser and Lacan took their inspiration from Marx and Freud, argues Fox, poststructuralists, of whom we could count Foucault, Derrida, Deleuze and Lyotard turned to Nietzsche. Indeed Sim (1996) argues that the poststructuralist reaction to Marxism manifested itself in an outbreak of nihilistic philosophy in the 70's which rejected order, rationality and instead demanded, after Nietzsche, a revaluation of all values. A classic example of this is Deleuze and Guattari's (1983) Anti-Oedipus. Thus we start to see the rejection of universal theories of knowledge to a more rhizomic approach to philosophy. Lyotard's greatest break with Marxism can be seen in his book *Libidinal Economy* (1974, 1993).

> We must come to take Marx as if he were a writer, an author full of affects, take his text as a madness and not as a theory, we must succeed in pushing aside his theoretical barrier and stroking his beard without contempt and without devotion... (Lyotard, 1993, p 95)

As Best and Kellner (1991) note, *Libidinal Economy* turns Marx against Freud and Freud against Marx and Nietzsche against both of them. The argument in *Libidinal Economy* is complex, but goes something like this; the body is a site of libidinal forces, these forces are not something that we can control, but are something we can literally just experience. The energy that drives people is the Freudian pleasure principle. We are the site of affect and desire, and desire is not something that can be systematised, but a force that roams around within discourse. This is of course counter to Jacques Lacan's claim that the unconscious is structured as a language. So, contrary to Lacan's ideas, Lyotard is arguing that it is language itself, particularly when set within an expert or scientific discourse which stifles desire; in other words, language becomes the Freudian reality principle. Philosophy, therefore should counter this stifling of desire. The goal of libidinal economy argue Best and Kellner (1991), is to describe the flows and intensities, and territorialisations of desire, and to liberate this desire to full intensity. Traditional theories, even critical theory has the effect as we have seen of stifling desire. 'Libidinal economy thus offers a new type of theory and practice that is purely affirmative, that attempts to provide the outlines of a new (anti)theoretics and politics of desire' (Best and Kellner, 1991, p 154). Lyotard talks of the Tensor, which forms a conduit through which desire generates libidinal effects. I think this is best read after Sim (1996) who argues that libidinal economy is ' to be understood as the state which calls into question all efforts at 'grand narrative' closure, the state to which we can do no more than bear witness' (Sim, 1996, p 25). There is also a further factor with Libidinal Economy, that of the question of the body in philosophy. Certainly *Libidinal Economy*, like Deleuze and Guattari's *Anti-Oedipus*, puts the body back in centre stage. As the body is the site of libidinal energy and the discharge of this energy, any philosophy that fails to take account of the body at a libidinal level will fail to understand reality. As Best and Kellner note, Libidinal Economy is Lyotard's most extreme attempt to go beyond all previous theories; in fact he attacks all previous theories to the extent that he traps himself in a theoretical dead-end.

> *Economie Libidinale* thus seems to commit Lyotard to a naïve naturalism in which the expression, articulation, and effects of all desire, beyond good and evil, were valorized, making it impossible to distinguish between fascist and revolutionary, or regressive and emancipatory desire…it is also questionable whether one can escape theory and reason from within the highly theoretical discourse of Lyotard's Economie *Libidinale* with its abstractions, implicit claims to truth and validity, and complex rhetoric and linguistic demands. (Best and Kellner, 1991, p 158)

Lyotard's idea of Libidinal Economy, as Fox (2003) notes, with its emphasis on plurality, fragmentation, desire and intensity, is often put forward as an antidote to our obsession with reason and rationality, but Lyotard himself was later to refer to it as that 'evil book, the book of evilness that everyone writing and thinking is tempted to do' (Sim, 1996, p 16). It was, put simply, for Lyotard, the work of a writer at the end of his tether.

The Postmodern Condition (1984) is considered by many as the seminal text on the postmodern era. Subtitled *A Report on Knowledge* Lyotard takes to task the discourses of modernity and attempts to produce a new epistemology that will make redundant the discourse of instrumental rationality that has dominated Western philosophical and sociological thinking. Sim (1996) argues that if one were to talk of a cult of postmodernism, then this book would be its bible (p 30). Lyotard's working hypothesis is fairly straightforward – 'that the status of knowledge is altered as societies enter what is known as the post-industrial age and cultures enter what is known as the postmodern age' (Lyotard, 1984, p 3). Thus, Lyotard argues, that as we see technological transformations, the nature of knowledge itself becomes transformed. So, for example the miniaturisation of computing technology and ready availability of high power machines means that information and learning are more accessible. We have an increase in the circulation of learning akin to the advancements in human circulation that came with the development of advanced public transportation. Research itself becomes dictated by technology, if knowledge is not translatable into computer format it will be discarded. The gist of this is that knowledge no longer has 'use value', but is a marketable commodity of exchange and this form of informational commodity is indispensable to productive power. In fact for Lyotard, it is the major stake in the worldwide competition for power. This will affect the privilege that nation-states have held as the purveyors of learning and knowledge. New forms of knowledge will bypass the state altogether. Indeed Lyotard argues, that is not difficult to imagine learning circulating in the same way as money on the global market: 'instead of for its "educational" value or political (administrative, diplomatic, military) importance; the pertinent distinction would no longer be between knowledge and ignorance, but rather, as is the case with money, between "payment knowledge" and "investment knowledge" '(Lyotard, 1984, p 6). In other words, knowledge used in everyday life to survive versus knowledge invested in a particular project to optimise its performance.

In what could be viewed as a thinly veiled attack on Habermas' thinking, Lyotard calls into question the nature of knowledge, or rather its legitimacy. Knowledge marks for Lyotard the site on which conflict between modern and postmodern ideas come to bear. The fight is basically between the big story and the little picture. Thus modernity is marked by what Lyotard refers to as the metanarrative or grand narrative, the totalising scientific discourse of Enlightenment thinking. Hence universal theories, for example, the scientific discourses, present to the individual some kind of truth or even guarantee of truth – this is the way it is, if you like. The legitimation crisis for Lyotard is summed up in a simple question – what legitimates the metanarrative itself? The Scientific discourse and legitimacy of science as a purveyor of truth is inextricably linked to what we know as ethics and politics; they both stem from the occident. Lyotard is claiming the same kind of argument that we saw in Foucault's work, the link between power and knowledge as two sides of the same coin: 'who decides what knowledge is, and who knows what needs to be decided' (Lyotard, 1984, p 9). The problem is, for Lyotard, that there are many forms of knowledge and narrative, other than the metanarrative; the metanarrative brings upon itself the crisis of legitimation. If we take traditional narrative, then it makes no claims of universal truth, they are, simply what they are – popular stories that exist in given societies that lend themselves to a whole series of language games. The narrator of the story is not an expert; a scientist, psychiatrist, or a judge; his or her only claim to competence is that he or she has heard it. The storyteller has authority in some sense by simply telling the story, but, in the same instance the listener also gains access to that authority by simply listening, and therefore being able to repeat. It is the narrative rather than the narrator that holds authority. This is clearly understood within given cultures, for example, the natural rhythm within a nursery rhyme, often makes it easier to recall from memory. This form of narrative and narration is quite simply legitimated by the fact 'they do what they do' (Lyotard, 1984, p 23). The opposite could be said of scientific knowledge; it burdens itself with legitimation, proof, verification, falsification. The scientific discourse differs significantly from the traditional narrative because it simply does not recognise that it is merely another story about the world. Back to Horkheimer and Adorno who claimed many decades before Lyotard that scientific discourses do not recognise themselves as mere projections from the mind of the scientist. In their critique of positivism (see chapter three) they argue that scientific methods of categorising and labelling nature are actually ways of dominating nature. Scientific categories are social constructions; they are made up by the scientist and emanate from the mind and imagination of the scientist. They have literally been made up, but now appear as if they are natural, as if they have always existed. In the same way, Lyotard argues that science does not conceive of its theories as being merely narrative, but something of far higher status – a universal truth. The opposite can be said of the narrative which is assigned to the low orders by the scientist:

> The scientist questions the validity of narrative statements and concludes that they are never subject to argumentation or proof. He classifies them as belonging to a different mentality: savage, primitive, underdeveloped, backward, alienated, composed of opinions, customs, authority, prejudice, ignorance, ideology. Narratives are fables, myths, legends, fit only for women and children. At best, attempts are made to throw some rays of light into this obscurantism, to civilise, educate, develop. (Lyotard, 1984, p 27)

So while narrative discourse sees scientific discourse as just another branch of the family of narrative, the opposite is true for scientific discourse and this for Lyotard is symptomatic of the entire history of Western cultural imperialism. Science is a set of narratives just like any other discourse, but refuses to recognise this, in order to maintain a culturally superior position. For Best and Kellner (1991), in Lyotard's sense of history there are three conditions for modern knowledge: first, they appeal to metanarratives to legitimate what are foundationalist claims. Second, there is an inevitable outgrowth of legitimation, deligitimations and exclusion, and finally, modern knowledge is marked by a desire for homogenous epistemological and moral prescriptions (Best and Kellner, 1991, p 165). So, modern discourses appeal to metadiscourses such as the narrative of Enlightenment progress, truth and emancipation to legitimate their positions, modern sciences legitimates itself in terms of health, well being, truth and progress. A rational discourse, for a rational time, to produce a rational course of action within the process of rationalisation, doing away with ignorance and superstition and bringing emancipation to the Western world. This of course has the effect of negating other cultures, other ways of life, different ways of seeing the world, and demonising that which does not appear rational. The problem with this world view is that it negates itself. The totalising and terrorising discourse of the metanarrative is unable to satisfy its own conditions of proof: It is not a case of 'I can prove something because reality is the way I say it is. But: as long as I can produce proof it is permissible to think that reality is the way I say it is', the problematic being ' what I say is true because I prove that it is – but what proof is there that my proof is true? (Lyotard, 1984, p 24). As Sim (1996) notes, 'science is a narrative which tries to pretend that it is not a narrative – and when one realises this, one has entered into the postmodern condition where the old rules no longer have any purchase to speak of' (Sim, 1996, p 40).

So to recap, in the *Postmodern Condition* Lyotard is arguing that in pre-modern or traditional times knowledge took on a certain narrative character imbued with myth, legend and storytelling. The authority lay in the actual narrative rather than the expert and had the effect of giving meaning to peoples lives and binding together society. Modern knowledge, or specifically scientific discourse does not recognise itself as a narrative and occupies a culturally superior position because it promises us a set of universal truths. The problem is, that much of science's cultural success is based within certain narrative myths itself, the idea of progress, liberation, total knowledge, and it is from these that it has gained its status with the promise of liberating us from disease, poverty and ignorance, while at the same time, controlling and taming nature. The rules of science give rise to what Mannheim (1960) would refer to as a self referential inconsistency, it only exists in relation to itself, scientific knowledge can only be proved by other scientific knowledge. In other words, what proof is there that my proof is true. This is not a bad thing if you are able to recognise it, science just becomes another set of narratives, but if it remains unseen it wanders into the realms of ideology, and hence we return to Lyotard's question: who decides what knowledge is, and who knows what needs to be decided? In other words, the scientific discourse is not value free, scientists decide to study certain things and for various reasons. Science remains therefore tied into cultural trends and values. As much as it would like to retain its objective status it quite clearly is not objective in the history of things. It is just as likely to form part of an interpretive narrative rather than an objective truth. So, if metanarratives are totalising, terrorising and exclusionary, what would we replace them with, what would a postmodern knowledge or science look like?

As you might expect, a postmodern science like postmodern knowledge rejects the metanarrative and involves the constant search for instabilities, heterogeneity, plurality and constant innovation in practice which involves the pragmatic construction of rules at a local level, thus suggesting a micro, rather than macro politics. Postmodern science is more concerned with the generation of paradox rather than any form of logical proof that is its own self referent. Lyotard therefore argues that:

> Postmodern science – by concerning itself with such things as undecidables, the limits of precise control, conflicts characterised by incomplete information, '*fracta*', catastrophes, and pragmatic paradoxes – is theorizing its own evolution as discontinuous, catastrophic, nonrectifiable, and paradoxical. It is changing the meaning of the word *knowledge*, while expressing how such a change can take place. It is producing not the known, but the unknown. And it suggests a model of legitimation that has nothing to do with maximized performance, but has as its basis difference understood as parology. (Lyotard, 1984, p 60)

Parology then, is the search for differences, paradoxes and instabilities. Lyotard is influenced by both chaos theory and catastrophe theory because they undermine the whole notion of the idea of the system because what they demonstrate is the untenable nature of accurate prediction or precise measurement. If we try to take society as a whole system, then complete control of it is impossible because this would necessitate an exact description of its initial state, but no such definition could ever be effected. Therefore, for Lyotard, this limitation 'only calls into question the practicability of exact knowledge and the power that would result from it' (Lyotard, 1984, p 56). So classical determinism works within the remit of the unreachable, but conceivable limit of a total knowledge system. As Sim (1996) notes, what Lyotard presents is a disturbing world picture which implies that all systems are inherently unmanageable because they are a paradoxical mixture of determinism and chance that resists ordering. In doing so, what Lyotard is arguing is that there is a complete lack of scientific basis to systems theory (Sim, 1996, p 42). The implication of this strikes at the very heart of modernity and modern social theory. The idea that Modernity as a series of systems that are responsive to human wants and needs is also untenable, but this fits nicely into chaotic notion of Parology. One cannot help thinking that Lyotard has fallen in the same trap that he sees in modernity, that of inventing a new way of thinking about science to correspond to his own view of modernity. A self referent? Arguing against Habermas, Lyotard claims that it is pointless, not possible, or even prudent to try to address the problem of legitimation by searching for a universal consensus in discourse or language as Habermas has done. This is because of two assumptions: first, the assumption that all speakers in the ideal speech situation can reach an agreement using a universal language game – no says Lyotard, language games are heteromorphous and there are many sets of pragmatic rules. In other words, we might not all be playing the same language game. Second and more damning, Lyotard argues that there is an assumption that the goal of dialogue is consensus. Not so, argues Lyotard; in his analysis of the pragmatics of science he claims to have demonstrated that consensus is only a particular state of discussion, not its end. Its end, for Lyotard is Parology:

> This double observation (the heterogeneity of rules and the search for dissent) destroys a belief that still underlies Habermas's research, namely, that humanity as a collective (universal) subject seeks its common emancipation through the regularization of the 'moves' permitted in all language games and that the legitimacy of any statement resides in its contributing to that emancipation. (Lyotard, 1984, p 66)

For Lyotard, Habermas' use of discourse as a weapon against the stable system has at its root a good cause, but the theory is bad because the idea of consensus is outmoded and suspect. We therefore have to arrive at a practice of social justice that is not linked to the idea of consensus and a good starting point is to recognise the heteromorphous nature of language games, the rules must be local and decided on by the current players and favour a multiplicity of finite meta-arguments. *The Postmodern Condition*, is then for Lyotard, an outline of a politics that would respect both the desire for justice and the desire for the unknown (Lyotard, 1984, p 67).

If we think about Lyotard's ideas critically then there appear to be several contradictions in his own work. Some I have already noted, but if we look at chaos and catastrophe theory, then as Sim (1996) notes, it is a moot point as to whether the many paradoxes they throw up are part of their objective, or just a barrier they have reached within the current state of knowledge. 'one generation's paradox being a later generation's solved problem, as is so often the case in scientific history' (Sim, 1996, p 41). Best and Kellner (1991) argue that Lyotard's work points to several problems in French postmodern theories. In rejecting the metanarrative as terrorising, and consolidating this idea in the *Differend* (1988) where Lyotard argues that different phrase regimes should given voice, we should celebrate difference and let the differend stand, listen to the silent voices, indeed the silencing of one voice over another to resolve conflict is in itself an act of terror. Lyotard himself is articulating a discourse which presupposes a dramatic break from modernity. In doing so, argue Best and Kellner, is Lyotard himself a concept of postmodernism, postmodernity, that presupposes a master narrative with a totalising perspective which marks the transition from one phase of society to another. Lyotard is also rather selective about which discourses are allowed to take part in his language games; he claims plurality on one hand, on the other he excludes 'from his kingdom of discourse those grand narratives which he suggests have illicitly monopolized the discussion... One is tempted to counter Lyotard's move here with an injunction to 'let a thousand narratives bloom' (Best and Kellner, 1991, p 172). In fact, argue Best and Kellner, Lyotard is caught in a double bind, we cannot make, or have normative critical positions, yet his war on the metanarrative and on totality does just that; if Lyotard was consistent with his own epistemology then he would not use the term 'post' at all because it involves the historical sequencing of thinking, returns to a kind of telos, in fact, it implies everything that Lyotard has been arguing against – a master narrative. How's (2003) critique is interesting. He notes, as we have seen, that Lyotard's objection to Habermas' theory revolves around the idea of language being inherently orientated towards consensus. In this Lyotard sees the development of another repressive metanarrative, that of common agreement. How argues, that from a sociological perspective it is not difficult to have sympathy with Lyotard's position, that of the recognition of different language games of different societies, but, he has fundamentality misunderstood Habermas' position, Habermas too, recognises that within the confines of modernity we can have plurality of language games, of different spheres of society, and this is a positive outcome of modernity. How also notes that when Habermas is talking about universal pragmatics, he is talking about what goes on behind the scenes. Whether we recognise it or not, he is not making some universal prescription about particular issues. Finally, How notes, that Habermas' notion of the ideal speech situation is a critical one in which genuine consensus requires all voices to be heard, in particular the dissenting ones, quite different from Lyotard's understanding (How, 2003, p 165).

So, this is the postmodern condition: the rejection of the metanarrative; the development of new forms of knowledge; the celebration of difference and diversity. We have seen the way in which the postmodern condition shapes new forms of knowledge while critiquing the positivistic sciences and the rationality of the social world. In the next section of this chapter I want to look at the work of Jean Baudrillard and move away from theories of knowledge to look at the implications that postmodernism has for the creation of self and the culture industry.

Simulacra and Simulation

It is difficult to know where to begin with Jean Baudrillard. On the one hand he has been described as the supertheorist of a new postmodernity, on the other, his arguments have been described as ludicrous:

> Elementary errors and wild arguments usually bring down the full weight of academic scorn. However, in Baudrillard's case they only seem to add to his charm. This the writer who, among other things, has claimed blithely that America is utopia; that the masses have disappeared; that symbolic exchange is the only reality; and that the proper role for women is the role of the temptress. Baudrillard, it seems, gets away with murder. (Rojek and Turner, 1993 p ix)

Scathing criticism indeed, but then Baudrillard is insistent on actually applying his postmodern theories and ideas rather than talking about the concept *per se*, sometimes controversial and often ironic. If we look at Baudrillard in a nutshell, then certain key themes arise. For Baudrillard, traditional Marxist analysis is simply not appropriate for analysing postmodern societies. The key dynamic of postmodernity is no longer the mode of production, but the mode of consumption and its relationship to identity (see *The Mirror of Production* (1975)). We no longer derive our identity from our occupation, but we buy it – identity is fluid and disembedded. In fact, our whole experience of the world is chaotic, a pastiche – hyperreality. Baudrillard's early works (*The System of Objects* (1968), *The Consumer Society* (1970), and *For A Critique of the Political Economy of the Sign* (1972, 1981)) largely deal with consumer society, new systems of mass consumption, the proliferation of consumer goods and the way in which these become tangled up in a complex web of objects and signs. The consumer is controlled in some sense by the object which attracts and fascinates controlling perception and behaviour. As Best and Kellner (1991) note, Baudrillard's first three books are sketches for developing a neo-Marxism that synthesises Marx with Semiology, but in his subsequent work he starts to distance himself from Marxist political economy.

As George Ritzer (1998) argues in the introduction to a later edition of *Consumer Society*, the book while demonstrating some of Baudrillard's later ideas on postmodern still has its roots firmly set in the modern. In the *Consumer Society* Baudrillard argues that we live in an age of profusion. The conspicuousness of consumption and abundance of objects means that we no longer relate to other human beings but to the profusion of objects that surround us. Daily life revolves around the reception of goods and messages. This represents for Baudrillard, a mutation in the ecology of the human species. Indeed we live in a new jungle of objects which range from household goods to street furniture and of course the constant celebration of the spectacle of the object in the mass media (Baudrillard, 1998, p 25). Profusion and piling high are the most striking features of consumer society, in the department store we move logically from one object to another, indeed there is a calculus of objects, but for Baudrillard the synthesis of profusion and calculus is the drugstore:

> The drugstore (or the new shopping centre) achieves a synthesis of consumer activities, not least of which are shopping, flirting with objects, playful wandering and all the permutational possibilities of these...it does not juxtapose categories of merchandise, but lumps signs together indiscriminately, lumps together all categories of commodities, which are regarded as partial fields of a sign consuming totality. In the drugstore, the cultural centre becomes part of the shopping centre. It would be simplistic to say that culture is 'prostituted' there. It is culturalized. (Baudrillard, 1998, p 27)

The point for Baudrillard is that we see in the drugstore the development of certain types of shopping experience and commodification of objects, and culturisation of culture This profusion has led to what Baudrillard describes as the drugstore as a town, a ski resort, they all borrow their model from the drugstore, the total homogenisation of everyday life. This is at the heart of consumption. The drug store features heavily in the development of the shopping centre and the city. At the same time we are in a vicious spiral of growth. Consumer society needs it; proliferation of objects, or should we say the destruction of objects. The more we demand the more is created the more we discard – the car being a classic example. As Kellner (1989) observes, Baudrillard's key point is that commodities are part of a system of objects that correlates to a system of needs. We have systems of objects and systems of needs, rather than objects in themselves. So, we might have refrigerator, washing machine, dishwasher, which says modern kitchen. We buy into a system of codes and fashion through the organisation of domestic products, and thus in society, consumption has become the centre of life (Kellner, 1989, p 13). The consumer society is still very modern as opposed to postmodern in its approach. In particular Baudrillard is still using a Marxist framework to criticise ideologies of growth and progress by using consumption as his empirical focus. In this book he conceptualises the development of consumer society in terms of the system of production. As Kellner notes: 'In developing his own theory, Baudrillard criticizes the standard mainstream view which conceptualizes consumption in terms of the rational satisfaction of needs with the aim of maximising utility. Against this view, Baudrillard posits a "socio-cultural" approach which stresses the ways in which society produces needs through socialization and conditioning thereby managing consumer demand and consumption' (Kellner, 1989, p 13). Baudrillard is arguing then, that we have what he calls the 'logic of social differentiation (1998, p 61) whereby individuals within society distinguish their 'self' and attain social standing by purchasing and using consumer goods. It is not that they are seduced into buying these goods as single entities or commodities, but the system produces a system of need, hence we buy the kitchen, the bathroom suite, or a certain style of décor for our house through which we differentiate ourselves in society. This then, for Baudrillard, is how we insert ourselves in society. In some sense it is similar to the Frankfurt School's critique of the culture industry and Marcuse's *One Dimensional Society*. Commodification represents a total social process, still very Marxist, but Baudrillard is starting to shift away from this framework as he starts to develop the notion that consumption replaces production as the nodal point through which society both organises itself and can be analysed. So, in *The Consumer Society* Baudrillard introduces us to the notion that the self is constructed in relation to the consumption of objects, but these objects form a system of needs by which we gain our status in society. We are not seduced in the same sense that we will find in his later work, rather, I feel that Baudrillard is saying that we buy into a lifestyle. I want now to turn to Baudrillard's postmodern turn and examine what probably is most oft cited works *Simulations* (1983) and *Simulacra and Simulation*. (1994).

'Simulation is no longer that of a territory, a referential being or a substance. It is a generation by models of a real without origin or reality: a hyperreal'. This is how Baudrillard introduces *Simulations* (1983) with the idea that that a territory now longer precedes a map, but the map precedes the territory, we live in hyperreal age, seduced by the images of hyperreality which hold us in their grip through obscene fascination. In the age of the mass media, the mass media creates reality – hyperreality, a pastiche of images and simulacra, simulations of simulations with no original. We no longer know what is real or not – *the desert of the real itself*. If the map was a simulation of the real then now it is the opposite. Simulators try to make the real coincide with their simulations. The charm and the magic of the cartographer skill in literally trying to make a map resemble the territory (remember these need not be maps) disappears with simulation. The real is produced argues Baudrillard, from miniaturised units, memory banks and command models; it need no longer be rational, as it is no longer measured against some ideal. 'It is nothing more than operational. In fact, since it is no longer enveloped by an imaginary, it is no longer real at all. It is hyperreal, the product of an irradiating synthesis of combinatory models in hyperspace without atmosphere, (Baudrillard, 1983, p 3). Thus for Baudrillard the age of simulation begins with the liquidation of all referentials; no longer do we have imitation, or signs of the real; we have the real itself which is a simulation. Baudrillard illustrates this by using the example of someone who feigns illness contra to someone who simulates illness:

> Someone who feigns an illness can simply go to bed and make believe he is ill. Someone who simulates an illness produces in himself some of the symptoms… Thus, feigning or dissimulating leaves the reality principle intact: the difference is always clear, it is only masked; whereas simulation threatens the difference between 'true' and 'false', between 'real' and 'imaginary'. Since the simulator produces 'true' symptoms, is he ill or not? (Baudrillard, 1983, p 5)

So, the simulation is the real because the person is ill. Baudrillard goes on to illustrate further with examples of medicine and the army but his point is that simulation outflanks classic reasoning because it submerges the truth principle. If someone can act crazy so well, then he must be mad, but are all lunatics' simulators? On to religion – God can be simulated, reduced to a set of signs, the whole system becomes a gigantic simulacrum, and an iconography sets the stage for an uninterrupted circuit of simulations. So, we have the notion that if modernity on one hand was dominated by production and industrialisation, on the other, in the postmodern era of simulations we have signs and information that are dominated by models and computerisation. Hyperreality is the blurring of any distinction between real and unreal. In fact, for Baudrillard, the hyperreal is more *real* than *real* because it is modelled. The real is no longer given, for example a moutainscape, but has been produced artificially (a model) as real, for Baudrillard, it is not unreal or surreal, but in some sense it is realer than real. A classic example for Baudrillard of the hyperreal is Disneyland. Disneyland comprises of entangled orders of simulation, illusions and phantasms – pirates, the frontier, future world which represents a microcosm of America, indeed an almost religious revelling in real America 'you park outside, queue inside, and are totally abandoned at the exit' (p 23). For Baudrillard all the values of America are encapsulated in miniature and comic strip form, as imaginary, to make us believe the rest of America is real. When in fact for Baudrillard places like Los Angeles are no longer real, but belong to the realm of simulations and the hyperreal. This is not a case of false representation (of reality), or an ideological misrepresentation, but a case of concealing that the real is no longer real.

> The Disneyland imaginary is neither true nor false; it is a deterrence machine set up in order to rejuvenate in reverse the fiction of the real. Whence the debility, the infantile degeneration of this imaginary. It is meant to be an infantile world, in order to make us believe that the adults are elsewhere, in the 'real' world, and to conceal that real childishness is everywhere, particularly amongst the adults who go there to act the child in order to foster illusions as to their real childishness. (Baudrillard, 1983, p 26)

Hyperreality extends to all areas of social and political life where models replace the real, so we have ideal homes, ideal sex, ideal relationships where the actual model determines the real. Simulations now constitute reality itself. We could look at many examples, reality TV, postmodern wars, even food does not escape…. Now you can buy an Indian takeaway in a brown takeaway bag from your local supermarket, it is a simulation of the food from a takeaway restaurant, but the food from the restaurant is a simulation, a model of Indian food. It is well known that Chicken Tikka Masala originated in the United Kingdom – a simulation of a simulation with no original – a simulacra.

One of Baudrillard's infamous works states that *The Gulf War Did Not Take Place* (1995), it was televisual spectacular; an event organised and mediated by the media. Our access to the reality of the war is through the media. He is not arguing that the media misled, or distorted the truth, rather that the war is a simulation of war based on a model that is portrayed through the reality of the press – graphic images of missiles finding their targets, tanks being 'busted', bridges being 'blown' which produce a hyperreality – TV no longer presents the world but defines it. In the hyperreal world we see the end of the Panopticon, the end of the gaze. It is redundant, we are no longer the real but we are the model – 'no more subject, focal point, centre or periphery: but pure flexion or circular inflection. No more violence or surveillance: only "information", secret virulence, chain reaction, slow implosion and simulacra of spaces where the real-effect comes into play' (Baudrillard, 1983, p 54). We have implosion, social boundaries collapse, the implosion of meaning in the media, the death of the social as people become more and more disillusioned

and resentful of the bombardment of messages from the media. People become more apathetic with constant calls to vote, buy this, buy that, the mass
becomes an almost silent majority where distinctions between class, politics
and culture disappear with the social; society is implosive.

Baudrillard's theory is pessimistic at its core. While in some sense Lyotard's
work can be viewed as positive, a celebration of a multi-layered world, and of
difference, Baudrillard's ideas suggest that we live in an exhausted and empty
world of manipulation, simulation and social implosion. Nothing new appears
on the horizon, just an endless precession of simulacra. This is of course a
huge critique of consumer society. Baudrillard intends to provoke and I feel
that he often uses irony to make his point become more and more provocative.
Forget Foucault (1987) is an open attack on Foucault's work in which he argues
what Foucault is describing is an obsolete era, power is dead, and that
we should forget Foucault all together because in our postmodern world of
simulation, media and modelling, Foucauldian theory is obsolete. He seems to
take the opportunity to distance himself from his other French contemporaries
by also being highly critical of Deleuze, Guattari and Lyotard rebuffing the
validity of micropolitics. Baudrillard moves on to metaphysics in the late
80's, but as Best and Kellner (1991) notes, his writings become a pastiche of
himself – 'His writings thus take on a postmodern style which pastiches his
previous texts, mixes together various subject matters, and eventually provides a frozen, glaciated hyperealization of texts more Baudrillardian than
Baudrillard, in which he endlessly reproduces his favourite ideas' (Best and
Kellner, 1991, p 132). Of course there have been some pretty damming critiques of Baudrillard's work, indeed whole volumes dedicated to critically
unpicking his ideas. For example, *Forget Baudrillard* (1993) contains a series of
papers that critically address Baudrillard's notions of what constitutes postmodernity, and his sense of history. In particular Porter (1993) draws our
attention to the fact that it is not just the twentieth century that has seen a proliferation of signs 'at least since the seventeenth century, capitalism has been
inseparable from the incitement of imagination, the creation of blitzes of spec-
ulation, fantasy, fiction, hyperstimulation' (Porter, 1993, p 6). Again Turner
(1993) argues that many of the configurations of the postmodern world were
present in the baroque society of the seventeenth century which makes the
idea of a unique break in modernity difficult to sustain (Turner, 1993, p 84).
Indeed Rojek (1993) argues that Baudrillard is not acting as some kind of harbinger of a postmodern state of affairs 'rather he is treading the well worn
paths of one type of modernist scepticism and excess – a path which has no
other destiny than repetition. His message of 'no future' does not transcend
the political dilemma of modernism, it exemplifies it' (Rojek, 1993 p 121–22).

Steven Best and Douglas Kellner (1991) provide the clearest and most com-
prehensive critique of Baudrillard's work arguing that while articles of the late
1980's provide some acute sociological insight, they also contain clichéd com-
monplaces, repetitions of pet ideas, and downright distortions and sophistries

– indeed 'This is symptomatic of Baudrillard's work in the late 1980's which combines some incisive observation with sheer nonsense and with racist, sexist, and misanthropic ravings. He does not provide any significant new perspectives or ideas and his project appears to have reached a cul-de-sac' (Best and Kellner, 1991 p 135). They argue that Baudrillard's work or analysis operates at an excessively high level of abstraction where human suffering is erased from the Baudrillardian universe. Citing Baudrillard's travelogue *America* (1988) Best and Kellner argue that Baudrillard fails to see some of the basic problems of life – poverty, inequality, the problems caused by homelessness, racism and sexism. Baudrillard's treatment of racial and sexual difference is insensitive and even grotesque, ignoring the very real problem of racism that is a common experience of most black peoples in America. Baudrillard's utopia is another person's hell. Indeed:

> Baudrillard's current positions are profoundly superficial and are characterized by sloppy generalizations, extreme abstraction, semiological idealism and oft repeated banalities, such as: we are in a 'post orgy condition' of simulations, entropy, fractal subjects, indifference, transvestism, and so on, *ad nauseum*. If he were merely expressing opinions or claiming to present a possible perspective on things, one would be able to enjoy his pataphysical meanderings, but Baudrillard's writing is increasingly pretentious, claiming to describe 'the real state of things', to speak for the masses, and to tell 'us' what we really believe (Best and Kellner, 1991, p 139).

Baudrillard constantly contradicts himself, arguing for hyperreality on the one hand, on the other claiming to know about the real conditions of today. He remains constantly clear about things while we remain confused. Indeed for Best and Kellner, despite offering postmodern critiques of totalising thought, Baudrillard represents totalising thought at its worst, claiming to have insight into the very heart of matters (Best and Kellner, 1991, p 140). Best and Kellner go on to many examples of the paradoxical nature of Baudrillard's work, including his views on the end of history, Eastern Europe and politics, noting that he has often dropped his most interesting work half way through to pursue some other avenue. I think that Mike Gane (1991) sums up the Baudrillardian position: 'He is not always capable of surprising and provoking us to the degree that he would wish, and some of his analyses are vulnerable to the most harsh of judgements. Yet the overall impression we are left with is of a consistency and persistence of critical imagination which produces, sometimes, remarkable insights. Some of his work is utterly self defeating, even hypocritical. But there is an undeniable vitality and creativity coupled with an undying fidelity not to utopian vision in a passive sense, but to a passionate utopian practice in theory' (Gane, 1991, p 157).

Thus, we have two versions of postmodernism: one shouts optimism, where we have the rejection of the metanarrative and the formation of new forms of knowledge that take into account the local, that celebrate difference and diversity – that show us a way forward and condemn the worse excesses of modernity, this is the social theory Jean François Lyotard. The other version, the Baudrillardian universe is pessimistic, there is no way forward, we live in a world of simulation, of hyperreality where the real is modelled, it is more real than the real where there is nothing new on the horizon. Society has imploded on itself. The implications for the self are on one hand that we can choose our *being* from a plethora of identities and differences, and on the other, that we, *ourself* become the real, simulacra, simulations of simulations. But if this is postmodernism, what are the implications for history?. Do we have also a new epoch of time that corresponds to this cultural condition?. In the next short section I want to briefly look at David Harvey's work *The Condition of Postmodernity* (1989).

The Condition of Postmodernity

David Harvey (1989) is clear right from the start of *the Condition of Post-modernity* as to his thesis which he sets out even before the preface. The argument follows thus: that there has been a change in political and economic practices since the early 1970's which is bound up with new dominant ways in which we experience space and time:

> While simultaneity in the shifting dimensions of time and space is no proof of necessary or causal connection, strong a priori grounds can be adduced from the proposition that their some kind of necessary relation between the rise of post-modernist cultural forms, the mergence of more flexible modes of capital accumulation, and a new round of 'time-space compression' in the organisation of capitalism. (Harvey, 1989, p vii)

These changes, argues Harvey, when we compare them to the basis, or rules of capital accumulation, appear not as a sign of a post-industrial society, or some new form of post capitalism, but as shifts in surface appearance. We could situate Harvey's work within the discourse of 'posts', but also within what has become an even bigger discourse, that of globalisation. Harvey is writing in contrast to authors like Daniel Bell (1976, 1979) who argue for a post-industrial concept of modernity. Post-industrial society differs significantly from earlier capitalist models in terms of the ordering of social structure. In post-industrial society there is a shift in emphasis from class and private property to the centrality of technology, science and culture. In other words, post-industrial society is organised around the ownership and accumulation of theoretical knowledge. 'What the concept of a post-industrial society suggests is that there is a common core of problems, hinging largely on the relation of science to public policy' (Bell, 1976, p 119). This is because in post-industrial society the axial principle is centred around education and scientific and governmental institutions where the source of innovation for Bell, is no longer the private business, but the university. The essential division in society is no longer between those who own the means of production and the proletariat, but the bureaucratic and authority relations between those who have powers of decision and those who do not. This applies to all forms of organisation – social, political and economic. Indeed for Bell there are three components to post-industrial society:

> In the economic sector, it is a shift from manufacturing to services; in technology, it is the centrality of the new science based industries; in sociological terms, it is the rise of new technical elites and the advent of a new principle of stratification. From this terrain, one can step back and say more generally that the post-industrial society means the rise of new axial structures and axial principles: a changeover from a goods-producing society to an information or knowledge society; and, in the modes of knowledge, a change in the axis of abstraction from empiricism or trial-and-error tinkering to theory and the codification of theoretical knowledge for directing innovation and the formulation of policy. (Bell, 1976, p 487)

So, while we have seen shifts in the type of working practices from industrial to service sector, there have also been shifts in consumption patterns where people have more leisure time, higher levels of spending power (through credit) and basically more time to play. While this new consumer society rejects the tenets of capitalist modernity, it still comes into conflict with the values of post-industrial society which although markedly changed from capitalist society still relies on central institutions – the nation state, central bureaucracy, national values. Post industrial society is therefore a society in transformation – the transformation from a society dominated by the production of *goods* to the production of *knowledge*. For Bell, this also brings about changes in the social structure with a new knowledge class based on the ethics of community where profit has no hold. The scientific class will eventually saturate society, not as technocrats, but to improve and build society as a whole with new values and principles of organisation. This can certainly be seen to fly in the face or what either Baudrillard or Lyotard claim. While describing certain functional changes in the organisation of modern industrial societies, Bell still places an emphasis on the scientific and technological grand narratives of modernity, indeed he sees a way forward in them. We can contrast this with the sociology of David Harvey, who we have briefly looked at and that of Frederic Jameson.

In the book *Postmodernism: Or, The Cultural Logic of Late Capitalism*, Jameson (1991) argues that we can contextualise postmodernity by viewing the development of capitalism in three stages. Thus we have *market capitalism, monopoly capitalism* and *multinational capitalism*. Multinational capitalism is what is wrongly called post-industrialism. We are now in what Jameson describes as 'late capitalism' which 'constitutes, on the contrary, the purest form of capitalism yet to have emerged, a prodigious expansion of capital into hitherto uncommodified areas' (Jameson, 1991, p 36) Jameson, unlike Baudrillard or Lyotard, claims that we can understand and map postmodernism within a neo-Marxist framework. Because, he argues, that postmodernism is not merely an aesthetic style or movement but a new stage of the cultural logic of late capitalism. This brings in a numbers of cultural shifts: a breakdown in the distinction between high and low culture; the almost absolute commodification of culture; the radical fragmentation of subjectivity – 'our insertion as individual subjects into a multidimensional set of radically discontinuous realities, whose frames range from the still surviving spaces of bourgeois private life all the way to the unimaginable decentring of global capital itself' (Jameson, 1991, p 413) and finally, the emergence of the postmodern 'hyperspace', what Jameson describes as an alarming disjunction point between body and built environment. In other words, postmodern buildings that confuse, where you cannot find your way around, or hotels where it is not obvious where the shops are, and even if you find one, you are unlikely to be as lucky again (p 44). Of course, this is the language of Lyotard and Baudrillard – the radical breakdown of the subject, simulations and simulacra, fragmentation, and not only hyperreality but hyperspace. Differences also come to light, rather than a radical rupture. Jameson sees postmodernism as a logical development, a stage of capitalism. His use of neo-Marxism puts him in the realm of a totalising discourse that is at loggerheads certainly with Lyotard and Baudrillard's ideas. Finally, Jameson does appear to use specific examples to make broader claims about what really are complex institutions and practices in society. David Harvey, in my opinion offers a more coherent reading of the condition of postmodernity. The central ideas in the book of the same name are the notions of time-space compression, post-Fordism and flexible accumulation.

Basically, Harvey is arguing that the postmodern age sees a transformation in the labour and production markets from Fordism to post-Fordism. Fordism is typified by the production line manufacturing seen in many car plants but also used to make many products in very large quantities. The product of this is of course vast amounts of identical things – any colour you like as long as it is black. On a more serious side the production line was subject to over production, lags between purchasing materials and selling the end product and a lack of flexibility in terms of product choice and design. Flexible accumulation is a direct confrontation with the rigidities of Fordism:

> It rests on flexibility with respect to labour processes, labour markets, products, and patterns of consumption. It is characterised by the emergence of entirely new sectors of production, new ways of providing financial services, new markets, and, above all, greatly intensified rates of commercial, technological, and organisational innovation. (Harvey, 1989, p 147)

This has seen a shift in product choice, with shorter production runs and flexible machine tooling that allows variable products to be manufactured. It is characterised by niche markets and rapid consumer demand for technological innovations. It has also seen a sea change in the labour market with flexible patterns of working practice in what is termed the *core periphery* model. A core of highly skilled full time employees central to the future of a particular company exists at the centre of the workforce while on the periphery we see two labour groups. First, is a team of full time employees but whose skills are readily available in the labour market. This group is characterised by a high turnover of employees which enables the workforce to be reduced relatively simply. The second periphery includes part time workers, fixed term contract staff, and sub contractors, all expendable at very short notice. This makes for the notion of the flexible firm and is increasingly becoming the standard model of employment is the postmodern condition. This flexibility is heightened and enhanced by the concept of time-space compression.

Time-space compression is a relatively straightforward concept with huge ramifications many of which I will discuss in the following chapter on globalisation. If we think of the map of the world, then it has shrunk considerably in the last 500 years. In fact, the world is fifty times smaller than in the sixteenth century. How so? Well, if we take the average best speed of a sailing ship in the 1500's then it is something like ten miles per hour. The average speed of a jet airliner in 2004 is at least, if not more than five hundred miles per hour. Time is re-organised to get over the constraints of space – we have the shortening of time and the shrinking of space. Maps literally shrink the world over time in relation to the increasing speed of transportation. Space compresses the earth to a global village of communication networks and economic and ecological interdependencies – *the present is all there is* (p 240). The implication of this postmodern condition is that manufacturing can be global. Think of aircraft with their engines manufactured in one country, the wings in another, the tail in another, and so on. Money can be moved around at the press of a button. Business decision making has shrunk with satellite communication networks and declining transport costs. There are of course terrible social, political and economic consequences of this form of capital accumulation which I will discuss in the following chapter, but for Harvey, this is the condition of postmodernity. This seems miles away from Baudrillard's world of simulations and simulacra and probably miles from the huge number of people in the world who have no access to basic human needs like clean water, fuel and food, let alone a passport to travel around the global village.

Summary and Conclusion

I think it is better to think in terms of *modernism(s)*, rather than postmodernism *per se*. We have postmodern architecture, postmodern art, postmodern theory; we have phases, postmodernity, post-industrial society; ways of organising labour – post-Fordism, and new ways of organising time. There are certain similarities in all postmodern theories: the rejection of the grand or metanarrative; an emphasis on difference, plurality and diversity; a distinct suspicion of scientific knowledge and a rejection of universal claims of truth. There is the notion that we have the death of the subject and the birth of the decentred self in which we select our identities from a whole range of possible choices that are available in the postmodern consumer society.

In Lyotard's work we see a careful philosophical critique of the status of knowledge. Like Daniel Bell, Lyotard draws our attention to new forms of learning, but unlike Bell, Lyotard argues that new forms of knowledge and learning will bypass the state altogether. Indeed this is precursor to the globalisation debate in the next chapter as Lyotard envisages learning circulating as money has done, and still does, on the global market with the introduction of new technologies. In his critique of the metanarrative we can see a parallel between the postmodernism of Lyotard and Foucault. The totalising scientific discourse of Enlightenment thinking is suffering a crisis of legitimation. This is because science refuses to see itself as simply a narrative; it burdens itself with objectivity, proof, verification, and in so doing, it claims a higher form of knowledge that demonstrates some kind of objective truth. The problem is quite simply what legitimates the metanarrative itself? Here again we have the Foucauldian link between power and knowledge – who decides what knowledge is and who knows what needs to be decided. The rational discourse for a rational time has failed to ask itself the simple question – what proof is there that my proof is true? Certainly something that Kuhn (1970) has tried to address and Lyotard builds on by demonstrating that science is not value free. Lyotard introduces us to the idea of Parology, a postmodern science that searches for paradoxes, differences and instabilities in which there is an emphasis on the local or micro. This is because a macro overview, or taking society as a system is untenable for Lyotard. Once again we see a referent to Habermas as Lyotard claims that the idea of modernity as a series of systems that are responsive to human wants and needs is untenable. It is not possible to address the problem of legitimation by searching for a universal consensus in language because of the numerous sets of pragmatic rules. It is assumed that the goal of dialogue is consensus; not so argues Lyotard. Consensus is only a particular state of discussion, not an end. I have outlined some of the problems with Lyotard's work, not least that we could argue that ultimately his radical break from the modern simply produces yet another totalising discourse and that he has fundamentally misunderstood Habermas' universal pragmatics. Yet despite this, Lyotard at least offers us some hope; a positive view of the future where difference is more than tolerated, but celebrated, Lyotard shouts optimism. This could hardly be said for the work of Baudrillard.

Baudrillard's work on consumer society has certain linkages with Horkheimer and Adorno's culture industry. There is more of an emphasis on the construction of self and the way in which we literally insert ourselves into society by buying a whole series of products, buying into a dream if you like. But this is modernist Baudrillard. Postmodern Baudrillard hurtles us into the realm of hyperreality where the charm and magic of life have all but disappeared to be replaced by the work of the simulators. We have simulations of simulations with no original referent – simulacra. The point is that we no longer have imitation or a sign of the real – the real itself is a simulation. Disneyland is the classic example, it is realer than real, it is the hyperreal. The implications for the self are obvious; we have ideal homes, ideal sex, ideal relationships in which the media no longer presents the world but defines it. What we see for Baudrillard is an implosion of society. Social boundaries collapse, meaning implodes in the media, we have the death of the social. People become more disillusioned, apathetic and resentful, buy this, vote that. Society becomes silent and distinctions between class and politics disappear. I think in Baudrillard's work, if we read between the lines, is deeply critical and ironic, and perhaps, like Weber before him he is proffering us a warning about the shape of things to come in the hope that we do not accept them. That we do not become simulations of simulations. If Foucault didn't convince us of the construction and often absurdity of the creation of self, then certainly Baudrillard hammers this message home even further. The same could be said of another theme running through this book, that of rationality. Lyotard probably offers us the damning critique of modernist rationality and science; indeed again, in the concept of the Differend he warns us that rationality is not always a good thing.

I have outlined the work of what we might call theorists of postmodernity – Harvey and Jameson provide an introduction in some sense to the next chapter on the globalisation debate. They differ from Baudrillard and Lyotard in the sense that they still map out postmodernism within a neo-Marxist framework. There is also a very real emphasis on space. In Jameson's work we have the concept of hyperspace in Harvey's time-space compression. There is a real emphasis on the changing nature of both labour markets and production processes, but also the way in which new technologies have literally shrunk the world. In the next chapter I want to address the phenomena of the shrinking world by looking at what have become known as the globalisation debate. I will examine the way in which time and space has been reorganised in the light of global networks of communications, banking and military power and ask a series of questions: Do we really live in a globalised world, or is it better to think of this in terms of 'some' people leading a global 'lifestyle'? Is globalisation just another term for the 'westernisation' of culture? Are 'new' forms of global economic and industrial systems simply new forms of cultural and economic imperialism – a form of postcolonialism? Is America the new empire of fear? Finally does the global really impact on the local at a level that changes the world and what are implications once more for the construction of our identity?

Summary of Key Concepts and Terms

Postmodernism: Reference to a cultural trend in art and architecture. In social and political theory there is a shift from realism to relativism; a rejection of universal truths and knowledge systems that lay claim to this; there is a critique of the logical unfolding of history; an emphasis on the fragmented and decentred nature of the self; finally an emphasis on the relationship between power and discourse

Postmodernity: a new phase or epoch in history in which the cultural referents we refer to as postmodern are a symptom of this change.

The Postmodern Condition: Jean François Lyotard. Marked by the rejection of meta-narratives and development of new forms of knowledge with an emphasis on the local which reject totalising discourses. The celebration of difference and diversity.

Metanarratives: A theory or theories that make universal truth claims, and claims to universal knowledge. Exemplified by the rational scientific discourse of modernity which tends to be totalising and terrorising, negating other cultures and ways of life while quashing the individuality of members of society.

Parology: Postmodern science which searches for differences, paradoxes and instabilities as an alternative to the grand or metanarrative

Consumer Society: Baudrillard's analysis of modern consumption in which commodities form part of a system of objects that correlates to a system of needs. We buy into a system of codes and fashion through the organisation of products – consumption becomes the centre of life. We distinguish our 'self' and attain our social standing by purchasing and consuming goods – we literally insert our 'selves' into society.

Simulacra. The world becomes made up of simulations of simulations where there are no original referents. The simulation of simulation is a simulacra.

Hyperreality: In a world made up of simulacra there is a blurring of the distinction between real and unreal. Hyperreality is more real than real because it is modelled, made of a pastiche of simulations. In particular, the media creates hyperreality by showing a pastiche of images, a simulation for example of a war in which the television no longer presents reality but defines it. Baudrillard's classic example of hyperreality is Disneyland.

Post-industrial society: Differs significantly from earlier capitalist models in terms of the ordering of social structure. Emphasis shifts from a class basis and the ownership of private property and production to an emphasis on the centrality of technology, science and culture. Shift from the production of goods to the production of knowledge.

Flexible Accumulation: confrontation with the rigidities of Fordism, emphasis on flexibility in the labour markets, marked by new flexible regimes of labour (core-periphery), niche markets and flexible production (post-Fordism).

Time-space compression: New technological innovations in travel mean that we have the shortening of time and the shrinking of space. Jet aircraft have literally made the world smaller. Time is reorganised to get over the constraints of space. The earth becomes a global village where the present is all there is.

Indicative Reading

Key Texts

Baudrillard, J. (1994). *Simulacra and Simulation*. Michigan: University of Michigan Press.
Harvey, D. (1989). *The Condition of Postmodernity*. London: Blackwell.
Jameson, F. (1991). *Postmodernism Or, the Cultural Logic of Late Capitalism*. London: Verso.
Lyotard, J-F. (1984). *The Postmodern Condition: A Report on Knowledge*. Minneapolis: University of Minnesota Press.

Secondary Texts

Bauman, Z. (1993). *Postmodern Ethics*. London: Blackwell.
Best, S. and Kellner, D. (1991). *Postmodern Theory: Critical Interrogations*. London: Macmillan.
Farrell Fox, N. (2003) *The New Sartre*. London: Continuum.
Jencks, C. (1977). *The Language of Post-modern Architecture*. New York: Pantheon.
Lash, S. (1990). *The Sociology of Postmodernism*. London: Routledge.
Lyon, D. (1999). *Postmodernity* (2nd ed.). Buckingham: Open University Press.
Rojek, C. and Turner, B. (eds) (1993). *Forget Baudrillard?* London: Routledge.
Sim, S. (1996). *Jean Francois Lyotard*. London: Havester Wheatsheaf.

7
Shrinking the World: The Globalisation of Modernity

Introduction

In this chapter I want to outline some of the key theorists and ideas in the globalisation debate. This will not be an exhaustive overview – the literature is too large and is still growing. In some sense it is akin to the postmodernism debate where we have moved from looking at the ideas of a particular key theorist to that of phenomena. Globalisation can be viewed as social-cultural, political and economic phenomena. First, we have idea that we saw in David Harvey's (1989) work that socially and culturally the world has become smaller, people now talk quite readily of a global village. Second, the world political map has changed, we now have major decisions that are made in a way that they transcend the nation state. We now have power blocs, rather than individual countries, NATO for example. Third, we have the economic: world money exchanges, finance and capital. This is all made possible by the technological advancements of modernity: high speed travel, computerisation, the internet and e-mail. No longer do we have to wait for weeks for a letter to arrive from the other side of the globe, communication is instantaneous with e-mail, satellite phones and advanced infrared technology. And if this fails, then we can always hop on a plane and fly to our destination is a relatively short time. The benefits of this global world are not just obvious for the capitalist entrepreneur but for the ordinary person in the (Western) street. We have more choice in the realm of the economic in terms of what we can consume. Products which would have gone rotten when shipped by boat are now moved by air. We can choose from a range of global identities. Clothing is available from around the world; indeed even our holiday is more likely to involve a global destination like India rather than a trip to the seaside. We can obtain money from an ATM anywhere in the world using our credit card. At home we can sit in front of our satellite television sets and watch our favourite sport in real time, wherever the venue is in the world. We seem to be truly globally connected; well the people who have the privilege to be in this position, but how do we theorise this and what are implications for the rest of the world (West and Rest)? Who pays for our enjoyment of this global cultural lifestyle? The globalisation debate seems to follow two clear strands – economic globalisation and the cultural. I will focus on the cultural while recognising the importance of the economic. In this first section, I want to look at the work of Anthony Giddens (1990, 1991) before going on to cast a critical eye over the theories of Roland Robertson (1992) and Martin Albrow (1996) who theorise the transition from modernity to a global condition. I then go on to look at the work of and Arjun Appadurai (1990) who adds further emphasis to the cultural flows of globalisation and David Held (1996) who theorises the future of the nation state.

The Globalisation of Modernity

Anthony Giddens (1990) argues that modernity is inherently globalising, and this is evident in the characteristics of modern institutions, in particular their *disembeddedness* and *reflexivity*. What does Giddens mean by disembeddedness and reflexivity? For Giddens, in the late modern age it not sufficient to talk about, or invent new terms such as postmodernity; rather we need to look at the nature of modernity itself where the actual consequences of modernity have become more radicalised and universal. The dynamism of modernity for Giddens lies in the separation of *time* and *space*. If we look at pre-modern or traditional societies then social relations are embedded in time and space. For the peasant, time is based in the agricultural calendar – the seasons. In terms of identity, status is ascribed at birth and there is little social mobility. In some sense there is little idea of space beyond boundaries, beyond a series of villages for example. Day to day life always linked time to space. Although in pre-modern times we have the agrarian calendar, the calculation of time and space is variable and imprecise. In other words, nobody could precisely tell the time of day, but instead made reference to time through 'where', or natural occurrences (Giddens, 1990, p 17). Something happens though to change this way of life:

> The invention of the mechanical clock and its diffusion to virtually all members of the population (a phenomenon which dates at its earliest from the late eighteenth century) were of key significance in the separation of time from space. The clock expressed a uniform dimension of 'empty' time, quantified in such a way as to permit the precise designation of 'zones' of the day e.g., the 'working day'. (Giddens, 1990, p 17).

So, with the invention of the mechanical clock, time is no longer seasonal and intimately connected with 'where', but becomes universal. Empty space suggests time to be filled, in other words it allows projection and a more precise zoning of activity. But time was still connected to space and place until we see a shift in the social organisation of time through the development of a standard worldwide calendar and the standardising of time across regions. As Giddens notes, in the latter part of the nineteenth century different areas within a state may have different times and this is made even more chaotic at the borders between states. In Britain we had railway time. Now the world is zoned from Greenwich Mean Time (since 1884 GMT). Giddens argues that the emptying of time is the precondition for the emptying of space. Think of place as a locale, as a physical setting, a geography of the social. In pre-modern time space and place more or less coincide, as I said earlier there was little recognition of space beyond the boundaries of the locale. In modernity however, space is removed from place in that there is a reduction in the social distance between communities on one hand; on another a given community can be influenced by a distant locale. In Giddens reasoning here we start to see the germination of the globalisation of modernity. Time and space are *distanciated*. Put quite simply, the sense of social distance between communities is reduced in that we can imagine a space without referring to our own locale. This then is what Giddens refers to as *time-space distanciation*; indeed the separation of time from space enables its recombination into social activity. The classic example is the timetable, a time-space ordering device which allows the complex co-ordination of transportation across vast tracts of time and space. This then, for Giddens, is the prime condition for what he calls the process of disembedding. Modernisation disembeds the Feudal as space and place are eroded. There are huge opportunities for change as we break free from the constraints of local habits and practices. This is where our old friend rationality makes a reappearance, in that the separation of time and space enables the distinctive rationalised organisations of modernity to appear and function in a way that would not be impossible in pre-modern times. With a standardised dating system, the notion of history appears in a systematised form and enables previous civilisations to be inserted into the schema of time and space. In addition to the mapping of the world, Giddens argues that time and space are recombined to form a genuinely world-historical framework of experience and action (Giddens, 1990, p 21).

For Giddens, Modern institutions are therefore disembedded. But what does he mean by disembedded and what are the mechanisms at work here? In terms of disembedding, Giddens quite literally means the lifting out of social relations from a local to a global context in which social relations are restructured across infinite spans of time and space. Giddens identifies two disembedding mechanisms; the first is the creation of symbolic tokens, the second, the establishment of expert systems. Symbolic tokens are media which can be passed around without regard to the specific persons or groups; they have a universal feel, they enable people to move from one local context to another, thus making the world appear to shrink – Giddens uses the example of money a common currency 'Money permits the exchange of anything for anything, regardless of whether the goods involved share any substantive qualities in common with one another' (Giddens, 1990, p 22). Indeed with credit cards we do not need to even share a common currency, we can move around the world and the currency is converted for us by the bank. The expert system, for example scientific technical knowledge is not context dependent but establishes social relations across vast tracts of time and space. Expert systems disembed social relations by the very nature of the non specific contextual form. For example, the modern medical model dominates the globe; it is an expert system in which the polio vaccination is the same in America as it is in the Sudan. It is an overarching perspective in which other medical perspectives are labelled alternative, viewed as witchcraft or simply ridiculed. By their nature they also drag us in to a labyrinth of risk and trust. We have to trust in the knowledge of the system as we cannot possibly attain the knowledge of all things in that system ourselves. Again Giddens takes us through the multiple risks and acts of trust we go through by just getting in a car and driving to an airport to board a plane. We cannot possibly know whether that aircraft is in a fit state to fly, we have to take the risk and trust in an expert system. In high modernity, trust and risk are inseparable.

A third distinctive element of modern institutions for Giddens is their reflexivity. In comparing modern and pre-modern or traditional cultures, Giddens notes that there is marked difference in the sense of reflexivity. In pre-modern cultures reflexivity is largely concerned with the reinterpretation and clarification of tradition. In modern times reflexivity takes on a different guise. Reflexivity is introduced into the very systems of modernity and the reproduction of those systems to the point where thought and action are constantly examined and refracted back on one another:

> The reflexivity of modern social life consists in the fact that social practices are constantly examined and reformed in the light of incoming information about those very practices, thus constitutively altering their character....In all cultures, social practices are routinely altered in the light of ongoing discoveries which feed into them. But (my emphasis) only in the era of modernity is the revision of convention radicalised to apply (in principle) to all aspects of human life, including the technological intervention into the material world. (Giddens, 1990, p 38).

In modern times we literally have reflection on the nature of reflection itself – reflexive modernisation. We moved from an age of tradition to reason, but for Giddens the reflexivity of modernity actually subverts reason because we believe in the certainty of our knowledge, in particular the scientific world view. But we can never be certain that knowledge will remain constant, it could be wrong, it could change, it could be reinterpreted – 'in the heart of the world of hard science, modernity floats free' (Giddens, 1990, p 39). So, Giddens would argue that modernity is deeply sociological. For, example, anyone embarking on marriage now will know that divorce rates are high; this may effect both the decision to marry as well as related things like property and belongings. People are reflexive, they think about these practices, they have some sociological knowledge. These are not merely facts about divorce rates, but knowledge that enables a reflexive decision to be made. Giddens example of the way in which even the lay person has some sociological knowledge is slightly tenuous to say the least, assuming a broadly middle class ideal of what people know, or want to know, but what it does demonstrate is the way in which we increasingly live in an information age. Giddens is arguing that the accumulation of knowledge does not mean that we are more able to control our fate as Enlightenment thinkers hoped; we simply have more knowledge from which we can be reflexive.

Giddens argues that if we take all these things together – the separation of time and space; the development of disembedding mechanisms, and the reflexive appropriation of knowledge, then we draw an analogy between modernity and a careering juggernaut. The *double hermeneutic* in which knowledge reflexivity is applied to system reproduction invariably means that the goal posts are for ever changing. Reflexive appropriation of knowledge is both energising and unstable, and at the same time extends out to huge spans of time and space egged on by the disembedding mechanisms which facilitate this progress. Capitalist society therefore for Giddens is inherently globalising. It is marked by a set of institutions, or institutional clusters which Giddens maps out in a circular diagram:

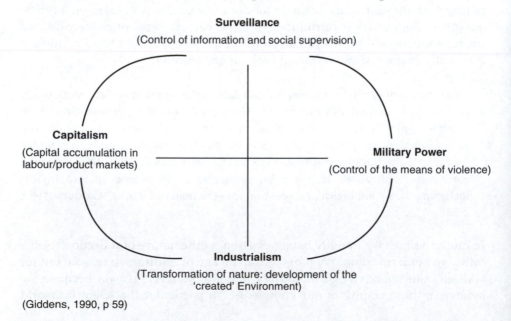

Surveillance
(Control of information and social supervision)

Capitalism
(Capital accumulation in labour/product markets)

Military Power
(Control of the means of violence)

Industrialism
(Transformation of nature: development of the 'created' Environment)

(Giddens, 1990, p 59)

The four institutional dimensions of modernity are interlocking and support each other. Modernity marked by the institutional dimension of capitalism involves the insulation of the economic from the political in a world of competitive labour and production markets. As we have seen in Foucault's work, surveillance plays a crucial role in the modern world and is fundamental to the working of most organisations and the production of knowledge and therefore power, in particular the governmentality of the nation state. Military power points outward at other nation states but relies on surveillance to operate successfully. Military power and war have increasingly become industrialised, and then of course industrialism is intrinsically linked with capitalism. This is more than a circle for Giddens; we could call it a web, as there is a clear link between surveillance and industrialism, of capitalism and military power. For Giddens, capitalism and the nation state are responsible for promoting and accelerating the expansion of modern institutions across the world and have been affected by all four institutional dimensions that I have described. So, nation states have concentrated administrative power, capitalist production has led to a massive expansion in wealth and military might and this has all been underpinned by the dynamic nature of modernity – time-space distanciation, disembedding and reflexivity. Modernity is then, inherently globalising for Giddens.

Giddens goes beyond international relations theory and systems theory (which I discuss in the next section) by considering political economy, or the world capitalist economy as just one of four dimensions of globalisation. Again we have the circular diagram:

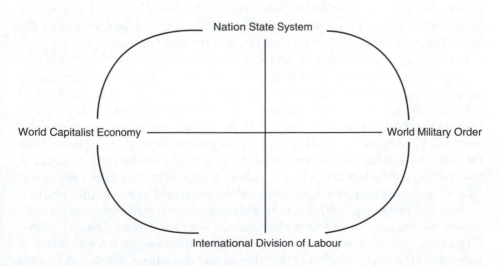

(Giddens, 1990, p71)

Thus we have the four dimensions of globalisation: first, the world capitalist economy. The main centres of power are capitalist states but transnational corporations within those states cross the boundaries of states and expand across the world. So a business corporation may have its base in one state, but extend their operation across the globe. As Giddens points out, the largest transnational corporations have immense economic power and budgets which are bigger than some nations. There is truly a world capitalist system in late modernity. The sheer wealth of transnational corporations enables them to operate outside the remit of nation states, particularly within developing countries, but there are some important ways in which their power cannot equal that of states. Thus, second we have the nation state which features a monopoly of the control of the means of violence within there own territory and for some, extending globally. Just think of the military might of the United States of America. The power of the nation state grows precisely because of the internalisation of state relations, in that resources are shared and pooled so more and more surveillance can be exerted over populations. Giddens calls this the dialectical nature of globalisation. On the one hand, a joint effort between states diminishes individual sovereignty, but on the other, the combined power increases influence within the state system. So, for example we have agencies of the United Nations. The third dimension is industrialism and the international division of labour. Local industries are increasingly becoming incorporated into the international division of labour. Trading on the world market has been particularly extended in the service sector. 'One of the main features of the globalising implications of industrialism is the worldwide diffusion of machine technologies' (Giddens, 1990, p 76). Finally, we have the world military order. The globalisation of military power is marked by the increasing use of alliances between states which empowers each member of the alliance; thus we have the industrialisation of war and flows of weaponry around the globe. We start to see globalised war where local conflicts become matters of global involvement as in the case of the NATO alliance in the former Yugoslavia, and the first Gulf war.

Finally Giddens manages to address the cultural aspects of globalisation noting that mechanised technologies of communication have dramatically influenced all aspects of globalisation. First the introduction of mechanical printing, the telephone, satellite and now the internet have contributed to making the local global, and global local. People become more aware of world events as the complex web of the media infiltrates all aspects of our lives. Thus for Giddens, globalisation is a result of the processes of modernity. It has little to do with postmodernism which Giddens rejects as just another metanarrative. It is in effect a globalising of the Western world view on life, politics, culture and technology. What Giddens does however, is to recognise globalisation, not only as an economic phenomena, but also as a major social transformation. Indeed, if we wanted to define globalisation, then for Giddens it represents 'the intensification of worldwide social relations which link distant localities in such a way that local happenings are shaped by events occurring many miles away and vice versa' (Giddens, 1990, p 64). In the next section of this chapter I want to look at the work of Martin Albrow and Roland Robertson who start to add a more cultural dynamic to the globalisation debate.

Theorising the Global Age

In the Global Age (1996) Martin Albrow notes that despite all the talk and excitement about new ages, postmodernism, as we have seen in the previous chapter has never been able to escape modernity; it always defines itself in terms of its relationship to modernity and therefore is probably just another phase of it. Albrow suggests that the only way we can move on is to go beyond the concepts of modernity and postmodernity and recognise a new reality – the Global Age (Albrow, 1996, p 2). Albrow argues that theorists such as Giddens (1990), Robertson (1992) and Ulrich Beck (1992) have all recognised substantial social transformations but still hang onto the idea of the continuity of modernity. For Albrow theorising means confronting our new reality however, in some way supplanting modernity with globality:

> Fundamentally the Global Age involves the supplanting of modernity with global-ity and this means an overall change in the basis of action and social organisation for individuals and groups. There are at least five major ways in which globality has taken us beyond the assumptions of modernity. They include the global environ-mental consequences of aggregate human activities; the loss of security where weaponry has global destructiveness; the globality of communication systems; the rise of a global economy; and the reflexivity of globalism, where people and groups of all kinds refer to the globe as the frame for their beliefs. (Albrow, 1996, p 4).

If we take all these things together argues Albrow, then they represent the challenge to what we call modernity, and therefore to one of its most enduring institutions, the nation-state. Citizens now transgress the boundaries both real and conceptual of the nation state in what is now a social transformation which threatens the very institutions of modernity. Forget modernity argues Albrow, and watch the global age open up a whole new world to us. I will return to Albrow later on in this chapter but first I want to examine the work of Roland Robertson and the rejection of systems theory. We have seen this in the work of Lyotard's Parology, where the world viewed as a whole, or as a system is unknowable. Lyotard's is an epistemological critique, whereas Robertson is critical of the focus on the economic and material. This focus ignores the importance of values, meaning and symbols, and we have to con-sider the response of the individual to the emerging global system. So, what is systems theory? Probably one of the best known proponents is Immanuel Wallerstein (1984).

Systems theory places an emphasis on the nation state in which we have a bounded configuration of states and national cultures integrated into a system by the global dynamics of capital accumulation. Throughout the history of the capitalist world economy, the system has not enjoyed a constant development, but development has occurred in wavelike spurts of expansion and contraction. There are periods when production in the world economy outstrips demand for goods and products leading to a redistribution of world income to the lower strata of the world economy. This redistribution expands the market within what Wallerstein terms the core zones and leads to the incorporation of new zones on the periphery (Wallerstein, 1984, p 6). Wallerstein's basic argument is that there is a link between the economic and political in which this cyclical effect of capitalism causes class conflict in core countries which actually strengthens the position of the worker, both in terms of employment rights, and standard of living rises, at the same time new lower stratas are incorporated into the system evening out the world distribution of income. Thus we have expansion promoting production which in turn promotes expansion. Thus for Wallerstein we have musical *chairs* of competing nation states:

> In the course of periods of stagnation, the system undergoes a shakedown, in which the producers of weaker efficiency are eliminated. This is what accounts for the musical chairs game at the top. The 'old' dominant enterprises (and the states in which they are located) find their costs steadily rising, because of the costs of amortizing 'older' capital investment, combined with rising labour costs resulting from the growing strength of worker's organization. 'Newer' enterprises (and the states in which they are located) thus constantly overtake 'older' enterprises in the quasi-monopolistic world market. (Wallerstein, 1984, p 7)

This game of musical chairs in not restricted to the core states, but also to what Wallerstein describes as the semi-peripherical states who also play the game becoming attached to core states or powers in moments of expansion. They then act as transmission belts and political agents of imperial power. Because they do not have the same economic or political power they are often cut of again by core states to return to the position of the imperial, or should we say colonial oppressed. This is what Wallerstein is describing then, the rise and fall of empires and the economic and political ties that develop into a global system. Hence we have the global division of labour divided along the lines we saw in Harvey's (1989) work in the previous chapter. At the centre is a core of powerful nation-states, for example, the United States of America, Europe and Japan. We then have a semi periphery of newly industrialised countries, in particular south East Asia, and on the periphery the third world. This forms an integrated system of exploitative trading relations between autonomous states with distinctive national cultures. As Robertson (1992) has noted Wallerstein's systems theory was a direct response to modernisation theories which only looked at societies comparatively. As opposed to seeing them as a system of relations on a global scale, they tended to focus Western societies as major reference points.

In response to systems theory, Robertson attempts to develop a flexible model of the global as a whole. This model has more emphasis on the notion of self and culture. 'I think in terms of four major aspects... These are *national societies*; *individuals*, or more basically *selves*; *relationships between national societies*, or the *world system of societies*; and, in the generic sense, *mankind*, which to avoid misunderstanding, I frequently call *humankind*' (Robertson, 1992, p 25). Robertson is concerned in the 'broadest' sense with the way in which the world is ordered, but he takes into consideration flexibility in his totality. Robertson's views can be seen to be slightly at odds with Giddens, in that he argues that globalisation cannot be seen as an outcome or consequence of modernity, or western project. In the increasingly globalised world there is a heightening of 'civilizational, societal, ethnic, regional and, indeed individual, self consciousness' (Robertson, 1992, p 27). Globalisation as a topic of academic debate should be understood in terms of the problem of the form in which the world becomes united. Robertson offers us a 'minimal phase model' of globalisation which indicates some of the major constraining tendencies in recent history in relation to the world order and compression of the world. Robertson's historical and temporal model can be outlined thus:

Phase I: The Germinal Phase. Europe fifteenth to eighteenth century. Growing of national communities and downplaying of medieval 'transnational system. Growth of the Catholic Church. Accentuation of concepts of individuality and humanity. Beginning of modern geography and the spread of the Gregorian calendar.

Phase II: The Incipient Phase. Mid Eighteenth to late Nineteenth century Europe. Formation of the homogeneous, unitary state. Formal international relations; standardised citizenship; concrete conception of humankind; increase in legal conventions and agencies dealing with international and transnational regulation and communication. Beginning of the problem of who gets admitted to international society and who does not.

Phase III: The Take-off Phase: 1870's–1920's. Singular form of globalisation centred on four reference points: national societies, generic individuals, a single international society, and singular conception of self. Increasingly global conception of a 'correct' and 'acceptable' national society. Inclusion of a number of non Europeans societies into international society. Globalisation of immigration restrictions. Huge increase in the number and spread of global communications. Development of global competitions and prizes (Olympics, Nobel). Implementation of world time and near global adoption of Gregorian calendar.

Phase IV: The Struggle-for-Hegemony Phase. !920's–1960's. Disputes and wars about the dominant globalisation process seen in take-off phase. Establishment of League of Nations and United Nations. High point of the Cold War (conflict within the modern project) The idea and nature of humanity focussed and shaped by the Holocaust and the actual use of an atomic bomb.

Phase V: The Uncertainty Phase: 1960's –.present. Heightening of Global consciousness. Moon landings, Earth Summits, Kyoto agreement. End of the Cold War. Number of global institutions and movements increase. Enormous advances in global communications. Concepts of individuals rendered more complex by gender, sexual, ethnic and racial considerations. Global civil rights. Idea of global humankind enhanced, particularly through environmental movements. Rising of interest in world civil society. Consolidation of global media system.
(Robertson, 1992, pp 58–59)

Although this provides a brief sketch of the development of the global system, Robertson's key points are that there is a logic to the globalisation process which operates in relative independence of strictly societal or socio-cultural processes. Globalisation has not developed out of an inter-state system; it is far more complex than that. Robertson is some sense builds on Wallerstein's theory, not rejecting it out of hand, far from it, but he adds a cultural dimension to the globalisation debate. The global field, for Robertson, is a socio-cultural system which has emerged from the compression of civilisational cultures, national societies, intra and cross national movements and organisations, sub societies, ethnic groups and individuals to name but a few. The compression of these groups on one hand can be constraining, but on the other hand differentially empowering. As Ulrich Beck (2000) notes, the workings of globalisation can lead to an intensification of a mutual interdependence between national boundaries; we go from separate worlds to transnational interdependence. What Robertson does however, is go beyond this by stressing how deeply the awareness of the world as single place has become in our everyday reality. Globalisation of the world and conscious globalisation which is reflected in the mass media are two sides of the same process. Globalisation is not just about interdependence though, it is about how world horizons open up in the cross cultural production of meaning and cultural symbols (Beck, 2000, p 47). Thus we are introduced by Robertson to the idea of *glocalisation*. Local and global are not mutually exclusive, the global and the local, the universal and the particular are inextricably intertwined. The local is an aspect of the global in as much as the global is a drawing together of local communities:

Globalization – in the broadest sense, the compression of the world – has involved and increasingly involves the creation and incorporation of locality, processes which themselves largely shape, in turn, the compression of the world as a whole. Even though we are, for various reasons, likely to continue to use the concept of globalization, it might well be preferable to replace it for certain purposes with the concept of glocalization. (Robertson, 1995, p 40)

So, on the one hand we have a growing worldwide emphasis on the uniformity and *universal* nature of institutions, organisations, signs and symbols; think of McDonald's, MasterCard, trends in clothing like denim jeans. On the other we have the local and *particular*, the emphasis on local cultures (which may be celebrated worldwide) and identity, but these are not in contradiction with each other, they are in some sense interlocking facets of the global age. As Beck (2000) notes though, it's not hard to imagine the glocal world disintegrating into conflicts: 'One only has to think of a division of the world triggered by *exclusion* of those 'without purchasing power' – perhaps the future majority of mankind – and hence a *Brazilianisation* of the world' (Beck, 2000, p 51). Although these forms of glocality emphasise a gloomy future, Beck argues they also may signal new forms of communality, for example the transnational Shell boycott. Indeed for Beck we may be witnessing the beginnings of a history of global civilisation 'in which globalization becomes reflexive and thus gains a new historical quality that justifies the term 'world society' (Beck, 2000, p 51). In the next section I will examine the work of Arjun Appadurai who builds on Robertson's cultural emphasis in the study of globalisation.

Global Cultural Flows

Arjun Appadurai (1990) extends Robertson's cultural analysis of globalisation to talk about landscapes of people, finance, media, technology and ideology in an assessment of cultural global flows. Appadurai argues that today's world involves interactions of a new order. Whereas in the past cultural transactions have involved either warfare or religion, or both, we now live in an age of global cultural processes in which the imagination as social practice is crucial: 'The imagination is now central to all forms of agency, it is itself a social fact, and is a key component of the new global order' (Appadurai, 1990, p 256). What Appadurai means by this is that imagination has become an organised field of social practices, a form of negotiation between individuals and globally defined possibilities. So for example we can see in the current war on terror there is a pastiche of imagination and empirical fact that is operating on a global level (see Clarke 2002, Clarke and Hoggett, 2004). This is a negative example, but the imagination also enables people in a global world to think of possible futures and broader horizons, no matter how bad their lot is. For Appadurai the new global cultural economy can no longer be thought of in terms of core periphery models, consumers and producers, or migration theory, rather the global cultural economy is chaotic, rhizomic and disorganised. There are disjunctures between economy, culture and politics which Appadurai analyses by pointing to five global cultural flows. Beck has described these as the cornerstones of imaginary worlds (Beck, 2000, p 53); Appadurai calls them the building blocks of the imaginary world – *ethno-scapes, mediascapes, technoscapes, financescapes* and *ideoscapes*. Appadurai uses the term *scape* to point to the fluid and irregular characteristics of these land-scapes, which in turn characterise global capital as much as they characterise international clothing styles (Appadurai, 1990, p 257). For Appadurai:

> These terms with the common suffix – scape also indicate that these are not objec-tively given relations that look the same from every angle of vision, but, rather they are deeply perspectival constructs, inflected by historical, linguistic, and political sit-uatedness of different sorts of actors: nation states, multinationals, diasporic com-munities, as well as sub national groupings and movements (whether religious, political, or economic), and even intimate face-to-face groups, such as villages, neighbourhoods, and families. Indeed the individual actor is the last locus of this perspectival set of landscapes, for these landscapes are eventually navigated by agents who both experience and constitute larger formations, in part from their own sense of what these landscapes offer. (Appadurai, 1990, p 257).

We therefore have a set of global cultural flows of irregular and fluid land-scapes which are deeply perspectival constructs which are building blocks of imagined worlds, that is multiple world views constituted from numerous cultural keys.

Ethnoscapes are the landscapes of persons. They constitute, for Appadurai, the shifting world we live in. There is a global flow of people: tourists, im-migrants, refugees, exiles, guest workers, all forms of moving groups and in-dividuals who more than ever affect the politics of, and between nation states. Appadurai is not arguing that there are no longer stable groups of kinship, rather that these stability's are shot through 'with the woof of human motion' as more and more groups deal with both the fantasy and reality of wanting, or having to move. The point for Appadurai is that these fantasies and realities now operate on much larger scales 'men and women from villages in India think not just of moving to Poona or Madras, but of moving to Dubai and Houston... refugees from Sri Lanka find themselves in South India as well as Switzerland'. For Appadurai as the nature of capital and technology changes, and nation states shift policies on refugee population, these groups have to adapt, they cannot afford to let their imagination rest too long.

Technoscapes are the global configuration of technologies that are fluid and move across all boundaries at high speed throughout the world. They pierce previously impervious boundaries and cross national borders in different configurations. As Appadurai notes, a steel complex in Libya for example, may also involve interests around the world – India, China, Russia and Japan providing new technological configurations. These configurations are no longer driven by economies of scale, or market rationality, but by increasingly complex relationships among money flow, political possibilities and the avail-ability of skilled and unskilled labour. 'So, while India exports waiters and Chauffeurs to Dubai and Sharjah, it also exports software engineers to the United States – indentured briefly to Tata-Burroughs or the World Bank, then laundered through the State Department to become wealthy aliens, who are in turn objects of seductive messages to invest their money and know-how in federal and state projects in India' (Appadurai, 1990, p 258).

Financescapes refer to the fact that global capital is more difficult to follow than ever before. Although traditional measures from the World Bank still apply, Appadurai notes that it is very difficult to make a comparison between wages in Japan or the United States, or property prices in New York or Tokyo without trying to unpick the complex fiscal and investment flows between the two economies. Global flows of capital have become more mysterious, rapid and volatile than ever. Huge amounts of money are moved at blinding speed between national boundaries, and the slightest fluctuation in interest rates or time fluctuations can have absolute implications. 'The critical point is that the global relationship among ethnoscapes, technoscapes, and financescapes is deeply disjunctive and profoundly unpredictable because each of these landscapes is subject to its own constraints and incentives (some political, some informational, and some technoenvironmental)' (Appadurai, 1990, p 259). Each then acts as a constraint and a parameter in relation to the other. Thus, for Appadurai even the simplest model of global political economy would have to take into account the deeply disjunctive nature and rela-tionship between human movement, technological flow and the transfer of finance.

Mediascapes further refract these disjunctures. They are related to the land-scape of images and refer to the electronic ability to distribute and disseminate information – television, film, newspapers, and periodicals. The image of the world is created by these media through documentaries, news programmes and current affairs or entertainment shows. They produce hundreds of images, narratives and ethnoscapes that are beamed across the globe. It is a profound mixture of politics, commodity and news. ' what this means is that many audiences around the world experience the media themselves as a com-plicated and interconnected repertoire of print, celluloid, electronic screens, and billboards' (Appadurai, 1990, p 259). The lines between the realistic and the fictional landscape are blurred, and the further away the audience is from the city, the more likely they are to construct a fantasy object, or an imagined world – the city as paved with gold. So, for Appadurai, mediascapes, whether they are produced by private or state controlled interests produce strips of reality out of which scripts can form imagined lives. They help to construct stories of *Other* or *Imagined* lives and could be the basis for the movement of peoples.

Ideoscapes are political images that often represent the state, or state ideologies, or counter ideologies. 'These ideoscapes are composed of elements of the Enlightenment worldview, which consists of a chain of ideas, terms, and images, including *freedom, welfare, rights, sovereignty,* and the master term *democracy*. The master narrative of the Enlightenment (and its many variants in Britain, France, and the United States) as constructed with a certain internal logic and presupposed a certain relationship between reading, representation, and the public sphere' (Appadurai, 1990, p 260). But for Appadurai the internal coherence of this master narrative has now loosened as nation states organise their political cultures around new frames of reference and different keywords. So, linguistically the differential Diaspora of keywords involves problems of both a semantic and pragmatic nature, something to think about in terms of Habermas' communicative action. Words need careful translation as their meaning changes from context to context throughout the globe; for example, democracy sits at the very centre of ideoscapes, but has very different meanings in different countries. We thus have a kaleidoscope of terminology as states seek to pacify populations whose ethnoscapes are in motion and whose mediascapes may cause severe problems for ideoscapes. The ideoscape is further complicated, fluid as it is, by the injection of new meaning into terms like democracy, by intellectuals in different parts of the world.

These are then the scapes that for Appadurai form the basis of global cultural flows, and it is the growing disjuncture between these scapes that forms the globalised world. The sheer speed, volume and scale of these flows mean that the disjunctures are central in global politics. Deterritorialisation is now one of the fundamental aspects of global life as populations migrate and move around the globe as guest workers. On the one hand it creates exaggerated attachments to politics at home (Appadurai uses the example of Hindus from India) through new networks of finance and religious identifications, on the other, deterritorialisation creates new markets for film makers and travel agents who thrive in the business of those dislocated populations with a need for contact with their homeland. Indeed mediascapes construct imagined homelands that are so fantastic that they create the basis for new forms of ethnic conflict. People, money and commodities are ceaselessly chasing each other around the world:

> These tragedies of displacement could certainly be relayed in a more detailed analysis of the relationship between the Japanese and German sex tours to Thailand and the tragedies of the sex trade in Bangkok, and in other similar loops that ties together fantasies about the Other, the conveniences and seductions of travel, the

economics of global trade, and the brutal mobility fantasies that dominate gender politics in many parts of Asia and the world at large. (Appadurai, 1990, p 262).

This has also had implications for nation states that are continuously embattled. Nations try to co-opt states, states try to become nations. Appadurai argues that in general, separatist transnational organisations who often use methods of terror exemplify nations in search of states. Often imagined communities will seek a state that they can call their own, for example, Tamils, Basques. States on the other hand often try and monopolise the moral resources of a community. Nation states use media scapes to pacify and control separatist groups, often using the notion of difference to unify and homogenise. This leads Appadurai to conclude that the nation and state are now so often at each other's throats that we have lost the hyphen between nation and states (nation-states). In returning to where he started – ethno-scapes, Appadurai argues that the central paradox of ethnic politics is primodia have become globalised, whether of language, skin colour or kinship – 'that is, sentiments, whose greatest force is in their ability to ignite intimacy into a political state and turn locality into a staging ground for identity, have become spread over vast and irregular spaces as groups move yet stay linked to one another through sophisticated media capabilities' (Appadurai, 1990, p 263). In other words, ethnicity which used to be assigned at a local level, however vast that locale, is now a global force which slips between the cracks of states and borders.

Appadurai argues that there has been a major and deep change in the relationship between production and consumption in the global economy. Commodity fetishism has replaced by two new descendants – *production fetishism* and *the fetishism of the consumer*. Production fetishism is an illusion created by transnational production that masks the exchange of transnational capital, earnings and far away workers. It appears as if things are produced locally when they are produced in a system of transnational networks. This obscures not the social relations but the relations of production that are often transnational. The local becomes a fetish in which the global is disguised. The fetishism of the consumer is where the key player is the producer but this is masked so that the consumer feels that he or she is the actor, when for Appadurai, he or she is actually the chooser. In this sense the consumer has transformed by mediascapes into a sign. The central feature of global culture today for Appadurai is a mutual contest between sameness and difference in a situation of radical disjunctures between different sorts of global flows.

So, to sum up, Appadurai provides a focus on the globalisation of culture which goes beyond the work of theorists such as Giddens and Robertson although still retaining some economic basis. Appadurai introduces us to the global imagination and the way the shrinking of the world allows us to think of new horizons. The argument is very postmodern; it is where we have flux and flow, uncertainty and difference and an emphasis on the local. The global flow of images, as we have seen also in Baudrillard's theory, keeps the cultural economy flowing. It is hard to imagine how we might use this as an analysis rather than a description, but in many places Appadurai provides food for thought, in particular the discussion of the changing nature of the nation state which I want to turn to briefly now.

The End of the Nation State?

The nature of the nation state has been central to all the globalisation debates that we have looked at thus far. Giddens (1990) talks of the increasing power that nation states possess, particularly in terms of the monopoly of the means of violence. Power grows because of the internationalisation of state relations through the pooling of resources. On one hand the nation state grows more powerful, on the other it starts to loose its sovereignty. System theorists see the nation state in terms of bounded configuration of states and national cultures that make up the system of the global dynamics of capital accumulation. Robertson (1992) prefers to talk about national societies while Appadurai (1990) talks about the loss of the hyphen between nation and state in his discussion of the conflict between nations, sometimes imagined, and states. Perhaps the leading figure in this discussion has been David Held (1988, 1996) who focuses on the erosion of national sovereignty and the long term decline of the nation state. Held prefers to think in terms of a *cosmopolitan* model of democracy in relation to ever decreasing state power. The question for Held is 'has sovereignty remained intact while the autonomy of the state has diminished, or has the modern state actually faced a loss of sovereignty' (Held, 1988, p 69). By sovereignty, Held means the power and control a nation state has over its own future in a given territorial space. A state must therefore be able to take final decisions and enforce laws within the state boundaries; a loss of sovereignty implies a loss of control over the direction of national policies. This is about setting policies and autonomy is about achieving goals once that policy has been set. The autonomy question is important because in the increasingly globalised world it becomes harder and harder for a state, particularly a weak one, to achieve objectives without the influence from other states altering the outcome. Held (1988) identifies a number of dimensions of globalisation which point to disjunctures or gaps between the power of the nation state to actually determine its own future and actual practices between state and economy at a global level.

Disjuncture 1: The World Economy

There has been a sea change between the formal authority of the state and the way in which production is organised in the global world. This puts limits on the power and authority of nation states. Increasingly, as we have seen, there have been huge changes in the organisation of production and distribution across global networks and core periphery production methods, with components being produced in multiple countries and assembled in another. Post-Fordism has also seen a growth in the exploitation of labour in third world countries where there is little regulation from either the state or trade unions. For Held, two aspects of the new international economic order are central:

> The internationalisation of production and the internationalisation of financial transactions, organised in part by fast growing multinational companies. Multinational corporations plan and execute their production, marketing and production with the world economy firmly in mind. Even when multinationals have a clear national base, their interest is in above all global profitability, and their country of origin may count little in their overall corporate strategy: the 'national loyalty' of multinationals is of an instrumental rather than a sentimental kind. (Held, 1988, p 70)

Supporting the global flows of production and distribution are banks which have increasingly become global organisations themselves. Because of new information and communication, technologies banks are able to respond immediately to any changes in markets irrespective of their spatial location. Although there has been a massive increase in trade since the post war period, governments have increasingly lost autonomy over national economic programmes. As Held notes, some countries can isolate themselves from transnational economic networks by re-creating boundaries and alliances, and extending national laws. The tension between the political and the economic is likely to be different in different spheres and between them 'West-West, North-South, East-West'. Although it is unlikely that the idea of national economy has been superseded, the increasing internationalisation of production, finance and global money flows is eroding the capacity of the state to control its own economic future, for example we seen various arguments around a single European market and the use of the Euro in most countries in Europe.

Disjuncture 2: Hegemonic Powers and Power Blocks

This is a feature of Held's (1988) original formulation of disjuncture in the nation-state which he drops in later work presumably because of the collapse of the former Soviet Union and the end of the cold war. The argument goes that there is disjuncture between the idea of the state as a military actor and the formation of hegemonic power blocks. The dominance of superpowers like the USSR and USA and of alliances like NATO can severely restrict and constrain the decision making and action of other nations. This disjuncture is no longer a point of analysis as there is only one superpower – the USA, which dominates the world both economically and in terms of military might in the new empire of fear (See Clarke and Hoggett, 2004).

Disjuncture 3: International Organisations and Political Decision Making

The notion that there is a perpetual form of public power embodied within an individual state is now defunct argues Held. This is because we now have a vast array of international regimes and organisations which have been created to manage huge areas of transnational activity through trade, to the oceans, the skies and space. The formation of these transnational decision making organisations has led to changes in the way that world politics is structured. So, we have new forms of multilateral and multinational politics with collective decision making between governments, international governmental organisations (IGO's), pressure groups and non-governmental organisations (NGO's). Held cites as an example the international earth summit in Rio in 1992 in which many organisations were represented on a global scale, not just nation states. Another is the International Monetary Fund which can dictate a government's economic policy as a precondition for a loan. As Held notes: 'In pursuing a particular line of economic policy, the IMF may insist as a condition of its loan to a government that the latter cut public expenditure, devalue its currency and cut back on subsidised welfare programmes' But argues Held, we also have to note that the IMF often intervenes at the request of a particular government, or political faction within the state. This cannot be directly interpreted as a loss of sovereignty, rather a striking example of the tension the idea of a sovereign state and the nature of decision making at an international level (Held, 1996, p 346).

The European Union (EU) is another example of the way in which international organisations can undermine state power. The difference with the EU however, is that it has the power to make laws which can be imposed on member states and also the power to make and enact policy. As Held notes, again we have pro's and con's. Although the individual autonomy of the member state is eroded, economically the state benefits. It is, argues Held, a case of the willing surrender of aspects of sovereignty which has helped the survival of the European nation state. For Held, these developments have helped in a move from a state centred international system of high politics to new forms of geo-governance. A striking example of this is the globalisation of military technology and the rising density of technological connections between states. This puts into question the very idea of national security (Held, 1996, p 348).

Disjuncture 4: International Law

International law subjects both governments and NGO's to new forms and systems of legal regulation and rights and duties that transcend the claims of nation states. For example, with the problem of genocide that we looked at in some detail in chapter three, the Nuremburg Tribunal established the international genocide convention that ensured an international framework of basic humanitarian values that reaches beyond individual nations and states. As Held notes 'The legal framework of the Nuremburg Tribunal marked a highly significant change in the legal direction of the modern state: for the new rules challenged the principle of military discipline and subverted national sovereignty at one of its most sensitive points: the hierarchical relations within the military' (Held, 1988, p 71). A further example is the European Convention for the Protection of Human Rights and Fundamental Freedoms (1950) which was committed to a radical legal innovation which enabled in principle, individual citizens to initiate proceedings against their own governments, which as Held notes, no longer leaves the state free to treat its own citizens as it sees fit (Held, 1996, p 349). The question will remain though, as to whether nations and states, or nation states see fit to abide by international law, or indeed take any notice of it at all. It would seem that even the biggest nation state of them all – the USA has been in contravention of international law in its treatment of Al-Qaeda suspects, this is even before we start thinking again about the atrocities in Kosova, Sierra Leone and Rwanda.

Disjuncture 5: Culture and Environment

This final disjuncture argues that in an increasingly global world it becomes more and more difficult to sustain and foster national identity. I think this has been particularly well articulated by Appadurai (1990) which I looked at in some detail in the previous section, but for Held we can see some remarkable developments in recent times which undermine the effectiveness of nation states to uphold a unitary identity. These include the spread of English as the dominant language of elite cultures, the globalisation of telecommunications, the explosion of satellite links, and the immense growth in internet usage. We have seen development of multinational multimedia empires and huge increase in tourism. These all facilitate ways of transmitting different cultural ideas around the globe and linking nations and peoples in different ways. Sixty–ninety per cent of box office receipts in Europe come from foreign films, but Held is quick to point out that this is largely the story of American dominance (Held, 1996, p 350). It is however for Held, environmental problems and issues that give the clearest example of a global shift in human organisation that exerts some of the most fundamental pressures on nation states. For Held, there are three issues at stake: first, shared problems with global implications. Environmental change, global warming and pollution are all shared global problems: second, interlinked problems associated with demographic expansion. Intensive farming, the devastation of the rainforests has implications for bio diversity and the possible extinction of some species. Third, transboundary pollution as exemplified by acid rain and in a more extreme case, nuclear waste from the fallout at Chernobyl. In response to these issues argues Held, there has been an interlinked process of cultural and political globalisation which manifests itself in the emergence of green movements and scientific and intellectual networks that transverse national boundaries.

So, to sum up for Held, not unlike many of the theorists that we have examined, the international order and its role in the nation state is changing quite significantly. Although we have some form of global interconnectivity for some time, Held argues that there has been a further internationalisation of domestic activities and an intensification of both decision making at an inter-national level and global politics. The disjunctures he describes have altered the way in which the nation states can and do operate. Sovereignty is now divided along the lines of a number of agencies, national, international and regional, and they become restricted by this plurality. Held argues that the modern theory of the sovereign democratic state presupposes the idea of a community which governs itself and looks to its own future. This idea is chal-lenged by the nature of global interconnections to the point where it casts doubt on the future and meaning of national politics. Held advocates the development of a cosmopolitan democracy which would involve the develop-ment of administrative capacity and political resources at regional and global levels to complement those polities at local and national level (Held, 1996, p 353). Neither local or global are privileged. As Albrow (1996) notes: 'In this new state, globally, nationally and locally alike, democracy will work best at the point where the knowledgeable user of the institution can bring experience to bear on the decisions that affect him or her' (Albrow, 1996, p 182). For Albrow the nation state becomes a modest subsidiary in the context of global-ity as institutional developments take place across boundaries and people's identity and lives will conform less to national identifications. In the global age national culture becomes separated from the state apparatus, indeed for Albrow: ' For the global citizen it will be reassuring if leaders of the nation state can guarantee the train timetable without asking for patriotic pledges in return' (Albrow, 1996, p 183).

The Global and the Postcolonial Condition

Given that the nation state was at the heart of what we know as colonialism and empire, it seems pertinent to ask finally about the relationship between nation state, globalisation and postcolonialism. As Leela Ghandi (1998) notes, colonialism was the historical harbinger of the fluid global circuits that charac-terise modernity. The colonial encounter is one of an adversarial conflict between competing nationalisms: 'Colonialism owes at least some of its inheri-tance to the violent and expansionist energies of European nationalism… the history of decolonisation has generally, and perhaps more effectively, been articulated through the resistant counter-energies of anti-colonial nationalism' (Ghandi, 1998, p 122). For Ghandi, anti-colonial revolutionaries in the shape of Frantz Fanon (1986) and Mahatma Ghandi and post colonial critics in the shape of Edward Said (1995) see much use in the positive role of anti-colonial nation-alisms, albeit a transitory stage, in mobilising the oppressed former colonised people of the world. As Ghandi notes, the growing literature on globalisation insists that with growing economic and technological homogenisation of the world, national boundaries become redundant. Citing Appadurai's (1990) work which we looked at earlier in the chapter, Ghandi draws our attention to the unprecedented movement of people's and technology around the globe. In post colonial times we have a far more fluid world which in the language of globalisation throws up concepts such as Diaspora and hybridity (for a discussion of those excerpts see Clarke 2003). These terms, argues Ghandi, assist postcolonialism in its search for evidence regarding the mutual transformations between coloniser and colonised. They can supply a rich and positive vein of thought and ideas, but as Ghandi notes:

> The West remains the privileged meeting ground for all ostensibly cross-cultural conversations. Moreover, within the metropolis, multicultural celebrations of 'cultural diversity' conveniently disguise rather more serious economic and political disparities. (Ghandi, 1998, p 136).

This is one of the major problems with the globalisation thesis. We could ask ourselves several questions 'the globalisation of whose world?' Of western culture? Of America? Is America the new Empire as it has recently seemed to be happy with using the rhetoric of empire publicly? The problem is that the benefits of living in a global world do not benefit all people, only those who have the privileged access to it. In *Globalization and the Postcolonial World* (1998, 2000) Ankie Hoogvelt shows us the other side of the globalisation debate, of an oppressed and certainly exploited third world, of countries in which containment and exclusion rule. Indeed Hoogvelt argues that rather than a wider dispersal of economic wealth and trade between, or from core to periphery in the globalised age, we have seen a thickening of economic exchanges within the core, with a few relatively small nations graduating to core status. There has been a decline in economic interaction between core and periphery both in relation to world trade and to total population's participation in the network. (Hoogvelt, 2000, p 356). Tellingly Hoogvelt argues:

> ...the regime of privitization and deregulation imposed by the World Bank and IMF structural adjustment programmes, have created a climate of what is euphemistically called 'financial openness' in which the Third World bourgeoisie are less restricted and more enabled than ever before to channel their nation's wealth to the financial markets and institutions of core countries. (Hoogvelt, 2000, p 357)

The upshot of this is that while the bourgeoisie participate in the world market, or in the core of the world system, their countries cannot. Hoogvelt (2000) talks of the imploding nature of capitalism, in which there is an intensification of trade within the core and a selective withdrawal of linkages with the periphery. So this is the globalisation of the core – Japan, Europe and North America at the expense of the periphery – Africa, Latin America and large parts of Asia. Hoogvelt describes globalisation as rearranging the world order in a three tier structure of concentric circles which cut across national and regional boundaries. At the core, we have the 'bankable' world elites from all continents that represent around twenty percent of the world population. They are encircled by a larger fluid social layer of workers and families who labour in insecure employment markets under cut throat competition that is the global market. These people represent twenty to thirty percent of the world's population. They are constantly labouring under the relentless elimination of jobs by machines, 'and a driving down of wages and social conditions to the lowest global denominator' (Hoogvelt, 2000, p 258). The third concentric circle represents those, and is the largest group, who are excluded from the global system: 'performing neither a productive function, nor presenting a potential consumer market in the present stage of high-tech information driven capitalism, there is, for the moment, neither theory, world view nor moral injunction, let alone programme of action to include them in universal progress' (Hoogvelt, 2000, p 358). For Hoogvelt, containment and exclusion rule the global system.

Hoogvelt (2000) uses the word postcolonial to describe the way in which social formations have emerged which are the result of the interaction between globalisation and the aftermath of colonialism. She pinpoints four postcolonial situations or conditions. First, there is the condition of 'exclusion and anarchy' as exemplified by sub Saharan Africa. In the aftermath of decolonisation the state is too weak to provide a viable political alternative or a civil society from the fragments left over from colonial rule. The state fails to progress from a juridical state to an empirical state which means also a failure of state led development projects and an increasing dependency on overseas aid. Globalisation has overwhelmed these fragile political and social orders, and has made peripheral their economies. We therefore, argues Hoogvelt, have a zone of civil collapse and anarchy on the edge of the global system. A second postcolonial condition is that of the anti-developmental stance of fundamental Islam. Although we would have to question why Islamic countries want to develop along Western economic lines, Hoogvelt argues that the failure of the developmental project coupled with the exclusionary effect of globalisation has interacted with Islam to render a different social formation: 'It is one in which the politics of religious identity and lifestyle have gained pre-eminence in the private sphere without, however, yielding a political project to (re) create civil society and rearrange state-society relations' (Hoogvelt, 2000, p 359). Third, we have some success in East Asia where state run developmental policies have placed some economies in the global capitalist market, but even these are under threat from the constant 'gales' of globalisation. The final postcolonial condition that Hoogvelt draws our attention to is in Latin America. Because of its particular colonial history, argues Hoogvelt, Latin America has an intellectual tradition of absorbing, experimenting with and revolting against Western models of progress. 'This intellectual commitment has helped to politicise the process of impoverishment and exclusion as the counterpart of Latin America's dependent insertion into the global economy' (Hoogvelt, 2000, p 360). Latin America's postcolonial condition then is of a testing ground for neo liberal policies of globalisation, together with the wrappings of privatisation on the one hand, and on the other, democracy. Civil society has become an arena for political and intellectual renewal.

It is clear then from Hoogvelt's analysis that while we are enjoying the multi-faceted cultural identities of our globalised world, the rift between the rich and poor, elite and pauper is growing. So, the global system, or globalisation is for the privileged, the only effect it has on the poor is to make them poorer. Indeed it has been argued that globalisation can be counterposed with a term that has considerably great explanatory and descriptive power – *imperialism* (Petras and Veltmeyer, 2001, p 12). For Petras and Veltmeyer (2001) the globalisation debate obscures, rather than accurately describes what is going on worldwide. Globalisation, throws an ideological veil over the interests of an emerging group of transnational capitalists and their economic interests. In Petras and Veltmeyer's view, the existing world economic order is in the processes of being renovated to create optimal conditions for the free play of greed, class interest, and profit making. In doing so, this new world order presents itself as the driving force of progress and the only road available (Petras and Veltmeyer, 2001, p8).

Thus, we have two points of view, the globalisation of culture, which brings with it new opportunities for celebrating difference, selecting identities and dissolving boundaries between nation states. On the other hand we have global economic exploitation, the aftermath of colonialisation and a new type of capitalist elite who transgress the border of nations and states in the globalised world system. We thus have implications for both the rationality of the social world and identity. In the final section of this chapter I want to try and bring some of these ideas together to look at the implications for the main themes of this book, in particular the rationalisation process and the construction of social identity.

Summary and Conclusion

As we have seen the implications for what constitutes our notion of self and identity are potentially huge in this postmodern globalised world. We literally consume identities, taking them off the shelf and buying them as we would any other product, buying a dream or a series of dreams which rapidly turn into a series of simulations. In the globalised, as opposed to postmodern world we have seen a set of structural changes which directly affect the way we relate to our own self and others. For example, in early modern society we tended to live in small communities, often bounded by the constraints of time and space. There was an emphasis on the nuclear family and the notion of community. If we take some of the major industrial trades of the modernity; steelworking, shipbuilding, and coal mining, then in all probability you were as likely to follow in the footsteps of your father and do the same kind of job and mother would stay home and look after the children in the patriarchal arrangement of modern times. It would have been unlikely that you would travel beyond the fairly confined borders of your locale and as such identity is constructed in relation to your job, your father's job, and your immediate locality. Times have changed though. There is far greater social mobility; people at least in the Western world are far more likely to travel extensively. You are far less likely to go into the same profession as your parents and the nuclear family is being eroded as the locus of identity in high modernity. That is not to say that traditional forms of identity construction are to be discarded, rather that the focus from which we construct our multiple selves is constantly changing and identity is fluid. Access to high speed technologies and information systems means that we can see a plethora of different cultures and ethnicities, diasporas and ways of life that should surely have some influence on our sense of self. We simply have more access to information now, more choice in our lifestyle and less constraint in our social mobility.

Appadurai (1990) tells us how people in the global world now use imagination as a social practice, no matter how bad our lot is. We can still imagine possible futures and broader horizons. Anthony Elliott (2001) argues that postmodern selves are best seen as ways of managing in contemporary culture, blending different ways of living, mixing modern and postmodern states of mind: 'If, for example, the term 'globalization' can today be used to fashion identities framed upon a sense of economic interconnectedness, democratic cosmopolitanism, and a postnational way of belonging, it can also be easily deployed in a more defensive manner, the production of identities held in thrall to fundamentalism or the flag' (Elliott, 2001, p 150). For Giddens (1991), high modernity brings about questions of *ontological security* and *existential anxiety* in relation to the self. In other words, the world of high modernity often threatens our sense of continuity and order in events (ontological security), as well as questioning our very existence, both in relation to the self and other (existential anxiety) 'The sheer sense of getting caught up in massive waves of global transformation is perturbing' (Giddens, 1991, p184). There is now more of an emphasis on lifestyle, and this is not just lifestyle in terms of consumption, but also in the world of work, and as most of us spend most of our lives working this is important. Note the difference here, in relation to work, lifestyle is something we choose, it is not handed down. We literally go, for Giddens, through a series of tribulations of the self. We are faced with dilemmas that stem from the high modern world we live in and the reflexive project of the self. So, we are faced with forces that both unify and fragment; lifestyle options both create opportunities but also instil feelings of powerlessness; there is the question of authority and uncertainty, there are no dominant authorities in high modernity and the self must steer a way between commitment and uncertainty, and finally we have a personalised versus a commodified experience of self in which personal appropriation is influenced by the standardisation of influence on consumption (Giddens, 1991, p 201). The upshot of this is that we all live under the threat of meaninglessness. This is usually held at bay by our old friend rationality, through routinisation, rationalisation and basic trust we hold our world together, the question is, how far is this being eroded and what are the consequences in late, high, global society?

Despite our new world of global cultural flows, flux, difference and disembeddedness, the processes of rationality and rationalisation increasingly play a part in our everyday lives. If Giddens (1991) is to be believed we actually need some form of routinisation, and a way of making our activities seem rational to avoid plummeting into the depths of meaninglessness. On the level of theory, many of the explanations of the state of the global world still rely on rational systems and processes of economic rationalisation to describe the global nature of society. Rationality, as the bedrock of Enlightenment thinking has simply gone global. Whether this is through systems of law, technology or morality, the rational standardisation and routinisation of everyday life has attempted to reach all parts of the globe. And again, this not always a good thing. We have seen from Hoogvelt's work how the rational economic systems of global capitalism become oppressive and exclusionary. The philosophical nature of what it means to be reasonable, or to reason, is rapidly changing – Is hate reasonable or does reason make people hate? This is the dilemma we face in the wake of Sept 11th and the War in Iraq. Global terrorism has blurred the boundary between reason and paranoia. We no longer know who our enemy is, we no longer know if it is safe to get on board a plane or a train. Reason often goads people to hate and this comes from all directions whether it is the West imposing its global polices of imperialism and economic intrusion or the fear instilled in ordinary people by the activities of global terrorism. We have in some sense arrived at an impossible situation in which we no longer know what is a genuine fear or a paranoid phantasy. The preferred solution to this has been total annihilation, but the problem is that the terrorists cannot be annihilated because they cannot be found. The toppling of Saddam Hussein's regime has made no impact on global terrorism, and the same goes for the war in Afghanistan. The retaliatory attacks borne out of anger have encouraged rather than discouraged the activities of the terrorists.

To conclude, I have looked at some of the main theories of globalis(z)ation, and although not exhaustive I have tried to strike a balance between the social, cultural and economic. Giddens as we have seen does not believe that we live in a postmodern world, rather that we are in a time of high modernity which is inherently globalising. If we take together the notions of the separation of time and space, the development of disembedding mechanisms and the reflexive appropriation of knowledge, then, for Giddens we can view modernity as a careering juggernaut. Modernity is inherently globalising and is marked by a set of key institutions or clusters: capitalism, surveillance, industrialism and military power. When mapped onto the global system they transform into the four dimensions of globalisation: the world capitalist economy, the nation state, the international division of labour, and the world military order. Thus in Giddens work we see a rejection of postmodernism in favour of a modernist perspective on globalisation. Giddens, offers some comfort to sociologists in that while placing some emphasis on economics, he also sees globalisation as a major social transformation. Albrow on the other hand argues that while theorists such as Giddens, Robertson and Beck have all recognised some form of major social transformation in their conception of globalisation they still hang onto the idea of modernity, no says Albrow, lets move on and supplant modernity with globality. In some sense I view Albrow's thesis as a very noble attempt to get away from the tragic and oppressive face of modern times by looking to a new future which does away with the rational bureaucratic oppressive regimes of modern times: 'Globality does not require novelty, expansion, bureaucracy, male or white domination. But the vitality, richness, and variety of the Global Age depend on the care with which its citizens preserve and tend the other more valuable achievements which were to the credit of the old modernity' (Albrow, 1996, p 202). Funnily enough, this sounds just like Habermas' argument in chapter four.

Roland Robertson's ideas add a cultural slant to the systems theory of Wallerstein. Globalisation is not just about interdependence, but how world horizons open up in the cross cultural production of meaning and cultural symbols. Robertson introduces us to the idea of glocalisation – the local and the global, the universal and the particular are mutually exclusive but inextricably intertwined. The local is an aspect of the global and vice versa. So, on one hand we have the rationalisation of, and uniformity which is the universal, in particular, global institutions and organisations, on the other hand we have an emphasis on local cultures and identities which to and fro together on the tides of global networks. Which brings us Appadurai's global cultural flows, a sophisticated argument which knits together landscapes of people, technologies, finance, media and ideology in something like a total rhizomic global landscape, everything is in flux and flow, everything influences everything else, a very Deluzo-Guattarian, semi Nietzschean view of the world. I think that Appadurai's work is important to because he introduces us to the global imagination, the idea that in the shrinking world we can think above and beyond our local horizon to think of new horizons and futures.

No examination of the nature of globalisation would be complete without addressing the nature and function of the nation state in our post times. Using the work of David Held I have looked at the way in which the power, autonomy, and sovereignty of the nation state is increasingly undermined by global disjunctures, transnational practices and international alliances. The nation state had its origins in colonialisation and this loops back to globalisation. It would seem that although the individual power of some nation states has eroded to the point that they are no longer world players on the military and economic stage, other nation states dominate. The economic and political power of the United States of America is unrivalled in the twenty first century, to the extent that it dwarfs any of its nearest rivals. This power is now so visible that even conservative Americans are using the word 'empire' to describe this unsurpassable ascendancy. This could lead us, as I have indicated, to ask such questions as whose global world? Are we just seeing new forms of imperialism and empire in which a core elite based on the old countries of the modern world continue to grow from strength to strength at the expense of those people on the periphery? Access to the benefits of the globalised world still seems the privilege of a small percentage of the world's population; while the rich get richer, the poor remain poor. In the final chapter of this book I want to address whether we live in an information society or disciplinary society and how these concepts may be linked. What are implications for everyday existence in a society that generates information globally? Can we usefully think of the idea of an information industry that has in some sense superseded the culture industry? And how do notions of information, disinformation, and networks feed into the idea of a risk society? Finally, how do these ideas of information and risk society interact with the globalisation debate, notions of rationality and the construction of the self. The question that we need to ask ourselves is 'who is taking which risk, on whose behalf, and to what end?'

Summary of Key Terms and Concepts

Anthony Giddens: Time-Space Distanciation: The separation of time and space to provide temporal and spatial zoning: timetables maps, world time.

Disembedding Mechanisms: The lifting out of social relations from a local context to span large time space distances. Includes the creation of symbolic tokens such as money and expert systems, for example in healthcare.

Reflexivity: The reflexive appropriation of knowledge becomes part of the system of reproduction and moves away from tradition.

The Double Hermeneutic: When knowledge reflexivity is applied to system reproduction there is both instability and new forms of energy. The goal posts are always changing as we reflect on our practices.

Institutional Clusters of Modernity: Capitalism (capital accumulation in labour and product markets; Surveillance (control of information and social supervision); Military Power (Control of the means of violence); Industrialism (Transformation of nature: Development of created environment) All these institutions are interlocking and support each other.

Four Dimensions of Globalisation: world capitalist economy, nation state system, world military order and international division of labour. Again, all these dimensions are interlocking and support each other.

Roland Robertson: Four major aspects of Globalisation: National societies; individuals and selves; relationship between national societies or the world system of societies; humankind. These are key areas of emphasis in developing a flexible model of the globe as a whole.

Arjun Appadurai: Global Cultural Flows:

Ethnoscapes: Landscapes of persons, the global flow of people, tourists, guest workers, immigrants, moving groups and individuals

Technoscapes: global configurations of technology that are fluid and move across boundaries at high speed around the globe.

(cont'd)

Financescapes: Rapid and volatile movement of capital around the globe. Huge amounts of money are moved at a blinding speed between national boundaries and slightest fluctuation of interest rates can have absolute implications.

Mediascapes: Landscape of images and the electronic ability to disseminate information. Helps to construct stories of Other or imagined lives.

Ideoscapes: Political images that represent the state composed of elements of the Enlightenment worldview.

David Held: Disjunctures in the Power of the Nation State

The World Economy: The organisation of production and distribution across global networks bypasses regulation by states or trade unions. The increasing internationalisation of production, finance and global money flows erodes the nation states capacity to control its economic future.

International Organisations and Political Decision Making: World politics has been restructured by the formation of transnational decision making organisations. We have a move from a state centred international system of high politics to new forms of geo-governance.

International Law: Internal law subjects governments to new forms and systems of legal regulation that transcend the claims of the nation state.

Culture and Environment: In the global world it becomes increasingly difficult to sustain national identity, particularly with the globalisation of media and telecommunication which undermine the effectiveness of the nation state to uphold unitary identity. Environmental issues and the politics that surround them give the clearest example of a global shift in human organisation that now exerts some of the most fundamental pressures on the nation state.

Ankie Hoogvelt: Globalisation as Rearranging the World Order

Hoogvelt argues that we can view the world order in terms of a three tier structure of concentric circles which cut across national and regional boundaries.

At the Core: The bankable world elites from all continents who represent just twenty percent of the world's population.

2nd Tier: A larger fluid social layer of workers and families who labour in insecure employment markets under cut throat competition in the world market.

At the Periphery: The largest group who are excluded from the global system, performing no productive function or representing a potential consumer. These people are excluded from any form of programme of action to include them in universal progress.

Indicative Reading

Key Texts

Albrow, M. (1996). *The Global Age*. London: Blackwell.

Appadurai, A. (1990). Disjuncture and Difference in the Global Cultural Economy. In Seidman, S. and Alexander, J. (eds), (2001). *The New Social Theory Reader*. London: Routledge. pp 253–265.

Giddens, A. (1990). *The Consequences of Modernity*. London: Polity.

Giddens, A. (1991). *Modernity and Self Identity: Self and Society in the Late Modern Age*. London: Polity.

Held, D. (1996). *Models of Democracy* (2nd ed.). London: Polity.

Robertson, R. (1992). *Globalization: Social Theory and Global Culture*. London: Sage.

Secondary Texts

Beck, U. (2000). *What is Globalization?*. London: Polity.

Ghandi, L. (1998). *Postcolonial Theory: An Introduction*. Edinburgh: Edinburgh University Press.

Harvey, D. (1989). *The Condition of Postmodernity*. London: Blackwell.

Hoogvelt, A. (1998). *Globalisation and the Postcolonial World: The New Political Economy of Development*. London: Macmillan.

Wallerstein, I. (1984). *The politics of the World Economy: The States, the Movements and the Civilizations*. Cambridge: Cambridge University Press.

8

Risk Society and (Dis)Information: From Reflexive Modernization to Cybersociality

Introduction

It has become clear that whether we are looking at surveillance society, post-modernism or globalisation the role, speed, sheer scale and proliferation of information has become a central aspect of our societies. Whether this is information in regard to the gathering of social statistics, of governmentality, and social control as Foucault would argue, or perhaps used as the basis of disciplinarity, or ideologically as information-knowledge-power, there is no doubt that the availability of information about any aspect of anything is quite staggering. Just stop a minute to think about what can be retrieved by the internet search engine Google in a matter of nanoseconds. The high speed transmission of information around the globe forms part of international strategies of surveillance as Giddens would argue, of money, finance and capital (Appadurai), of culture, pastime and pleasure, as a way of constructing identities, as a way of destroying identities; the use of information is huge and increasing with the technological advancements of internet technology and high speed servers. People simply have a huge amount of information from which they can construct their lives, make decisions, take' risks, or simply indulge in the pleasure of knowing.

In this final chapter I want to examine the various ways that 'we' exist in late modernity and the ramifications this has for identity construction. In particular I will critically address Beck's (1992) Risk Society thesis and argue that although plausible in terms of sociological theory we have to question who in the world is able to engage either socially or politically with this phenomenon. This leads to the question of reflexive modernization. Through Beck, Giddens (1990) and Lash (1994) I explore the nature of the individualisation of society and again I question the dynamics underlying this process; whether this project of self is plausible for the majority of the world's population. In other words, have we moved from the classical model of industrial society where identity is largely built on tradition, or are we in a late stage of modernity where identity is fashioned by risk and selective biography? As Beck notes, the unremarkable prefix 'post' is a key word of our times, and as subjects we are witnesses to a key break within modernity itself, a break from classical industrial society to 'risk' society. I still feel that we have to question who takes what risk and on whose behalf. In the final sections I will look at the notion of an information or network society primarily through the work of Manuel Castells (1996) and Scott Lash (2002) and finally I want to address one of the key sites of social information and misinformation, the virtual world of cyberspace.

Risk Society

Ulrich Beck (1992, 1995a,b, 1996) argues that we now live in a risk society and that the social production of wealth is now accompanied by the social production of risk:

> The concept of risk is directly bound to the concept of reflexive modernization. *Risk may be defined as a systematic way of dealing with hazards and insecurities induced and introduced by modernization itself.* Risks, as opposed to older dangers, are consequences which relate to the threatening force of modernization and to its globalization of doubt. They are politically reflexive. (Beck, 1992, p 21).

It would seem that in the twenty first century we have become competent and reflective actors in assessing how numerous risks impact on our day to day lives. Risks come in every form from the use of mobile phones, through dietary concerns to the very real nature of the risk of terrorism. Is it safe to fly, is it worth the risk, what risk am I taking? We have become experts at managing, detecting and calculating risk in our everyday existence; we can engage with the risk, deny it, or resign ourselves to the consequences. Some risks however, are politically beyond, our control, in particular the global nature of climate change and pollution. This is because many global hazards are unforeseen or unintended consequences of other risks. We live not just in a risk, but a global risk society driven by high technology and science where nobody can really be sure of the dangers we face. As Beck notes, we have always lived in a world of risk; risk is not an invention of modernity. Travellers who set out to find the new world(s) accepted risks, but there is a fundamental difference argues Beck Columbus took a personal risk – 'not global dangers like those that arise for all of humanity from nuclear fission or the storage of radio active waste' (Beck, 1992, p 21). Therefore for Beck, the nature of risk has changed from something that denoted bravery and adventure to something that signals the destruction of the planet. Beck gives some graphic examples to illustrate the changing nature of risk. Forests have been devastated for years by intensive agricultural practices, but today this happens on a global scale and the devastation comes not from the physical intrusion of over zealous agricultural practices but from the effects of industrialisation. The death of forests occur globally as a result of pollution. This transcends the boundaries of nations and states as pollution knows no barriers. So countries with very little source of industrial pollutants may have their forests devastated by the global effects of industrialisation. In other words, a hazard or risk produced in one country is no longer confined to that particular country. The perception of risk has also changed. Again Beck comments:

> It was reported that sailors who fell into the Thames in the early nineteenth century did not drown, but rather choked to death inhaling the foul-smelling and poisonous fumes of the London sewer. A walk through the narrow streets of a medieval city would have also been like running the gauntlet for the nose. 'Excrement piles up everywhere, in the street, at the turnpikes, in the carriages...' (Beck, 1992, p 21).

The point for Beck is that hazards in past times assaulted the senses; they could not escape perception, whereas in our risk society hazards are hidden and often escape immediate perception, they are 'localized in the sphere of physical and chemical formulas' (Beck, 1992, p 21). So, we have toxins in food stuffs, the threat of nuclear fallout, acid rain. Think of mad cow's disease. Although it was largely contained in the UK, it had the potential for worldwide dispersal through networks of global distribution largely unseen in processed foods that contained meat products. Chemical pest control products get into the food chain via our quest for variety and demand for year round supply of, rather than the seasonal consumption of certain vegetables and fruits. This has created a demand for organic products, because we know that if we buy inorganic we are taking a risk. Beck notes that in the past hazards were connected to the under supply of hygienic technology, whereas now they have their basis in industrial overproduction. Beck's main point is that ecological and high tech risks have a new quality, in that the afflictions they cause, and the effect of their application is no longer tied to their place of origin – 'By their nature they endanger *all* forms of life on this planet' (Beck, 1992, p 22). These threats are beyond the framework of insurance and medical precautions because, for example an atomic accident is no longer an accident as the ramifications last for generations. Indeed the affected may include those who are not even born. For Beck this means the calculations of risk used by science and legal institutions simply collapse, it is no longer valid.

Beck distinguishes between risks and hazards in modern and pre-industrial society. He is at pains to point out that hazards in pre-industrial society may or may not be equal to those in modern society, but that is really not the point: 'Humanities' dramas, plagues, famines, and natural disasters, the looming power of gods and demons – may or may not quantitatively equal the destructive potential of modern mega-technologies. They differ essentially from "risks" in my sense as they are not the result of decisions, or more precisely, of decisions that focus on techno-economic advantages' (Beck, 1995, p 20). So there is no notion of risk in this sense in pre-industrial society, everything, so to speak, was in the lap of the gods. Hazards, dangers and catastrophes came from some other in the form of nature, god or demon. As we have tried to make society more rational, control nature and predict the future, incalculable hazards become calculable risks. Again think of the issues we looked at in chapter three where Horkheimer and Adorno talk at length about the attempt by man to make nature in its own image, to control and rationalise and project categories of classification onto the natural world. Rather than making ourselves like nature in order to protect and survive we try to make nature like ourselves. As society has become more rational, or better rationalised then the notion of the calculability of risk emerges. The idea of risk society, or world risk society is bound up with the notion of instrumental rational control which the processes of modern life incorporates at all levels, from individual risks in terms of credit management to the global risks of terrorism. For Beck then, risk society means an epoch in which the dark sides of progress start to dominate social debate, and central to any political analysis is the distinction between risks and threats:

> What marks a watershed, in my view, is society's confrontation with the possibility of an artificially produced self-annihilation. Unlike the risks of early industrial society, contemporary nuclear, chemical, ecological and biological threats are (1) not limitable, either socially or temporally; (2) not accountable according to the prevailing rules of causality, guilt and liability; and (3) neither compensable nor insurable... To use an analogy, the regulating system for the 'rational' control of industrial devastation is about as effective as a bicycle brake on a jetliner. (Beck, 1995, p 2).

Beck (1996) lists a typology of global threats. First, we have what he calls wealth driven ecological destruction and technological industrial dangers such as the hole in the ozone layer, the greenhouse effect and the unpredictable risks involved in genetically engineering plants and animals. Second, there are risks that are directly related to poverty. Poverty driven environmental destruction is not evenly spread around the globe like the wealth driven variation, it tends to happen in particular locations with world wide ramifications. The obvious example is the destruction of rainforests where seventeen million hectares are lost each year, but also there is the problem of toxic waste from obsolete technologies where the countries in question do not have the resources or political means to prevent the disastrous consequences of accidents and spillages. The final threat is from weapons of mass destruction, nuclear, biological or chemical. Beck argues that there is a growing threat from this type of weapon and the way in which they may fall into private hands outside the restrictions, guidelines and the control structure of the atomic pact of the superpowers. Indeed we have seen very recently the emphasis on weapons of mass destruction in the war on Iraq, leading to a near paranoia over their existence and deployment time. For Beck the reality is that all three types of threat may influence each other. A country or countries may go to war over scarce resources such as water. An ecological disaster such as flooding in Bangladesh may lead to emigration which in turn leads to war (Beck, 1996, pp 14–15). Various states could threaten to blow up their own, or other countries' nuclear installations to threaten regions with annihilation. Indeed for Beck 'There are no limits in our imagination to the horror scenarios that could bring the various threats into relationship with one another' (Beck, 1996, p 15).

The problem is that this only goes to confirm for Beck, the existence of a world risk society – a society where the traditional logic of risk management has been whittled away to reveal hard to deal with dangers. These dangers remove the traditional, or conventional means of safety calculation. The damage from these potential dangers loses all spatio-temporal dimensions becoming global and probably un-reversable. It is harder to pinpoint or blame individuals and therefore, any form of compensation or indeed insurance becomes impossible. Hence, argues Beck, there are no plans for aftercare should the worst happen. We could summarise the nature of world risk society as thus:

- There are series of global threats that are driven by wealth (ecological disaster as a result of techno industrial developments), poverty (driving deforestation) and war (in particular the acquisition of weapons of mass destruction).

- The risk associated with these threats is likely to lead to irreversible global damage that cannot be confined within the boundaries of nations, states or continents.

- The idea that we can compensate for, or insure against these dangers, nuclear or chemical, becomes impossible as traditional forms of risk management have been rendered obsolete.

- Safety calculation is no longer possible and any idea of accountability collapses. This makes plans for aftercare in the event of an incident unlikely.

Hence, Beck's contention that the regulating system for the 'rational' control of industrial devastation is about as *effective as a bicycle brake on a jetliner*.

Behind Beck's idea of risk society is the notion of *reflexive modernization*, a social theory that is not too dissimilar to the views of Gidden's and Habermas. Reflexive modernization is defined in contrast to modernisation by Beck, so, if modernisation means the disembedding and re-embedding of tradition by industrial social forms, then reflexive modernization involves the disembedding of industrial social forms and the re-embedding of modernity. In other words, one form of modernity undercuts and changes another in what Beck refers to as reflexive modernization:

> Reflexive modernization, then, is supposed to mean that a change of industrial society which occurs surreptitiously and unplanned in the wake of normal, autonomized, modernization and with an unchanged, intact political and economic order implies the following: a *radicalization* of modernity, which breaks up the premises and contours of industrial society and opens paths to modernity. (Beck, 1994, p 3).

So we have a new society without a revolution. This, argues Beck, is exactly that which was considered out of the question by Marxists and Functionalists. Essentially Beck is arguing that a more traditional view of the social theory of society sees change coming about through painful events, revolutions and upheaval. This need not be the case; indeed we can enter a new type of society without political interventions or decisions and with new wealth as well as new poverty. Beck argues that the reflexive modernization of industrial society arrives on 'cat's paws'. For example the boundary between non-work and work has become blurred in the temporal and flexibilisation of wage labour 'small measures with large cumulative effects do not arrive with fanfares' (Beck, 1994, p 3). Beck identifies two phases in transformation from industrial to risk society. First, there is the stage where threats are produced but do not become public or political issues. The ethos of industrial society still dominates, producing and legitimating more and more risks. The second stage is where it becomes an issue of public and political concern that the institutions industrial society not only continuously produce more threats, but more importantly, they are unable to control these threats. The hazards that industrial society produce become the very undoing of industrial society. The concept of reflexive modernization does not imply for Beck the notion of reflection, but *self confrontation* – self confrontation with the effects of risk society that cannot be addressed by the dynamics of industrial society or by its standards. The blindness of modernity to the hazards and risks it creates leads to a societal confrontation in which the political is reclaimed, or there is an attempt to reclaim politics and put it back at the heart, through sub politics, of everyday life. That is politics above and beyond the traditional institutions of modernity, of nation states. Beck cites the example of Greenpeace bringing the Shell Oil company to its knees in 1995, but it was not Greenpeace *per se* who achieved this, but a massive sub politic, a mass public boycott of Shell Oil (Beck, 1996, p 18). The problem however, is that no matter how reflexive people are, the good is often undone by what Beck refers to as 'organised irre-sponsibility' (See Beck, 1995b). In other words there is a constant denial of the dangers of risk society which are bypassed and diluted by the formal pro-cedures of rationality: 'it is the application of prevalent norms that guarantees the non-attributibility of systemic hazards: hazards are writ small as risks, compared away and legally and scientifically normalised into probable 'resid-ual risks', making possible the stigmatisation of protest as outbreaks of 'irra-tionality' (Beck, 1995b, p 64). As society becomes more aware and confronts the potential destruction of the planet, industrial fatalism returns to our old friend rationality as a form of denial.

For Beck, there are two sides to the same process of reflexive modernization; the first is globalisation, and the second is individualisation. This is the disem-bedding of social relations from tradition and the re-embedding, or reinven-tion of social relations. So, industrial society's ways of life are re-embedded with new ones, which for Beck, individuals must stage, cobble together and produce. In other words individuals create their own biography and sense of self:

> To use Sartre's term, people are condemned to individualization. Individualization is a compulsion, but a compulsion for the manufacture, self design and self staging of not just one's own biography but also its commitments and networks as pre-ferences and life phases change, but, of course, under the overall conditions and models of the welfare state, such as the educational system (acquiring certificates), the labour market, labour and social law, the housing market and so on. Even the traditions of marriage and the family are becoming dependent on decision making, and with all there contradictions must be experienced as personal risks. (Beck, 1994, p 14)

This is very Giddens, the idea that the standard biography becomes a chosen biography. The idea that intimate and public parts of people's lives once governed by tradition are now engaged with and disputed. Gender roles, notions of class are called into question, people now make their own decisions about their lives and futures as traditional ways of thinking and doing disinte-grate. There is a paradoxical side to individualisation though, in that, new ways of thinking and being bring in new ethics, responsibilities and obliga-tions. In other words today's liberation is tomorrow's incarceration. Certainly Habermas (2003) has shown us this in the dilemmas we face in the light of genetic testing and engineering. While we are free from the traditional con-straints of class, family and gender, we now have to cope with a whole new set of worries around companionship, ambiguity and isolation – 'someone who is poking around in the fog of his or her own self is no longer capable of noticing that this isolation, this "solitary confinement of the ego", is a mass sentence, that millions of people, in all the highly industrialized countries, are also pacing the prison cells of the self' (Beck, 1995b, p 40). Individualisation is the basis on which Beck describes a new modernity comprised of risks, hazards, globalisation and reflexivity and not least *ambiguity*.

Scott Lash (1994) asks us what a critical theory would look like in today's informationalised capitalist order. He argues that a critical theory can be found in the framework of reflexive modernity, but only when it is 'grasped radically against its own grain' (Lash, 1994, p 110). He develops Beck's and Giddens work in three ways. First, Lash argues for a new set of structural conditions of reflexivity. What underpins reflexivity is not the social, economic, political and ideological structures of Marxism, or the institutional, regulated social structures of functionalism, but argues Lash, the web of global and local networks of information and communication structures. In this way 'life chances' and class inequality no longer depend on a persons relationship to the mode of production, but instead on the persons place in relation to the mode of information. We have reflexive winners and reflexive losers: 'Life chances in reflexive modernity are a question of access not to productive capital or production structures but instead of access to and place in the new information and communication structures' (Lash, 1994, p 121). Lash argues that we have a transformed middle class who work in the information and communication structures and a reflexive working class who work for and with these structures who are the reflexive winners of post-industrial society. But we also have the reflexive losers, a third class who are excluded from information and communication structures: 'this third class who are downgraded from the classical proletariat of simple modernity are the 'reflexive losers', the bottom and largely excluded third of our turn-of-the-twenty-first-century 'two thirds societies' (Lash, 1994, p 130).

The second development is that of theory. Beck and Giddens notion of reflexivity argues Lash, is essentially cognitive in nature, situated in the tradition of Kant through to Habermas. Lash proposes an aesthetic, as opposed to cognitive form of reflexivity which is situated in the tradition of the earlier Frankfurt school. As we have seen in chapter three critique is of high modernity's totalising and terrorising regimes, of unhappiness where Enlightenment ideals have turned in on themselves, trapping, rather than freeing people. The *particular* here argues Lash is the aesthetic involving not just high art, but popular culture and the aesthetics of everyday life. Critique for Lash, after Adorno, is critique of the 'subject' from the point of view of the 'object', of the *universal* by the *particular*. Think of the mimetic, the signs of culture, the sound of the city. For Lash:

> This theory of reflexive modernity or any theory of reflexivity is reflexive in so far it concerns the mediation of everyday experience – whether this mediation is conceptual or mimetic. A theory of reflexivity only becomes a critical theory when it turns its reflection away from the experience of everyday life and instead on to 'system'. Aesthetic reflexivity – either of cultural forms or of experiencing individuals – is not conceptual but mimetic. It is reflexive in so far as it operates mimetically on every-

day experience; it becomes critical only when its point of mimetic reference becomes 'system', of commodities, bureaucracy, or reification of life forms. (Lash, 1994, p 140).

From this Lash concludes that society today probably has more to do with risks than insecurity, but risk society is not so much about the distribution of 'bads', rather it is about the mode of conduct centred on risk. Lash suggests that it might be that we could agree with Zygmunt Bauman and ignore the metaphysics of risk altogether, learning to live with contingency and ambivalence. This is because Bauman's thesis is both a mimetic critique of high modernity and at the same time the dark side of Enlightenment, it is an ethics of high modernity with Enlightenment as Id and Ego as the calculating subject. So, for Lash, the particular is understood as aesthetic, not just the universal of high culture. If we are being reflexive we need to focus on both universal and particular, but in particular – the particular. The third area that Lash builds on is the idea of individualisation. Reflexive modernization as we have seen places a strong emphasis on individualisation, a state in which the individual 'I' is no longer constrained by communal ties and constructs his or her identity from a plethora of biographical narratives. Despite this, argues Lash, we have seen the revenge of the repressed 'we' of ethnic cleansing, new forms of anti-Semitism and nationalist fragmentation in the former USSR. In focussing on community Lash moves from the aesthetic to the hermeneutic. A hermeneutic reflexivity of community involves the notions of habit, tradition, care and the ethics of care, as opposed to insecurity and risk. Community for Lash is first and foremost about shared meaning, but the big question is 'can a reflexive community exist in our time-space distanciated societies'? Yes, theoretically argues Lash, in the notion of care and an ethics of care, but he is not clear what this community would look like. It may be nearer than we think argues Lash as the middle class grows, more and more people are part of the expert systems that are now dominated by information and communication structures. Indeed we can be pessimistic and view everybody as individualised, or we can see chances open up for new forms of 'we' that are grounded in expert system and information and communication structures. These would be very different to traditional communities offering more possibilities for reflexivity, a hermeneutic reflexivity.

We have seen Giddens' (1990) contribution to the debate on reflexive modernization in chapter seven. For Giddens, reflexive modernization is about learning to live in a post traditional society. In high modernity we literally reflect on our reflections, or at least on the nature of reflection in a way that makes life deeply sociological. We have moved from an age of tradition to an age of reason in which the reflexivity of modernity actually subverts reason. We seem to believe in the certainty of many knowledge systems, but paradoxically, we know that knowledge is not certain, or fixed, it is forever changing or being reinterpreted. But, we think about our practices, in a way that enables us to make a reflexive decision about our future. This is tied in with the notion of trust and risk. We have to trust in expert systems to a certain extent because we cannot possibly attain the knowledge of all things in a system. So, even some of the simpler actions in everyday life, for example, driving to work, entail multiple risks and acts of trust. To sum up the debate thus far: we can see that for Beck, the driving force behind risk society is reflexive moderniza- tion which involves the disembedding of industrial social forms and the re- embedding of a different modernity. This does not happen in some form of revolutionary event; rather it is a silent, on 'cat's paws' – small measures with large cumulative effects. Individualisation – the disembedding of social rela- tions from tradition and invention of social relations means that people have to create and stage their own biographies, which is much the same as what Giddens is saying. The upshot of this is that we face new dilemmas, responsi- bilities and obligations. Lash, as we have seen, agues that the structural condi- tions of reflexivity are now underpinned by a global network of information and communication structures. Critique, for Lash, if we are to have a critical theory, rests in critique of the subject by object – universal by particular. We may have an alternative to risk society in the shape of the hermeneutic reflexivity of community based on care and the ethics of care.

Anthony Elliott (2002) makes a considered critique of the Risk Society thesis. First, after Turner (1994) Elliott notes that risk, anxiety and uncertainty have been characteristic of many civilisations, but in our present time is it really the ultimate worry of individuals in society. Does the means end rationality of risk really pervade our private lives? Does the concept of risk really capture the contemporary social condition? These are big questions that Elliott does not answer; rather he focuses on the way in which risk is perceived. For Elliott, Beck's model is rather too rationalistic, instrumental and calculative, it ignores the aesthetic the hermeneutic and the embodied nature of the self. It classically ignores the affective and psychodynamic dimensions of self and subjectivity. Second, Elliott notes that while Beck is arguing that global risks propel social reflexivity, and in doing so putting a great emphasis on reflexive institutional dynamism, we still have a parallel process of social disintegra- tion. This social disintegration has seen the spread of cultural, ethnic and gendered conflicts that seem to have little trace of personal and social reflexivity, a point that Lash had made earlier. Elliott argues:

> Beck's contention that contemporary societies are propelled toward self- confrontation, split between reflex and reflection, remains dubious. In what sense, for instance, can one claim that reflection-free forms of societal self- dissolution exist independently of the reflective capacities of human agents? For what, exactly, is being dissolved, if not the forms of life and social practices through which institutions are structured? How might the analytic terms of reflexivity, that is social reflexes (non-knowledge) and reflection (knowledge), be reconciled? (Elliott, 2002, p 302)

Indeed Elliott is arguing that an account of blind social forces, the cat's paw, is incompatible with, and renders incoherent, concepts of reflection and reflexivity. Maybe both Beck and Elliott have both missed the point and we have some form of social unconscious. The third major point that Elliott makes is that for Beck the individualisation of society leads to an erosion of class consciousness. In other words, we no longer channel our personal grievances into collective action and the basis of class itself is eroded. Not so, argues Elliott. While the processes that underlie reflexive modernization may be affecting social inequalities and changing the nature of them, it is implausible to argue that class has been transfigured. From this, and as a fourth point, Elliott argues that Beck's notion of power and domination is lacking because it fails to analyse 'the psychological, sociological and political forces by means of which the self-risk dialectic takes its varying forms' (Elliott, 2002, p 306). Indeed for Elliott the task of the sociological imagination should be to analyse the areas of privatisation, commodification and instrumentalisation that act as channels of risk management. A fifth point for Elliott is the way in which Beck's work on reflexivity fails to address the modernist and postmodern configurations which may be in some way implicit in social practices in contemporary times. For example, the notion of a standardised lifestyle that we can see in the work of Adorno contradicts the stress that Beck places on risk and uncertainty. More notably argues Elliott, Beck's theory does not sit well with that of the postmodernists, who of course would argue that if indeed we are in a new epoch this has just as much to do with new ways of thinking and socio-political changes, not simply risk, but a plurality of seeing and thinking about the world in which risk is merely one factor among many.

So broadly speaking we can see that while Beck proffers a fairly rationalistic techno version of risk society, other important authors such as Scott Lash are reminding him not to forget the aesthetic, the cultural and perhaps the emotional. Critics like Elliott urge more of a dialogue between modernist and postmodernist views of risk, globalisation and the creation of self. We are now nearing the end of our journey *From Enlightenment to Risk*, but before I conclude I want to look at the idea of an information or network society, primarily through the work of Manuel Castells, before going on to consider the notion of a virtual society, of cyberspace.

The (dis)Information Age and Network Society

Manuel Castells (1985, 1989, 1996, 1997, 1998) argues that a technological revolution which is centred on information technologies is reshaping the material base of society. For Castells (1996) what has developed is a condition of structural schizophrenia split between function and meaning in which patterns of social communication start to break down. When people stop talking to each other social groups and individuals become alienated, seeing each other as 'stranger' (see chapter 3), becoming more threatening and fragmented. For

Castells, this means that identity becomes more specific and difficult to share with others –'The informational society, in its global manifestation, is also the world of Aum Shinrikyo, of American Militia, of Islamic/Christian theocratic ambitions, and of Hutu/Tutsi reciprocal genocide' (Castells, 1996, p 4).

The crux of Castells' argument is not that technology is changing society, rather that a set of changes have facilitated a network society. So we have the collapse of communism and the end of the cold war; the economic restructuring of capitalism on a global basis (new forms of capital flexible labour); an increase in consciousness around ecological (and feminist) issues which we looked at in depth in relation to Beck in the previous section; the problematic associated with the nation state that we reviewed in the previous chapter; the rise of fundamentalism; the IT revolution, and the production of a global criminal economy that impacts on us all. Thus we see the emergence of a network society based on IT revolution, the restructuring of capitalism and changes in social consciousness (Castells, 1996, 1998). Castells argues that new information technologies are integrating the world into some form of global network of instrumentality. So we have seen the rise of the internet, multimedia, of virtual communities, networking across vast tracts of time and space. New electronic media do not depart from traditional cultures, they absorb them. Castells gives the example of the Karaoke explosion emanating from Japan, rapidly diffusing over the whole of Asia and now possibly a worldwide phenomena in a very short space of time. It appears the Karaoke machine continues the tradition of singing together in bars, which has been popular the world over, as much in Japan as in Spain or the UK, but what it actually does is to integrate this habit into a pre-programmed machine and drag us in to the world of the multimedia:

> The *Karaoke* machine is not a musical instrument: the singer is swallowed by the machine to supplement its sounds and images. While in the *Karaoke* room we become part of a musical hypertext, we physically enter the multi-media system, and we separate our singing from that of our friends waiting their turn to substitute a linear sequence of performance for the disorderly chaos of pub singing. (Castells, 1996, p 370)

So, even the humble Karaoke machine has made us more instrumental, (or irrational) in our behaviour as we are subsumed in global multimedia experience. For Castells, the multimedia supports a change in social and cultural patterns which are characterised by differentiation which segments users/viewers/readers/listeners. Markets are segmented by the preference of users and senders taking advantage of the global flows of information to identify interests. One expression of this differentiation is the virtual community. Thus we have an increasing social stratification between users, between those with the time and money to interact and access informational technologies, with the knowledge of how to use the system and extract information and those who are fed information – Thus, the multimedia world will be populated by two essentially distinct populations: 'the interacting and the interacted' (Castells, 1996, p 371). In other words, on the one hand we have people who are able to select their circuits of communication and on the other hand, those who are provided with their information. For Castells this is largely determined by class, ethnicity, gender and country. The multimedia by nature of the integrated system starts to blur the boundaries of the contents that they are presenting; something argues Castells that was already starting to take place in mass television production. So, different communication modes borrow codes from each other so that a game of football starts to resemble an action movie for distant viewers. In this way, the easy switching between communication modes reduces the mental distance between cognition and sensation; indeed we have to think less about what we see. Are we really becoming passive consumers of the culture industry? This for Castells, results in messages being mixed with symbols, blurring the codes and creating a multifaceted semantic context made of random mixtures of various meanings – Baudrillard's pastiche of hyperreality. The most important aspect of the multi-media for Castells in the information age is that everything is captured within its domain; it is tantamount to ending the separation between audio-visual-printed-popular-learned-culture-entertainment-information-education-persuasion. Indeed for Castells:

> Every cultural expression, from the worst to the best, from the most elitist to the most popular, comes together in this digital universe that links up in a giant, a historical supertext, past, present, and future manifestations of the communicative mind. By so doing, the construct a new symbolic environment. They make virtuality our reality. (Castells, 1996, p 372).

What is significant for Castells in the world of new communication systems is not the inducement of virtual reality but its construction. Virtual being so in practice, real, actually existing, thus argues Castells, reality, as experienced, has always been virtual, because it is always perceived through symbols which frame practice with some form of meaning. Castells is critical of those who argue that new electronic media does not represent reality because this assumption is based on the notion of a real uncoded experience that never existed – all reality is virtually perceived. For Castells what marks the new information age is a system that generates real virtuality – 'It is a world in which reality itself (that is, people's material/symbolic existence) is entirely captured, fully immersed in a virtual image setting, in the world of make believe, in which appearances are not just on the screen through which experience is communicated, but they become experience' (Castells, 1996, p 373). The new information networks are inclusive in that they provide all kinds of cultural images and delights. But they function to undermine the symbolic power of traditional senders to the system: religion, morality, traditional value and ideologies. So, the preacher needs to re-encode himself in the internet zone where networks are more efficient than the traditional face-to-face situation of the transmission of cultural and religious values. Castells argues that this is the final stage of secularisation as the co-existence of chat-lines and pornography on demand with transcendental messages within the same system means that the charismatic religious prophet loses his superhuman status. Paradoxically, the mass consumption of religion undermines religion in the information society – 'societies are finally and truly disenchanted because all wonders are on-line and can be combined in self-constructed image worlds' (Castells, 1996, p 375).

On the flip side of this, the new communication networks have radically transformed space and time. That is to say, localities for Castells become disembodied from their cultural, geographical and historical meaning and re-integrated into a system of functional networks – we have a space of flows rather than a space of place. For Castells, the *space of flows* and *timeless time*, that is time erased so past, present and future become past-present-future in the same message, are the very basis of a new culture – the culture of real virtuality 'where make-believe is belief in the making' (Castells, 1996, p 375). Thus we have global networks of information flows through networks of corporations and firms. Global cities connect with each other, information nodes connect at a local and regional level, but the territories between the cities or nodes increasingly become irrelevant. Castells points to Mexico City where two thirds of the megapopulis play no role in the functioning of Mexico City as a business centre. The concept of *timeless time* for Castells leads to blurring of the lifecycle. All living beings have a biological clock, rhythms, and we ignore this at our peril. For most of history human rhythmicity was constructed in relation to nature; go with the flow, the season, night and day. With the triumph of reason and medical science we have shifted bio-social lifecycles to socio-biological models as infant mortality and extended life have become possible. Castells argues that in the network society this has shifted again, there is a breaking down of rhythmicity, either biological or social associated with the lifecycle. Old age has changed from the last phase of life to a highly diverse universe of early retirees, late workers, average retirees, and elders. The third age is reconfigured as *exit from the labour market* and no longer signals the effective end of life People are now expected to live another third of their life after retirement from work. Simultaneously reproduction is coming under increasing control, with genetic technologies. In effect we see a major change in the nature of the lifecycle – social arrhythmia. The implication of this is the annihilation of time, or human biological time and the arrival of virtual time, the timeless time of the information society.

For Castells, dominant functions and processes centre in the information age around the network. While Castells acknowledges that networks as a social organisation have existed in other times and places the information technology paradigm has allowed the network to proliferate. The network is a set of interconnected nodes, for example the international stock exchange markets that connect with the network of global financial flows. The network of networks and the provider of all types of information, the internet, is connected by thousands of nodes and joined by millions of flows of information. A networked social structure is dynamic, flexible and global, open to innovation and change without threatening stability. Our relationship to nature has changed as well. In this society it is no longer the case that we have to dominate nature in order to survive everything nature throws at us. For Castells, in the new age culture supercedes nature. Nature is only revived as a cultural form, for example, the environmental movement revive nature as an ideal cultural form. Indeed for Castells, in the information age, life is marked by the autonomy of culture vis-à-vis the material bases of our existence. We may not like what we see when look in the mirror of historical reality, as we are alone at last in our human world (Castells, 1996, p 478).

In terms of identity and identity construction Castells largely follows, or agrees with Giddens who understands the self as reflexive in terms of an individual's life history or potential biography. However, in network society this increasingly becomes problematic because of the separation in different time space-frames between power and experience. Reflexive life planning 'becomes impossible, except for the elite inhabiting the timeless space of flows of global networks and their ancillary locales' (Castells, 1997, p 11). Similarly, intimacy based on trust calls for a reconfiguration of identity in the context of the networking logic of the dominant institutions and organisation of that network. Castells argues that identities are no longer constructed on the basis of civil societies, but as a prolongation of communal resistance giving examples of Islamic and Christian fundamentalism. Indeed, for Castells:

> For those social actors excluded from or resisting the individualization of identity attached to life in the global networks of power and wealth, cultural communes of religious, national, or territorial foundation seem to provide the main alternative for the construction of meaning in our society. These cultural communes are charecterized by three main features. They appear as reaction to prevailing social trends, which are resisted on behalf of autonomous sources of meaning. They are, at the onset, defensive identities that function as refuge and solidarity, to protect against a hostile outside world. They are culturally constituted... (Castells, 1997, p 65)

In other words, they are marked by a community of believers (religious), or the icons of nationalism (national), or the geography of locality (territorial). These specific codes mark the values and meaning ascribed to each cultural commune. They are a defensive reaction against globalisation, against networking and flexibility, and against the breakdown of the patriarchal family. They become the source of meaning and identity construction and the production of new cultural codes that are plucked from historical material; they are in some sense akin to Anderson's (1983) imagined communities, the counter to information society. If we return to the work of Scott Lash (1994, 2002), we start to see the idea of a disinformed information society.

For Lash (2002) there are two types of information in the information society. The first type is tied up with rationality, knowledge and the idea of a knowledge rather than work intensive society. So, for Lash information society is a knowledge society, that is discursive knowledge as exemplified by training, by distanced reflection, by problematisation. This means that labour power in the information society contributes ideas rather than material products *per se*. For Lash the workers of information society produce papers justified through discursive argument. The worker becomes informational in a shift from material processing to information processing – 'it brings particulars under universals (concepts, propositions) and produces new particulars' (Lash, 2002, p 142). For Lash we have moved from economies of scale to *economies of scope* as the reflexive consumer demands choice and difference, or at least to be different from one another. Consumers now consume through the lens of reflexivity rather than habit, production is more flexible, we have shorter runs, more prototypes, and more models. In other words, in the information society the production process, particularly in design, research and development, begins to marginalise the labour process – a move from commodities to singularities. The result of this is that competition in the market becomes less of a matter of cheapest, fastest, most, but of the idea of the prototype. Machines, cars, software, and thus we are in the realm of intellectual as opposed to material property. Intellectual property is about the future and has to do with the prototype. Real property accumulates, intellectual property circulates globally, and this means things tend to fly out of control. For Lash, this why society is always a *dis*information society.

The second form of information is not so much about information society, but information culture. It is about the unintended consequences of the first type of information, information overload, spinning out of control. An example is the newspapers, they are here today, gone tomorrow, they have little to with universal knowledge, no meaning outside of real time. News and information displaced from temporality are literally garbage. The point for Lash is this kind of information literally spirals out of control, it is ubiquitous and in the age of the informational city 'goods, lifestyles and design are ephemeral' (Lash, 2002, p 145). So, we find this not just in digital messages or newsprint, but in the whole of the consumer capitalist city where turnover is fast and duration is short. In music, adverts, TV, internet, even fast moving consumer goods are information. Lash points out that even in earlier twentieth century adverts there would at least be some indication of what something was worth and how you would use, now we just have, as seen in Baudrillard's work a pastiche of images. We are Giddens 'experts' in consuming and understanding fast moving branded goods. This leads Lash to outline the key points of information and disinformation:

- Information type 2 is an unintended consequence of information type 1. The information society has as its unintended consequence the information culture. The rational control of reflexive accumulation results in the out-of-control anarchy of information diffusion

● Information type 1 works through a logic of binaries, without it the chaos of information type 2 would not be possible

● Modernity is ordered, but modernity's consequences are disordered

● Therefore the consequences of order are disorder

● The classification, ordering and simplicity of information society result in the uncontrollable complexity of information culture

● The consequences of accumulation are circulation. The stockpile results in the junk pile, the result of this is real jobs, junk jobs and McJobs
(Lash, 2002, p 146).

Lash therefore concludes that disinformation is partly a side effect of informationalisation, but Lash warns us that it would be a mistake to think that the information society is fundamentally disinformed, as information and disinformation are a contradictory pair and undecidable. Disinformation can as easily become information, as information can become disinformation, and at the centre of the contradiction between information and disinformation is *the idea*. For Lash, the materiality of capitalism has led to the domination of its opposite – the idea – ideas circulate, assets accumulate. The crux then of Lash's argument is that highly rational formulations lead to the most irrational of consequences. The information society is both rational and irrational in the same breath. The 'idea' is the unit of content of the information, society, age, order, and for Lash in the idea, rationality and irrationality are juxtaposed in the highest tension. We can no longer step outside the global communication flows to find critique – 'The critique of information is in the information itself' (Lash, 2002, p 220).

Some are critical of the information society thesis. For example, Frank Webster (1995) is critical of abstract notions of the information age, preferring to see explanations of informationalisation in terms of historical continuities, for example, the work of Giddens and Habermas. For Webster, certainly authors such as Castells are too abstract, turning away from the real world and delving into technological determinism. Webster is critical of Castells for insisting the information revolution will transform the way we live (Webster, 1995, p 213). Chris May (2002) argues that many aspects of our globalised information society remain remarkably to similar to previous models of interaction: 'economics is still recognizable as modern (or perhaps late) capitalism; despite forecasts of increased "virtualization", politics, communities and other aspects of social existence remain located in the material world; states continue to play an active and important role in our lives' (May, 2002, p 149). Of course the problem remains, as with globalisation that the effect of information society is variable depending on your socio-economic status, spatial location, gender and social status. It is still a world of have's and have-not's in which some people have access to multiple information and communication technologies that improve the standard of their life and enable them to access information instantaneously. There is a flip side to this, in that work encroaches on lifeworld, hours become extended and unpaid. On the other hand, we have Lash's reflexive losers who are excluded from information and communication structures. We could also consider the intergenerational use of information and new technologies, and the way in which the use of technology has changed. The mobile phone for example started life simply as exactly what it is, a phone that is portable. It is now used as a social accessory, notebook and camera. People would be lost without their small objects of desire. The most important thing we have to ask ourselves is not whether things have changed because they certainly have, despite the protests of traditionalists. We do live in a new age of information. The central questions are *who have things changed for, who lives in the new information age, and as Lash intimates, who is excluded?*

Cyberspace and the Virtual Self?

The logical step forward from the notion of network society is to argue that we are now living in a cyber society where social interaction takes place in cyberspace and we start to see the development of the virtual self. David Lyon (2002) argues that the idea of cyberspace, like the notion of information society is a construct, a product of the imagination which allows us to address some of the significant features of today's world. Lyon argues that while Castells brings to our attention the global flows of information networks, and in doing so highlights the way in which power, privilege and life chance are distributed in the global world, Castells often fails to open the 'black box' of cyberspace to explore inner social meanings (Lyon, 2002, p 24). For Lyon, whatever way we analyse the information society, one thing is clear, we are increasingly becoming dependent on 'those' machines (computers) in our everyday life. This is apparent at home, work, in the way in which we organise our entertainment, travel, banking, there is a huge, unseen, taken-for-granted information network supporting our everyday lives. Lyons' point is that it is the *experiential*, rather than the statistical or commercial analysis of information society that gives rise to the possibility of something we call cyberspace. In other words, how do we *experience* information and communication networks in our everyday lives on a day-to-day basis? How do we become wrapped in the media?

Cyberspace is about ambiguity, paradox and contradiction argues Lyon. First, it is crucial to note that cyberspace can only be experienced by an embodied person who is positioned in a locale, no matter how distant the separation of time and space. Cyberspace erodes the modernist project of territorial boundaries and the control of spaces on the one hand, but we can *only* take advantage of internet banking if we have a bank account and access to electronic modes of communication, for all the hype about the freedom of the internet there are many who are excluded 'It produces polarization, not a homogeneous global village' (Lyon, 2002, p 25). After Castells, Lyon notes that 'spaces of flows' tend to dominate the 'spaces of places'. In other words, certain areas of high connectivity are often focused on a node like the City of London, and often surround by areas where flows of connectivity are relatively low. The effect is, that experience of 'here' and 'there' varies considerably in the information society and cyberspace. So second, while Castells elites may enjoy and experience cyberspace as a space of relative freedom, others are excluded. Lyon is sceptical about the emancipatory potential of cyberspace in the broader sense. In acknowledging that the internet was created by the military as a nuclear proof network, we also have to acknowledge, that as with all things military, the internet was created within a culture of command. Although new technologies frequently display characteristics unintended by their creators, Lyon notes:

> All purposes of information technologies relate to the various instrumental control motifs of modernity, and all freedom from these is hard to conceive, at least for people whose lives are touched, directly or indirectly by those technologies...There can be very little doubt that, by their very constitution, information societies are surveillance societies. (Lyon, 2002, p 26).

For Lyon, even though we might find it comforting to know that the computer operating international airlines schedules is not a chaotic complexity of informational flows, rather an instrumental and controlling information system which avoids aircraft crashing, there can be little doubt that the internet, both externally and internally is characterised by control and surveillance. The fourth area of ambiguity follows from this, in that cyberspace is both dystopian and utopian at once. On the one hand we have the notion of better, free, wished for communities, where equal access and democratic communication are the order of the day, but we have also seen that cyberspace can also be controlling and a site of surveillance. A fifth area of ambiguity argues Lyon is that of the question of cyberspace and (un)reality. Indeed the expression 'yesterdays dreams becoming today's realities' seems to have been inverted in cyberspace argues Lyon. Citing the example of Baudrillard's response to the Gulf War that we examined in Chapter 6, Lyon argues that the reality of yesterday is supplanted by simulations and the hyperreal – the dreams of today. This is of course not limited to cyberspace but the media as a whole. Different types of unreality present themselves – multi-user dimensions (MUDs) where players immerse themselves to the point that the world of the game becomes real.

Lyon talks of cybersociality, the use of electronically mediated communications as a means of introducing liquidity and fluidity into social relationships.

He is at pains to point out that just because we use e-mail to communicate it does not mean that we do not talk to each other face-to-face. Interaction does not take place in a social vacuum, but in space where social expectations are already in place. The internet, e-mail and digital technologies just provide further possibilities for social interaction. What we can take from this I feel is that we live *with* rather than *in* cyberspace – 'Cyberspace is all about the experience of multiple, mediated interactions, which, remember, is still the preserve of a small minority of the world's population' (Lyon, 2002, p 33). This kind of argument leads Steve Woolgar (2002) to propose five broad rules for apprehending, or getting hold of, and understanding the notion of a virtual society. The five rules are thus and I feel that they have been fairly implicit in the work of Castells, Lash, Lyon and Webster, and would form a strong basis for a social theory of virtual society and for further research:

- The uptake and use of new technologies depend crucially on local social context

- The fears and risks associated with new technologies are unevenly socially distributed

- Virtual technologies supplement rather than substitute for real activities

- The more virtual the more real

- The more global the more local
(Woolgar, 2002, pp 14–20)

All these areas overlap, for example we have looked in quite some depth at the nature of globalisation and the use of information technologies and communications. The way in which one might try and escape the local and move to a globally transformed identity very much rests on the specific ways in which technology is managed locally – restrictions on internet usage in China for example. It is to the question of identity in cyberspace that I want to turn to finally – can we have a cyber/virtual identity, and if so, how are these formed?

I think there are problems around trying to analyse that nature of cyberspace and its potential for identity construction. This is because of many of the reasons we have discussed, for example a large part of the world does not have access to the technologies we have been talking about, and I also agree with Lyon that interaction does not take place in a social vacuum when using e-mail, the web, chat rooms or groups. The problematic is really how far the experience of cyberspace actually affects our identity once we have shut the computer down. Sure it can give us snapshots of the rest of the world, other cultures, lifestyles, ways of life, but will this affect our identity anymore than a two week holiday in Morocco, or a business trip to Europe. My feeling is that the internet plays more a part in representing what we feel our identity to be, rather than constructing it *per se*. In some sense, the computer may have become more of a part of our everyday lives than just a tool, but in general we use it to find out things, obtain knowledge about things, and to transmit knowledge. The best example I can think of is that of the personal homepage, which interestingly is usually constructed around real and concrete examples of our identity, rather than anything virtual. Again, I would argue that we live with, not in, cyberspace. I think when Ben Agger (2004) writes in *The Virtual Self* that the internet can help reconfigure identity through knowledge and thus forming community, he is being slight optimistic in his view. I do not think that the internet, as Agger argues creates virtual selves. I think identity construction is more fluid and contingent than that. It may enrich our lives, but it does not create our selves. It may be a telling feature of the book that it was written in N. America, one of the most connected and affluent societies in the world, that in general it fails to reflect on the internet have-not's and the position of privilege that the author writes from. I think it is better to think about what our online identity says about us as Tim Jordan (2002) notes, rather than what being online does to our identity. It is well known that you can easily pose as the opposite gender, politic, religion, whatever, when online, but is this really what people do on a day-to-day basis. I would argue that online WebPages, e-mail addresses, preferences say more about you, than influence your identity. Perhaps we could say that our online identity is simply different, but as Jordan argues:

> Identity is both present in cyberspace and is different to non-virtual space; the only mistake here would be to assume that the powers flowing around offline identities are absent online, instead of identifying the particular forms of identity which exist in cyberspace and through which cyberpower takes hold. (Jordan, 2002, p 122).

So, online identities for Jordan are constructed by different markers, our e-mail address says more about us than our clothes which the recipient of an e-mail, for example, cannot see. But, in some sense we are still promoting our identity in a different way, rather than cyberspace constructing our self. To return to the personal homepage. David Bell (2001) argues that the homepage presents the self through a number of devices – biographies, links to other sites, photographs; they all provide information about who we are, or how we would like to present our self as to the public. So, in some sense, as Bell argues, we can present previously hidden aspects of our identity, but also censor what we choose not to reveal, in other words the author of the homepage has total control of the identity that he or she wishes to portray and project out to others. For Bell, some of the common themes of identity online include visibility and invisibility, modes of self-presentation used by participants, issues of otherness and 'passing' in the sense of Garfinkel's ideas (Bell, 2001, p 135). We can quite literally pass for who we want to be in cyberspace. There is no doubt what-so-ever that computers and information networks

play a significant role in our lives today, they have become part of the furniture in homes and because of the miniaturisation of technology we can literally carry around a camera, telephone, and digital communication device all in
one pocket. There are some convincing ideas that point to the way in which
identity can be portrayed and manipulated through online presence, but this
seems more to do with the way in which we *present* our self online, rather than
the way in which we construct our identity in everyday life. In some sense
also, there is a slightly sinister side to online identity particularly in relation to
what remains invisible.

Summary and Conclusion

This chapter builds on the globalisation debate to look at the different ways in
which we exist in late or high modernity, in particular our relation to risk, the
way in which we develop strategies for living in the new world of information
and communication technologies, and the new choices we may have in the
construction of who we are and how we present this to others. I take a slightly
cynical approach to both globalisation and the possibilities for identity construction because I believe that the opportunities offered are very much first
world, and very much Western. In other words, the use of information and
communication technologies may be emancipatory for some, but not for the
majority of the inhabitants of the globe. The same goes for the nature of risk;
very few people are actually able to engage politically or socially with the
risks that they are being exposed to, either because they do not have the information, do not live in a democratic country (although this makes little difference sometimes), or they are socially and economically excluded from
choice. This is not to say that Beck's thesis is not a valuable piece of sociological theory. It is. Beck certainly shows us the changing nature of our engagement with the world, in particular the move from very plausible local risks
and hazards that have assaulted our senses to global risks that do not immediately attract our perception, for example acid rain, toxins in food stuffs, the
hole in the ozone layer. The main point for Beck, as I have indicated, is that
ecological and high tech risks have a new quality, in that their effects and
afflictions are no longer tied to their place of origin. The risks associated with
global threats (ecological disaster, poverty, war) are likely to lead to irreversible global damage that will not, and cannot be confined within the
boundaries of nations, states, or even continents.

Underlying Beck's Risk thesis is the notion of reflexive modernization. Very
much a Habermasian, Beck argues that the transformation of industrial to risk
society in high modernity is very much the result of a cumulative, stealth
driven and unplanned set of measures which result in the radicalisation of
modernity. There are two sides to this process – globalisation and individualisation, and we are condemned to this compulsion – the manufacture and
staging of self biographies, networks of preferences, and life phase change.

While this frees us in some sense from the confines of tradition, it also throws up new worries and ambiguities – the prison cells of the self. As this book is essentially about contemporary critical theories of society, it is important to address the nature of theory itself, something that Scott Lash does very successfully in building on the work of Giddens and Beck. Lash argues that a critical theory can be found in the framework of reflexive modernity, but, only when grasped against its own grain. So, new information and communication technologies may have its winners, but there are losers as well. Those excluded from these networks of information and communication make up for Lash, about two thirds of society. Theory should contain not just a cognitive form of reflexivity, but also an aesthetic. If we intend to be reflexive we need to look at both the *universal* and the *particular*, that is, the aesthetic. Although reflexive modernization has placed an emphasis on individualisation we have seen the return of the repressed 'we' in the form of ethnic conflict, anti-Semitism and nationalism. We need to start thinking about the notion of a reflexive community and an ethics of care argues Lash. This will enable new and reflexive forms of 'we'.

I feel that while Beck offers us a fairly rationalistic techno model of late modernity, authors such as Lash, and I would agree with him, give a gentle reminder that we should not forget the aesthetic and the emotional. I feel this is particularly important as we start to think and talk about information and network societies. Castells has shown us how the construction of identity becomes increasingly problematic in the network society as reflexive life planning becomes almost impossible with the exception of elites in society. Those excluded from the individualisation of identity, which after all, we are told is attached to the global networks of power and wealth, form both sites of new identity construction and resistance to global capitalism which often result in violence and terror. In other words we have a divided world. This division seems at the moment, if we are to believe the politicians, to lie along the lines of the division of East and West, or perhaps more alarmingly, the West and the rest. There is in Lash's writing on information society an idea that has been central in the writing of this book. The idea that the most rational of formulations can lead to the most irrational of consequences; again the critique of information, for a critical theorist, is in the information itself. I have argued that the most important question we have to ask ourselves in an age of global information and communication networks, it not whether we live in a new age, call it what you will, there is certainly a pastiche of ideas and theories that are circulating which could be called postmodern, the same goes for the notion of risk, and of a network society. The question is however, *who* have things changed for, *who* lives in this new society, and *who* is excluded.

I have also provided a brief discussion of cyberspace and the idea of the virtual self. If we return to Baudrillard then there is no better place than the internet to see the symptoms of postmodern hyperreality, the construction and pastiche of simulations and simulacra, the fragmentary chaos of a postmodern world in which difference is celebrated and the virtual becomes real. We have to remember though that on one hand the internet may erode the modernist project of territorial boundaries, but on the other it was created by a command culture, and thus we are back in Foucault's surveillance society where every key stroke is logged and every connection leaves a trail of data, information society is undoubtedly a surveillance society. I have been even more sceptical in my portrayal of the idea of a virtual self, I do not want to go back over my argument, but suffice to say, I feel at this moment in time, an online identity is more to do with the way in which we choose to present our self online, and a lot less to do with the construction of identity in everyday life, the sinister side of this is that which remains invisible. I think at the very most what has been produced with new form of information and information technology is a form, after Lyon, of cybersociality.

Summary of Key Terms and Concepts

Beck: Risk Society: Risk is defined as a systematic way of dealing with hazards and insecurities induced and introduced by modernization itself. Hazards in pre-industrial society came from some other, nature, Gods or Demons. Therefore there is no notion of risk in pre-industrial society. Everything is in the lap of the Gods. Risk in modern society focuses on techno-economic advantage.

World Risk Society

- There are series of global threats that are driven by wealth (ecological disaster as a result of techno industrial developments), poverty (driving deforestation) and war (in particular the acquisition of weapons of mass destruction).
- The risk associated with these threats are likely to lead to irreversible global damage that cannot be confined within the boundaries of nations, states or continents.
- The idea that we can compensate for, or insure against these dangers, nuclear or chemical, becomes impossible as traditional forms of risk management have been rendered obsolete.
- Safety calculation is no longer possible and any idea of accountability collapses. This makes plans for aftercare in the event of an incident unlikely.

Reflexive Modernization: *The disembedding of industrial social forms, and the re-embedding of another modernity. A radicalization of modernity which is the result of a cumulative, stealth driven set of measures. The reflexive part does not refer to reflection but self confrontation of risk.*

Individualization: The compulsion for the manufacture, self staging and design of one's own biography, commitments and networks as preferences. A move away from traditional forms identity construction, as people now makes decisions and choices about their lives. The standard biography becomes a chosen biography.

Network Society: Castells argues that new information technologies are integrating the world into a global network of instrumentality. Technologies such as the internet, multimedia, even virtual communities network across vast tracts of time and space. What marks the new information age is a system that generates real virtuality.

Space of flows: Localities become disembodied from their cultural, geographic and historical meaning and re-integrated into a space of flows rather than a space of place.

Timeless time: Time erased so that past, present and future all become present in the same message. This leads to a blurring of the lifecycle, arrhythmia, as biological time disappears and virtual time arrives.

Information/disinformation: Lash argues we now have two types of information. The first, marked by rationality, training, knowledge, producing papers. The second type of information refers to information culture which has produced an overload of information circulating around the world. The unintended consequence of the information society is the information culture, of disinformation. This is not to say that society is fundamentally disinformed, rather that disinformation and information are contradictory pair, one days information is another days disinformation. Disinformation can quite easily turn into information.

Cybersociality. Lyon's idea that electronically mediated communications add a certain liquidity and fluidity in social relations, not supplanting formal face-to-face communications, but adding further possibilities for social interaction.

Virtual Society Woolgar's Rules for understanding Virtual Society

- The uptake and use of new technologies depend crucially on local social context
- The fears and risks associated with new technologies are unevenly socially distributed
- Virtual technologies supplement rather than substitute for real activities
- The more virtual the more real
- The more global the more local

Indicative Reading

Key Texts

Beck, U. (1992). *Risk Society: Towards a new Modernity*. London: Sage.
Castells, M. (1996). *The Information Age: Economy, Society and Culture. Vol 1: The Rise of the Network Society*. London: Blackwell.
Giddens, A. (1990). *The Consequences of Modernity*. London: Polity.
Lash, S. (2002). *Critique of Information*. London: Sage.
Woolgar, S. (ed.) (2002). *Virtual Society: Technology, Cyberbole, Reality*. Oxford: Oxford University Press.

Secondary Texts

Agger, B. (2004). *The Virtual Self: A Contemporary Sociology*. London: Blackwell.

Armitage, J. and Roberts, J. (2002). *Living with Cyberspace: Technology and Society in the 21st Century*. London: Continuum.

Beck, U., Giddens, A. and Lash, S. (1994). *Reflexive Modernization: Politics, Tradition and Aesthetics in the Modern Social Order*. London: Polity Press.

Bell, D. (2001). *An Introduction to Cybercultures*. London: Routledge.

Elliott, A. (2002). Beck's Sociology of Risk: A Critical Assessment. *Sociology*. 36 (2). pp 293–315.

Lyon, D. (2002). Cyberspace: Beyond the Information Society? In Armitage, J. and Roberts, J. (2002). *Living with Cyberspace: Technology and Society in the 21st Century*. London: Continuum. pp 21–33.

9

Critical Psycho-Social Studies: A Conclusion

The purpose of this book has been to outline and critique contemporary sociological and critical theories, and in particular what they have to say about rationality and the construction of the modern self. Thus we have gone on a journey from Weber and the early work of the Frankfurt School to notions of postmodernism and globalisation and the implications these ideas have in the analysis of the construction of our self identity. I have been more than sceptical about the notion of the virtual self in my analysis of network and information society and feel that activities in cyberspace have more to do with how we present a side of our self, rather than how we construct an identity.

One of the key elements of modern societies is the almost obsessional basis of the logic of capitalism, the constant tension between that which is perceived as rational, and, or irrational, and something that is often overlooked, the role of emotion in the creation of our everyday lives. This is where I would argue that a psycho-social perspective adds depth to contemporary critical theory, an idea that has developed from Horkheimer and Adorno's early writing based in philosophy and psychoanalysis and is now gaining ground in mainstream ESRC research projects. I will address this later in this chapter. If we return to Weber, then, his work stands as a fateful warning about becoming obsessional about material things, a forerunner to notions of culture industry and postmodern consumption patterns. Indeed Weber has shown us how seemingly irrational ideas become rationalised at a societal level. Weber anticipated the ideas of later writers by showing how self disciplinarity led to the creation of the rational actor in his study of the Protestant Ethic. These writers include Foucault, but earlier than this, Marcuse was able to see in Weber's ironic statements and ironic warning about the trajectory of capitalism. This is really where we start the critique of modernity, rationality and positivistic thinking and method. The Frankfurt school point to the frantic development of production and the quest for the control of nature by man; the stealth like intrusion of irrationality in the capitalist social world, where rational procedures and methods are used for the purposes of greed, to justify hatred and to carry out genocide. Thus we have a huge critique of Enlightenment ideals, of the very notion of what it means to be a rational human being, and of the notion of popular culture. In critiquing culture Adorno in particular shows how it is permeated with ideologies and illusional dynamics which have a quite dramatic impact on the construction of self. Adorno questions quite rightly whether we are products of our own interests or simply automatons, pseudo individuals who are manipulated and indoctrinated by the dynamics of the capitalist culture industry. Adorno, quite clearly opens up the doors for the postmodern critics of culture who build on his work in numerous ways.

In developing a critical theory, both Horkheimer and Adorno draw on the ideas of Freud. But, in doing so they also highlight some clear issues in sociological analysis with the demise of religious practice and the increasing secularisation of society. There are also implications for sociology of the body, in that Horkheimer and Adorno draw our attention to the way in which the increasing rationalisation of society draws us away from our very essence, from our body and our 'natural' self. The sanitised world does away with the animal in us as notions of disgust and revulsion develop as part of the civilising process. They also show how the social constructions of positivistic thinking become naturalised as science or discourses of science in much the same way that Foucault describes the development of expert discourses. The problem at the very heart of this critique is that we are no longer free in an Enlightenment sense; we are dominated by discourse, by capitalism and by ideology. We are no longer able to reflect, or to practice self reflection, the self is a product of manipulative ideology that results in the hatred of the Other.

While Horkheimer and Adorno are pessimistic at their core, Jurgen Habermas is intent on rescuing the Enlightenment project and has done so, in fact still doing so, for a good many years in which he engages the postmodernist and post-structuralist view of the world with his notion that we can be free and emancipated – modernity is simply an unfinished project. The key to Enlightenment as we all know is not the kind of reflexivity advocated by Giddens et al, but sustained self reflection on our practices and methods. Originally Habermas advocated a method through the use of psychoanalysis and the self reflection model pointing to the role it could play in uncovering distorted meanings and expressions in everyday life. He extends this argument in the theory of communicative action, reasserting the Enlightenment view that systematic self reflection on human nature through communication is ultimately liberating. In some sense Habermas is trying to rescue the rational project of modernity by arguing that there is a form of communicative rationality lodged in our very essence as a communicative species. The problem with Habermas' ideas I have argued, is not so much that they are abstract and dense, we can quite clearly see for example notions of lifeworld and system in our everyday interactions with work, organisations and social, rather, Habermas is open to misinterpretation. Habermas' ideal speech situation is quite literally that, an ideal, and once we accept that then the theory becomes useful. Of course Habermas will not let go of his search for a substantive rationality and cynics of course will claim that his ideas are a recipe for endless talk. We see in Habermas' work though the kind of critical reflexivity found in psycho-social thinking, a reflexivity that Habermas claims that theorists such as Foucault lack.

I remain ambivalent about Foucault's work; on the one hand *Madness and Civilisation* is one of the best critiques of modern psychiatry that I have read, but on the other, Foucault for me, returns to the pessimism of Horkheimer and Adorno and does not show us anyway forward. Again, after Habermas, Foucault's work does not appear to be postmodern, but anti-modern. Foucault also fails to recognise some of the gains made in modernity through the instrument of law, concentrating of the effects of domination rather than some of the positive effects of 'progress'. At heart of this negative view is the relationship between power and knowledge through discourse in which Foucault argues that claims to legitimacy based on power/knowledge oppress the mad, the deviant, and the insane. Different groups with different discourses struggle for power over one another. I think we can hardly dispute this, conflict abounds, but we also have to recognise, if we were to follow Habermas, that in the very discourse that Foucault talks of, there is an element of communicative rationality in language that promotes consensus and understanding. It is easy to be critical of Foucault, but I feel that in the same way that Habermas is concerned with the idea of rationality, the same could be said of Foucault. The two theorists just approach the idea in different ways. While Horkheimer, Adorno and Habermas tend to look at the bigger picture, Foucault concentrates on specific instances to reveal different forms of rationality that have different effects and relationships to one another. The most important aspect of Foucault's work for me is he asks 'at what price' has the modern rational self been defined by experts and expert systems? Thus turning on their head popular conceptions of how the mad have been treated and defined over the ages. In particular he draws our attention to the way in which the self is constructed in relation to 'not me', and the way in which our imagination starts to run riot when we start to perceive for example, who, and what, are behind the walls of confinement. In some sense I would argue, that in Foucault's work we start to see the notion of a psycho-social approach to critical theory. Although Foucault would probably not approve, the premise of the creation of Cartesian man is based in not rational, but irrational ways of thinking about Others. In particular, it has an imaginative feel. It is in some sense a clear example of the way in which one person's irrationality becomes another's rationality and vice-versa. Certainly this is the case in Foucault's examination of the social construction of sexuality and notion of Bio-power where we are left wondering about where we derive our sense of identity from, and if we have a choice of who we are, how do we make that choice? Or, more importantly how much of that choice is made for us. Once again, Foucault demonstrates that Enlightenment ideas of emancipation do not readily make good partners with the idea of a rational society and this has specific ramifications for the construction of self.

One of the problems with contemporary social theories of society is that they tend to focus on a Western world view and a Western idea of what constitutes irrationality and rationality. Ok, so we could argue that of course this is the case because we are studying the institutions of modern industrial society. But in the notion of postmodernism and globalisation we start to see theories applied to the global condition and I feel this is where things start to go awry. I have argued that it is more appropriate to think in terms of modernism (s) rather than postmodernism per se. So, we could argue that we have certain types of postmodern theory, architecture, art; we have new ways of organising labour and new ways of organising time. There is the idea that we have the death of the subject and the birth of the decentred subject. We can select our identity from a range of possibilities. But, I would question, as I have with the globalisation debate about who has actually got access to these new forms of self construction. It seems that in tandem with fragmentation we also see the return of old types of traditions, ethnic conflicts and calls for allegiance to imagined communities. In other words theoretically we may be in a world of postmodern thinking, a critique of totalising metanarratives like science, but practically the world of the modern still reigns strong. Lyotard's emphasis on a postmodern science that emphasises paradox, difference and instability is commendable in the way in which it advocates optimism, a world in which difference is more than tolerated, but celebrated. This is more than can be said for Baudrillard's work which relegates self and construction of self to the depressing world of hyperreality. Self becomes no more than a reflection of consumer society in which the simulation rules the day. The implication is, that we have ideal selves, ideal homes, ideal relationships, in which the media defines the world that we live in. I have argued, however, that I feel that Baudrillard is being ironic at a level that is similar to Weber's fateful warning about rationalisation. Take notice lest the self becomes a simulation of a simulation.

David Harvey has shown us how the map of the world has shrunk over the last five hundred years. Time-space compression means that the globe is fifty times smaller that in the sixteenth century. Again, we would ask the question: who it is smaller for? As we have seen the shortening of time and the shrinking of space the increasing speed of transportation compresses the world into a global village. *The present is all there is,* but course there are terrible economic and social consequences for those people who do not belong to countries that have privilege to part of these networks. So, while people live in an idealised global village, others have no access to basic human needs, let alone a passport to join in with the fun. The globalisation debate in some sense places more emphasis on social structure than postmodern ideas. In other words, changes in employment, the organisation of time and space through transportation and technological advancements and how these directly affect the way in which we relate to self and others. There is, it is argued, a move away from traditional forms of identity construction and far greater social mobility. We no longer adopt the identity, through work and locale of our parents, identity is constructed in relation to the ever changing and fluid world. Despite this new era of global cultural flows the idea of rationality and the process of rationalisation are never far from our everyday lives. We are assaulted with so many images, systems, networks and fluidity's we actually need some kind of routinisation of our everyday lives to avoid plummeting into the abyss of meaninglessness. Many of the theories that try to explain the globalisation of modernity simply rely on the notion of rational systems and networks to describe the global condition. What we see is the globalisation of Western world views and the spread of Western cultural imperialism. Theory then focuses on the different ways in which we exist in the multi-named condition of high, late, or postmodernity. Again, analysing what we could call a network society or information age I have chosen to take a slightly cynical approach to both globalisation and the possibilities we have for identity construction. I feel that these opportunities are very much the privilege of people who have access to information and communication technologies, these may be emancipatory for some, but not for majority of the inhabitants of the globe. The same goes for the nature of risk, as very few people are able to engage either politically or socially with the risks they are being exposed to. We have to ask ourselves – whose global world?

I have attempted to show throughout this book the way in which notions of identity, rationality and irrationality are inextricably linked with each other. The most important thing we need to note, whether this be in discussing notions of the construction of the self, or community or nation, that one person's rationality is another person's irrationality and vice-versa. This I have argued is an even more pertinent idea in the wake of Sept 11th. The philosophical nature of what it means to be reasonable, or to reason, has accentuated by what would appear to be unreconcilable world views – is hate reasonable or does reason make people hate? The boundary between paranoia and reason has been blurred in the new world of global terrorism where we no longer know whether it is safe to get on a plane or simply walk into a building. We have arrived at an impossible situation in which we can no longer differentiate between genuine fear and paranoid phantasy – reason often goads people to hate. I have argued elsewhere (Clarke, 2003) what I feel that a critical sociological theory of racism would look like and want to build on this here to offer what I feel are the main strands of a contemporary critical theory of society. The first point I feel is to reiterate the notion of self reflection on methods and practice. In other words, why are we looking at a particular phenomenon, and not some other, and why are we using a particular method in studying it? Second, we must also confront issues in a reflexive, as well, as a reflective vein as Beck has told us. Third, we have to look at rationality and irrationality as two sides of the same coin; one person's rationality is another's irrationality and we cannot take it for granted that one or the other is better or worse, just a different way of viewing the world. Fourth, we cannot separate the psychological from the socio-structural. The structures of modern society are premised on the *ideas* of modern society, psychological dynamics fuel social structures and vice-versa. As a fifth point following on from the four, critical theory must necessarily have a psycho-social element. Finally, we have to take seriously the constructions and perceptions of the human imagination and emotion. We have to take them as concrete, even if they feel wrong. The way in which people imagine the world to be, and imagine the way that others exist in the world is central to the construction of identity. It does not matter that belief may be more fiction than fact, because the human imagination is central to identity construction, it is therefore concrete and has very real consequences for the world we live in. I would therefore summarise a contemporary critical theory as thus

- An emphasis on self reflection *and* reflexivity in both method and practice.

- A recognition in the analysis of rationality and irrationality of the relative nature of the concepts.

- The analysis of both the social and psychological structuring of society.

- Theory therefore must be psycho-social.

- A critical theory must take seriously the constructs of the human imagination and emotion.

- Both fact and fiction are concrete and have very real consequences for the social world.

These my seem like obvious points, but time and time again they are ignored, whether it be in Habermas trying to provide a rational explanation of terrorism through the analysis of distorted and violent communication, or in the globalisation debate where often the Western world view is mistaken for a global world view where the economic rather than cultural or emotional are privileged. Don't get me wrong, these are essential part of critical social theory, but they are a *part* and not a whole. In the same way that one person's rationality is another's irrationality, one person's fiction is another's fact. Information, as Scott Lash has told, can just easily be disinformation, and in today's world, without both sustained self reflection and confrontation it is very difficult to tell one from the other. Maybe Kant was right, we should free ourselves from our tutelage, and there is much lacking which prevents us from using our reason, but the problem is that we no longer live in an age of enlightenment, but an age of terror.

Bibliography

Adorno, T. (1967– Translated 1975). The Culture Industry Reconsidered. In Bronner, E. and Kellner, D. (1989). *Critical Theory and Society*. London: Routledge. pp 128–135.

Adorno, T. (1991). Freudian Theory and the Pattern of Fascist Propaganda *.The Culture Industry*. London: Routledge. pp 114–135.

Agger, B. (2004). *The Virtual Self: A Contemporary Sociology*. London: Blackwell.

Albrow, M. (1996). *The Global Age*. London: Blackwell.

Anchor, R. (1967). *The Enlightenment Tradition*. London: Harper & Row.

Anderson, B. (1983). *Imagined Communities*. London: Verso.

Appadurai, A. (1990). Disjuncture and Difference in the Global Cultural Economy. In Seidman, S. and Alexander, J. (eds) (2001). *The New Social Theory Reader*. London: Routledge. pp 253–265.

Arendt, H. (1964). *Eichman in Jerusalem: A Report on the Banality of Evil*. New York: Viking Press.

Ashenden, S. and Owen, D. (eds) (1999). *Foucault Contra Habermas*. London: Sage.

Austin, J-L. (1962). *How to do Things with Words*. Oxford Clarendon Press.

Bahr, E. (1994). 'The Anti-Semitism Studies of the Frankfurt School: The Failure of Critical Theory', in Bernstein, J. (ed.), *The Frankfurt School Critical Assessments*.London: Routledge. pp 226–233.

Baudrillard, J. (1968). *Le systeme des objects (The System of Objects)*. Paris: Denoel-Gonthier.

Baudrillard, J. (1970, 1998). *The Consumer Society*. London: Sage.

Baudrillard, J. (1972, 1981). *For a Critique of the Political Economy of the Sign*. St Louis: Telos.

Baudrillard, J. (1975). *The Mirror of Production*. St Louis: Telos.

Baudrillard, J. (1983). *Simulations*. New York: Semiotext(e).

Baudrillard, J. (1987). *Forget Foucault*. New York: Semiotext(e).

Baudrillard, J. (1988). *America*. London: Verso.

Baudrillard, J. (1993). *The Transparency of Evil: Essays on Extreme Phenomena*. London: Verso.

Baudrillard, J. (1994). *Simulacra and Simulation*. Michigan: University of Michigan Press.

Baudrillard, J. (1995). *The Gulf War Did Not Take Place*. Sydney: Power Publications.

Bauman, Z. (1973). *Culture as Praxis*. London: Routledge & Kegan Paul.

Bauman, Z. (1989). *Modernity and the Holocaust*. Cambridge: Polity Press.

Bauman, Z. (1990). *Thinking Sociologically*. Oxford: Blackwell Publishers.

Bauman, Z. (1991). *Modernity and Ambivalence*. Cambridge: Polity Press.

Bauman, Z. (1993). *Postmodern Ethics*. London: Blackwell.

Bauman, Z. (1997a). 'The Dream of Purity,' in *Postmodernity and its Discontents*. Cambridge: Polity Press, ch. 1.

Bauman, Z. (1997b). 'The Making and Un-making of Strangers', in *Postmodernity and its Discontents*. Cambridge: Polity Press, ch. 2.

Bauman, Z. (1998). *Globalization: The Human Consequences*. Cambridge: Polity Press.

Beck, U. (1992). *Risk Society: Towards a new Modernity*. London: Sage.

Beck, U., Giddens, A. and Lash, S. (1994). *Reflexive Modernization: Politics, Tradition and Aesthetics in the Modern Social Order*. London: Polity Press.

Beck, U. (1995a). *Ecological Enlightenment: Essays on the Politics of the Risk Society*. New Jersey: Humanities Press.

Beck, U. (1995b). *Ecological Politics in an Age of Risk*. London: Polity Press.

Beck, U. (1996). World Risk Society as Cosmopolitan Society: Ecological Questions in a Framework of Manufactured Uncertainties. *Theory, Culture & Society*. 13 (4), pp 1–32.

Beck, U. (2000). *What is Globalization?* London: Polity.

Bell, D. (1976). *The Coming of Post-Industial Society*. New York: Basic Books.

Bell, D. (1979). *The Cultural Contradictions of Capitalism*. London: Heinemann.

Bell, D. (2001). *An Introduction to Cybercultures*. London: Routledge.

Bendix, R. (1966). *Max Weber: An Intellectual Portrait*. London: Methuen.

Berger, P. and Luckmann, T. (1967). *The Social Construction of Reality*. London: Penguin.

Best, S. and Kellner, D. (1991). *Postmodern Theory: Critical Interrogations*. London: Macmillan.

Best, S. and Kellner, D. (1997). *The Postmodern Turn*. New York: Guildford Press.

Best, S. (1995). *The Politics of Historical Vision: Marx, Foucault, Habermas*. London: Guildford Press.

Bilton, M. and Sim, K. (1992). *Four Hours in My Lai*. London: Viking.

Bronner, E. and Kellner, D. (1989). *Critical Theory and Society*. London: Routledge.

Brubaker, R. (1991). *The Limits of Rationality: An Essay on the Social and Moral Thought of Max Weber*. London: Routledge.

Burchell, G., Gordon, G. and Miller, P. (1991). *The Foucault Effect: Studies in Governmentality*. London: Harvester-Wheatsheaf.

Castells, M. (ed.) (1985). *High Technology, Space and Society*. London: Sage.

Castells, M. (1989). *The Informational City: Information Technology, Economic restructuring and the Urban-Regional Process*. London: Blackwell.

Castells, M. (1996). *The Information Age: Economy, Society and Culture. Vol 1: The Rise of the Network Society*. London: Blackwell.

Castells, M. (1997). *The Information Age: Economy, Society and Culture. Vol 2: The Power of Identity*: London: Blackwell.

Castells, M. (1998). *The Information Age: Economy, Society and Culture. Vol 3: The End of Millennium*. London: Blackwell.

Chalk, F. and Jonassohn, K. (1990). *The History and Sociology of Genocide*. London: Yale University Press.

Chomsky, N. (1965). *Aspects of the Theory of Syntax*. Cam USA: MIT Press.

Clarke, S. (2002). 'From Aesthetics to Object Relations: Situating Klein in the Freudian Uncanny', *Free Associations* 8 (4) No 48: 547–60. Karnac Books.

Clarke, S. (2002). On Strangers: Phantasy, Terror and the Human Imagination. *Journal of Human Rights.* **1** (3) pp 1–11.

Clarke, S. (2003). *Social Theory, Psychoanalysis and Racism*. London: Palgrave.

Clarke, S. and Moran, A. (2003). The Uncanny Stranger: Haunting the Australian Settler Imagination. *Free Associations*. Vol 10 (2) No 54. pp 165–189.

Clarke, S. and Hoggett, P. (2004). The Empire of Fear: The American Political Psyche and the Culture of Paranoia. *Psychodynamic Practice*. Vol 10 (1). pp 1–18.

Comte, A. (1974). Aim of the Course. General Considerations on the Nature and Importance of positive Philosophy. In Andreski, S. (ed.), *The Essential Comte*. London: Croom Helm. pp 19–41.

Comte, A. (1974). Fundamental Characteristics of the Positive Method in the Study of Social Phenomena. In Andreski, S. (ed.), *The Essential Comte*. London: Croom Helm. pp 137–198.

Craib, I. (1989). *Psychoanalysis and Social Theory*. London: Harvester-Wheatsheaf.

Craib, I. (1998). *Experiencing Identity*. London: Sage.

Crews, F. (1993). The Unknown Freud. *New York Review of Books*. 18th November.

Crocker, L. (ed.) (1969). *The Age of Enlightenment*. London: Harper & Row.

Crowley, J. (2001). Profile: Tom Clancey. *New Statesman*. 24 September.

Dean, M. (1999). *Governmentality: Power and Rule in Modern Society*. London: Sage.

Deleuze, G. and Guattari, F. (1983). *Anti-Oedipus*. Minneapolis: University of Minnesota Press.

Dews, P. (1999). *Habermas: A Critical Reader*. London: Blackwell.

Diderot, D. and D'Alembert, J (eds) *Encyclopédie, ou Dictionnaire Raisonné Des Sciences, Des Arts et des Métiers*. Le Breton: Paris. (1752–1772).

Dilthey, W. (1976). *Selected Writings*. Cambridge: Cambridge University Press.

Douglas, M. (1966). *Purity and Danger*. London: Routledge.

Dreyfus, H. and Rabinow, P. (1982). *Michel Foucault: Beyond Structuralism and Hermeneutics*. London: Harvester-Wheatsheaf.

Durkheim, E. (1964). *The Division of Labour in Society*. New York: The Free Press.

Durkheim, E. (1964). *The Rules of Sociological Method*. New York: The Free Press.

Durkheim, E. (1970). *Suicide*. London: Routledge.

Elias, N. (1982). *The Civilising Process 1: The History of Manners*. Oxford: Blackwell.

Elliott, A. (2001). *Concepts of the Self*. London: Polity.

Elliott, A. (2002). Beck's Sociology of Risk: A Critical Assessment. *Sociology*. 36 (2). pp 293–315.

Evans-Pritchard, E. (1965). *Witchcraft, Oracles and Magic Among the Azande*. London: Clarendon Press.

Farrell Fox, N. (2003). *The New Sartre*. London: Continuum.

Fanon, F. (1986). *Black Skin, White Masks*. London: Pluto Press.

Flax, J. (1990). *Psychoanalysis, Feminism and Postmodernism in the Contemporary West*. Berkeley: University of California Press.

Foucault, M. (1961, 1967, 1995). *Madness and Civilisation: A History of Insanity in the Age of Reason*. London: Routledge.

Foucault, M. (1975, 1977). *Discipline and Punish: The Birth of the Prison*. London: Penguin.

Foucault, M. (1976). *The History of Sexuality Vol 1: The Will to Knowledge*. London: Penguin.

Foucault, M. (1984). *The History of Sexuality Vol 2: The Use of Pleasure*. London: Penguin.

Foucault, M. (1984). *The History of Sexuality Vol 3: The Care of the Self*. London: Penguin.

Foucault, M. (1980). *Power/Knowledge*. London: Harvester-Wheatsheaf. (ed.) Colin Gordon.

Fraser, N. and Nicholson, L. (1988). Social Criticism Without Philosophy: An Encounter Between Feminism and Postmodernism. *Theory, Culture and Society*. 5 (2). pp 373–394.

Freud, S. (1919, 1961). 'The Uncanny', in *The Standard Edition of the Complete Psychological Works of Sigmund Freud vol. XVII (1917–1919)*. London: Hogarth Press, pp 219–252.

Gadamer, H-G. (1989). *Truth and Method*. London: Sheed and Ward.

Garfinkel, H. (1967). *Studies in Ethnomethodology*. London: Prentice-Hall.

Gane, M. (1991). *Baudrillard's Bestiary: Baudrillard and Culture*. London: Routledge.

Garrett, S. (1993). *Ethics and Airpower in World War II*. New York: St Martin's Press.

Geertz, C. (1975). *The Interpretation of Cultures*. London: Basic Books.

Gellner, E. (1974). 'French Eighteenth Century Materialism', in *The Devil in Modern Philosophy*. London: Routledge. pp 113–148.

Gellner, E. (1985, 1993). *The Psychoanalytic Movement: The Cunning of Unreason*. London: Fontana.

Ghandi, L. (1998). *Postcolonial Theory: An Introduction*. Edinburgh: Edinburgh University Press.

Giddens, A. (1971). *Capitalism and Modern Social Theory: An Analysis of the Writings of Marx, Durkheim and Max Weber*. Cambridge: Cambridge University Press.

Giddens, A. (1976). 'An Introduction to the Protestant Ethic', in Weber, M. (1992), *The Protestant Ethic and the Spirit of Capitalism*. London: Routledge.

Giddens, A. (1990). *The Consequences of Modernity*. London: Polity.

Giddens, A. (1991). *Modernity and Self Identity: Self and Society in the Late Modern Age*. London: Polity.

Goldhagen, D.J. (1996). *Hitler's Willing Executioners: Ordinary Germans and the Holocaust*. London: Abacus.

Gordon, S. (1984). *Hitler, Germans and the 'Jewish Question'*. Princetown: Princetown University Press.

Grunbaum, A. (1984). *The Foundations of Psychoanalysis: A Philosophical Critique*. California: University of California Press.

Gutman, R. (1993). *A witness to Genocide*. London: Element.

Gutting, G. (1994). 'Foucault and the History of Madness', in Gutting, G. (ed.), *The Cambridge Companion to Foucault*. Cambridge: Cambridge University Press. pp 47–70.

Habermas, J. (1971a). *Towards a Rational Society*. London: Heinemann.

Habermas, J. (1971b). *Knowledge and Human Interests*. London: Heinemann.

Habermas, J. (1974). *Theory and Practice*. London: Heinemann.

Habermas, J. (1976). *Legitimation Crisis*. London: Heinemann.

Habermas, J. (1981, 1984). *The Theory of Communicative Action Vol 1: Reason and the Rationalization of Society*. London: Heinemann.

Habermas, J. (1985). *The Philosophical Discourse of Modernity*. London: Polity Press.

Habermas, J. (1987). *The Theory of Communicative Action Vol 2: The Critique of Functionalist Reason*. London: Heinemann.

Habermas, J. (1989). *The Structural Transformation of the Public Sphere*. London: Polity.

Habermas, J. (1992). *Between Facts and Norms: Contributions to a Discourse Theory of Law and Democracy*. London: Polity.

Habermas, J. (2003). *The Future of Human Nature*. London: Polity.

Halfpenny, P. (1982). *Positivism and Sociology: Explaining Social Life*. London: Allen & Unwin.

Hanfling, O. (1981). *Essential Readings in Logical Positivism*. London: Blackwell.

Harvey, D. (1989). *The Condition of Postmodernity*. London: Blackwell.

Hastings, M. (1993). *Bomber Command*. London: Papermac.

Held, D. (1980,1990). *Introduction to Critical Theory: Horkheimer to Habermas*. London: Polity.

Held, D. (1988). Farewell Nation State. *Marxism Today*. (December). pp 69–73.

Held, D. (1996). *Models of Democracy* (2nd ed.). London: Polity.

Hoggett, P. and Thompson, S. (2001). The Emotional Dynamics of Deliberative Democracy. *Policy and Politics*. Vol 29, no 3. pp 351–364.

Honneth, A. and Joas, H. (eds) (1991). *Communicative Action*. London: Polity.

Hoogvelt, A. (1998). *Globalisation and the Postcolonial World: The New Political Economy of Development*. London: Macmillan.

Hoogvelt, A. (2000). 'Globalisation and the Postcolonial World', in Held, D. and McGrew, A. (eds), *The Global Transformations Reader*. London: Polity. pp 355–360.

Horkheimer, M. and Adorno, T. (1947, 1994). *Dialectic of Enlightenment*. London: Continuum.

How, A. (2003). *Critical Theory*. London: Palgrave.

Hoy, D. (1986). *Foucault: A Critical Reader*. London: Blackwell.

Jameson, F. (1991). *Postmodernism Or, the Cultural Logic of Late Capitalism*. London: Verso.

Jarvis, S. (1998). *Adorno: A Critical Introduction*. London: Polity.

Jay, M. (1994). 'The Jews and the Frankfurt School: Critical Theory's Analysis of Anti-Semitism', in Bernstein, J. (ed.), *The Frankfurt School Critical Assessments*.London: Routledge. pp 235–246.

Jencks, C. (1977). *The Language of Post-modern Architecture*. New York: Pantheon.

Jencks, C. (1991). *The Post-modern Reader*. New York: St Martin's Press.

Jordan, T. (2002). 'Technopower and its Cyberfutures', in Armitage, J. and Roberts, J. (2002), *Living with Cyberspace: Technology and Society in the 21st Century*. London: Continuum. pp 120–130.

Kant, I. (1784). 'What is Enlightenment', in Beck, L. (1963), *Kant on History*. Indianapolis: Bobbs-Merrill.

Keat, R. and Urry, J. (1975). *Social Theory as Science*. London: Routledge.

Kellner, D. B. (1989). *Jean Baudrillard: From Marxism to Postmodernism and Beyond*. London: Polity Press.

Kelly, M. (1998). *Critique and Power: Recasting the Foucault/Habermas Debate*. London: MIT Press.

Kritzman, L. (1988). *Michel Foucault: Politics, Philosophy, Culture*. London: Routledge.

Kuhn, T. (1970). *The Structure of Scientific Revolutions*. Chicago: University of Chicago Press.

Laplanche, J. and Pontalis, J-B. (1973). *The Language of Psychoanalysis*. London: Hogarth Press.

Lash, S. in Beck, U., Giddens, A. and Lash, S. (1994). *Reflexive Modernization: Politics, Tradition and Aesthetics in the Modern Social Order*. London: Polity Press.

Lash, S. (1990). *The Sociology of Postmodernism*. London: Routledge.

Lash, S. (2002). *Critique of Information*. London: Sage.

Layton, L. (1998). *Who's That Girl? Who's That Boy?: Clinical Practice Meets Postmodern Gender Theory*. New York: Jason Aronson.

Leach, E. (1964). 'Anthropological aspects of language: animal categories and verbal abuse', in Eric H. Lenneberg (ed.), *New Directions in the Study of Language*, Chicago: University of Chicago Press.

Levi, P. (1979). *If this is a Man*. London: Abacus.

Lifton, R.J. (1986). *The Nazi Doctors: Medical Killing and the Psychology of Genocide*. London: Macmillan.

Lyon, D. (1999). *Postmodernity* (2nd ed.). Buckingham: Open University Press.

Lyon, D. (2002). 'Cyberspace: Beyond the Information Society?', in Armitage, J. and Roberts, J. (2002), *Living with Cyberspace: Technology and Society in the 21st Century*. London: Continuum. pp 21–33.

Lyotard, J-F. (1974, 1993). *Libidinal Economy*. London: The Athlone Press.

Lyotard, J-F. (1984). *The Postmodern Condition: A Report on Knowledge*. Minneapolis: University of Minnesota Press.

Lyotard, J-F. (1988). *The Differend: Phrases in Dispute*. Manchester: Manchester University Press.

Mannheim, K. (1960). *Ideology and Utopia*. London: Routledge.

Marcuse, H. (1964). *One Dimensional Man*. London: Routledge.

Marcuse, H. (1968). *Negations*. London: Penguin.

May, C. (2002). *The Information Society: A Sceptical View*. London: Polity.

Mead, G-H. (1962). *Mind, Self and Society*. Chicago: University of Chicago Press.

Merquior, J.G. (1991). *Foucault*. London: Fontana Press.

Michels, R. (1929). *Der Patriotismus*. Munich: Duncker und Humblot.

Mommsen, W. (1992). *The Political and Social Theory of Max Weber*. London: Polity.

Niewyk, D. (1997). *The Holocaust*. New York: Houghton Mifflin.

Outhwaite, W. (1994). *Habermas: A Critical Introduction*. London: Polity.

Paddison, M. (1996). *Adorno, Modernism and Mass Culture: Essays on Critical Theory and Music*. London: Kahn & Averill.

Parkin, F. (1982). *Max Weber*. London: Tavistock.

Parsons, T. (1949). *The Structure of Social Action*, Vol 1, 2. New York: Free Press.

Petras, J. and Veltmeyer, H. (2001). *Globalization Unmasked: Imperialism in the 21st Century*. London: Zed Books.

Popper, K. (1959). *The Logic of Scientific Discovery*. London: Routledge.

Popper, K. (1971). *The Open Society and its Enemies*. Princetown: Princetown University Press.

Popper, K. (1983). *Realism and the Aims of Science*. London: Hutchinson.

Porter, R. (1990). Foucault's Great Confinement. *History of the Human Sciences*. 3. pp 47–54.

Porter, R. (1993). 'Baudrillard: History, Hysteria and Consumption', in Rojek, C. and Turner, B.(eds) (1993), *Forget Baudrillard?* London: Routledge. pp 1–21.

Richards, B. (1989). *Images of Freud: Cultural Responses to Psychoanalysis*. London: Dent.

Ritzer, G. (1998). Introduction to Baudrillard, J. (1970, 1998). *The Consumer Society*. London: Sage.

Roberts, A. and Guelff, R. (ed.). (1989). *Documents on the Laws of War*. Oxford: Clarendon Press.

Robertson, R. (1992). *Globalization: Social Theory and Global Culture*. London: Sage.

Rojek, C. and Turner, B. (eds) (1993). *Forget Baudrillard?* London: Routledge.

Rojek, C. (1993). 'Baudrillard and Politics', in Rojek, C. and Turner, B. (eds) (1993), *Forget Baudrillard?* London: Routledge. pp 107–123.

Rouse, J. (1994). 'Power/Knowledge', in Gutting, G. (ed.). *The Cambridge Companion to Foucault*. Cambridge: Cambridge University Press. pp 92–114.

Rustin, M. (1991). 'Psychoanalysis, Racism and Anti-Racism', in *The Good Society and the Inner World*. London: Verso. pp 57–84.

Said, E. (1995). *Orientalism: Western Conceptions of the Orient*. London: Penguin.

Sartre, J-P. (1968). On Genocide. *Ramparts*, pp 37–42.

Sartre, J-P. (1993). *Being and Nothingness*. London: Routledge.

Sayer, D. (1991). *Capitalism and Modernity: An Excursus on Marx and Weber*. London: Routledge.

Schleiermacher, F. (1911). *Werke*. Leipzig: Felix Meiner.

Schroeder, R. (1992). *Max Weber and the Sociology of Culture*. London: Sage.

Schutz, A. (1932, 1972). *The Phenomenology of the Social World*. London: Heinemann.

Schutz, A. (1944). 'The Stranger: An Essay in Social Psychology', *The American Journal of Sociology*, XLIX (6), May: 499–507.

Searle, J. (1969). *Speech Acts*. Cambridge: Cambridge University Press.

Sedgwick, P. (1982). *Psycho Politics*. London: Pluto Press.

Sim, S. (1996). *Jean Francois Lyotard*. London: Harvester-Wheatsheaf.

Simmel, G. (1950). *The Sociology of Georg Simmel*. (Ed. and Trans.) Wolff, K. New York: The Free Press.

Smart, B. (2002). *Michel Foucault*. London: Routledge.

Stichweh, R. (1997). 'The Stranger – On the Sociology of Indifference', *Thesis Eleven* 51, 1–16.

Swingewood, A. (2000). *A Short History of Sociological Thought*. (3rd ed). London: Palgrave.

Tancock, L. (1966). Introduction to d' Alembert's Dream. Diderot, D. (1966). *Rameau's Nephew/D'Alembert's Dream*. London: Penguin. pp 133–147.

Turner, B. (1993). 'Baudrillard for Sociologists', in Rojek, C. and Turner, B. (eds) (1993), *Forget Baudrillard?* London: Routledge. pp 70–87.

Turner, B. (1996). *For Weber: Essays on the Sociology of Fate*. London: Sage.

Wallerstein, I. (1984). *The politics of the World Economy: The States, the Movements and the Civilizations*. Cambridge: Cambridge University Press.

Weber, M. (1921, 1978). *Economy and Society, Vol 1*. Berkeley: University of California Press.

Weber, M. (1930, 1992). *The Protestant Ethic and the Spirit of Capitalism*. London: Routledge.

Weber, M. (1991). *Essays in Sociology*. (ed.) Gerth & Wright Mills. London: Routledge.

Webster, F. (1995). *Theories of the Information Society*. London: Routledge.

Wiggershaus, R. (1994). *The Frankfurt School*. London: Polity Press.

Wilton, T. (2004). *Sexual (Dis)Orientation: Gender, Sex, Desire and Self Fashioning*. London: Palgrave.

Winch, P.(1974). 'Understanding a primitive society', in Wilson, B. (ed.), *Rationality*. London: Blackwell. pp 78–111.

Winch, P. (2000). *The Idea of a Social Science and its Relation to Philosophy*. (2nd ed.). London: Routledge.

Wiggershaus, R. (1994). *The Frankfurt School*. London: Polity Press.

Woolgar, S. (2002). 'Five Rules of Virtuality', in Woolgar, S. (ed.), (2002). *Virtual Society: Technology, Cyberbole, Reality*. Oxford: Oxford University Press. pp 1–22.

Zukier, H. (1996). 'The essential "Other" and the Jew: From anti-Semitism to Genocide', *Social Research* 63 (4), 1110–54.

Index